The Irish Social Services

John Curry

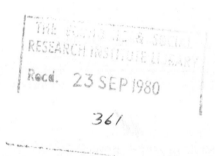
Institute of Public Administration
Dublin

Published by
Institute of Public Administration
59 Lansdowne Road
Dublin 4
Ireland

First Published 1980

British Library Cataloguing in Publication Data

Curry, John
  The Irish social services.
  1. Public welfare — Ireland.
  I. Title   II. Institute of Public
Administration *(Republic of Ireland)*
361'. 9417   HV250.3
ISBN 0-902173-97-9

Set in 11/12pt Baskerville and Printed by
Cahill Printers Limited Dublin

Contents

Acknowledgements

Preface

Chapter 1   **Introduction 1**
Factors influencing the social services 1;
social policy developments in Ireland 6

Chapter 2   **Income Maintenance 5**
Introduction 15; poverty 17; social insurance 23; social assistance 30; other income
maintenance schemes 38; administration
45; finance 50

Chapter 3   **Housing 60**
Introduction 60; administration 61; major
trends in housing output 62; factors in
planning housing needs 67; local authority
housing 69; private housing 76; private
rented sector 84; level of subsidy by tenure
group 85; housing conditions 88;
Appendix: Differential Rent Scheme 91

Chapter 4   **Education 94**
Introduction 94; first level education 96;
second level education 108; third level
education 120; adult education 130;
equality of opportunity in education 133;
public expenditure on education 136;
Appendix: circular on community schools
from department of education, October
1970 139; Appendix: schedule of annual
benefits payable under the higher
education grants for 1979 to students 143

Chapter 5   **Health Services 145**
             Introduction 145; administration 147;
             finance 152; services 154; eligibility for
             health services 176

Chapter 6   **Welfare Services 189**
             Introduction 189; the elderly 189;
             community servicese 191; the handicapped
             196; deprived children 203; voluntary
             organisations 214; social work 220

Chapter 7   **Some EEC Comparisons 224**
             Introduction 224; social policy 225; income
             maintenance 227; health services 233;
             housing 240; education 244

             Notes to Chapters 250

             Select Bibliography 265

             Index 271

Acknowledgements

It is a pleasure to thank all those who helped, either directly or indirectly in the preparation of this book. While it is not possible to mention all of them by name some merit special recognition. I am particularly indebted to Séamus Ó Cinnéide who first suggested the idea of a textbook for students and who gave me every encouragement along the way. Staff of the Institute of Public Administration have been of invaluable assistance, notably Jim O'Donnell, Tony Farmar, Frances Lawlor and Kathleen Harte; a special word of thanks to Brigid Pike who compiled the index. To my former colleagues John Blackwell and Paul Turpin I am grateful for constructive comments and suggestions on an earlier draft. My wife, Vera, has been both patient and supportive while the book was in preparation. My special gratitude to Yvonne Kennedy and Mary Ryan for typing the manuscript. Clarence Quinn-Berger has been a source of constant encouragement. Last but not least I am indebted to students in the Institute of Public Administration who have, unwittingly, been of inestimable help over the years.

To all of the above I am sincerely grateful but none are responsible for any errors or views contained in the following pages.

John Curry
April 1980

Preface

This book is based on lectures delivered to first year students attending the Diploma in Administrative Science course at the Institute of Public Administration. It was inspired by the fact that although excellent reports, articles or books exist on individual social services, there is no one book to which the students can be referred for an overview of these services. The purpose of the book therefore, is to provide an introduction to the range of social services in Ireland. While the book is primarily intended for students, it is hoped that it may be of interest to social administrators, voluntary workers or lay persons concerned with how the social problems of Irish society are defined and dealt with.

In a book of this nature, covering as it does such a large range of services, it is inevitable that there will be omissions, and that certain areas will not be given the emphasis some persons might require. This has been largely dictated by a desire to treat the subject matter not only as comprehensively but also as concisely as possible. Those interested in delving further should find the references to each chapter of benefit.

One of the disadvantages of a text book on social services is that developments occur so rapidly that the text quickly becomes outdated. This applies in particular to statistics. While these have been used freely throughout the book, the main intention in doing so was to give some idea of structure at particular points in time. The references will indicate the sources from which such statistics may be updated. Rounding errors occur on certain tables, for instance nos. 1 and 35.

Chapter 1

Introduction

Factors influencing the social services

The social services are those provided by the state or other bodies to improve the individual's welfare. They differ, therefore, from other public services which have the good of the community as their objective. The basic social services are income maintenance, health, education, housing and welfare or personal social services.

These services are important in Irish society for a number of reasons. Firstly, almost half of all expenditure by public authorities (central government and local authorities) is devoted to education, health, income maintenance and housing.[1] The proportion of gross national product devoted to these social functions in 1975 was 27.5 per cent, as compared with 15.8 per cent in 1965. Secondly, social services affect practically everybody in our society at some stage in their life. Almost one-third of the population depends solely or mainly on income maintenance payments[2] and at any time a similar proportion are attending a school or college of some kind.[3] Approximately one-sixth of the population lives in houses or flats rented from local authorities[4] and, with few exceptions, all private housing is subsidised to some degree from public funds. Approximately one in every six persons is treated in hospital every year.[5] Thirdly, there is a large work-force engaged in the direct provision or administration of the social services: in 1977-8, approximately 52,000 persons were employed in the health services and 40,000 in education.[6]

Kaim-Caudle has identified three major factors which influence the type and level of social services provided in a country: socio-demographic, economic and policy.[7] It is easy to understand how these factors have influenced and continue to influence the provision of social services in Ireland.

1

Socio-demographic factors

Changes in the total population determine to a large extent the state's commitment to certain areas of social provision. A declining population, for example, implies a reduction in housing expenditure, while an increasing population suggests the need for increased expenditure on education. In the 1950s when emigration from Ireland was running at 40,000 per annum it was deemed that our housing needs had been virtually met and consequently housing output was low (see Chapter 3). By the 1960s, however, the situation had been reversed and for the first time since 1841 the national population increased, emigration declined sharply, the demand for housing increased and housing output rose steadily.

Apart from trends in the total population the provision of services is also influenced by changes in the birth rate, marriage rate and death rate. An increase in the birth rate, for example, has obvious implications for child health services, educational facilities, children's allowance and other income maintenance payments where allowances are made for child dependants. Similarly, a decline in the death rate and an increase in life expectancy have a direct effect on the provision of pensions, community care facilities and institutional services for the elderly. In Ireland the birth rate in 1975 was 21.7 per 1,000 inhabitants, the highest of any country in the European Economic Community (EEC). Life expectancy has increased throughout this century and the number of persons aged 65 and over has continued to rise (see Chapter 6). The dependency ratio (the ratio between the working age-group, i.e. aged 15 to 64 years, and the groups aged under 15 and over 65) also affects the general level of services. In Ireland the ratio is 100 : 74 as compared with an average of 100 : 60 in the EEC.

In practice the burden of dependency is greater if the ratio is based on the active and non-active sections of the population, that is if the latter were to include those over 15 years of age either engaged in full-time education or unemployed. The ratio indicates the relative burden of providing services which benefit the young and the old. Those in the cash earning group will have to bear the burden, through direct or indirect taxation, of providing services for the dependent groups.

The distribution of population between urban and rural areas and the density of population also has important implications for the social services.[8] It is cheaper, for example, to provide certain services such as water supply in high density urban areas than in sparsely populated rural areas. Major specialised services such as hospitals will tend to be located in the larger urban areas, making access difficult for those living in remote areas. In 1971, just over half (52.2 per cent) the population in Ireland lived in urban areas (towns of 1,500 persons or over) and the population density ranged from 2,395 persons per square mile in Dublin to 48 per square mile in Leitrim. A further factor is that many rural areas contain disproportionate numbers of elderly persons, a legacy mainly of persistent and selective migration. This has implications for the provision of a number of services catering for the old.

Economic factors

The level of state commitment and of state investment in social provision is naturally influenced by the economic resources of the country. During a period of economic growth it is possible to improve social services, while in a recession it becomes difficult to maintain, let alone expand, services. The importance of the economic factor in Irish social expenditure is clearly illustrated by events of the past decade or so. In the second half of the 1960s and in the early 1970s economic growth was accompanied by increased expenditure on social services which resulted, among other things, in the introduction of free post-primary education, of new income maintenance schemes and the reorganisation of health services. More recently, however, and particularly since 1975 when the effects of a world-wide recession began to affect Ireland, there has been little expansion of services. Cutbacks or at best a retention of the status quo have been the order of the day. In 1976, for example, there were cutbacks in housing where state grants for new dwellings were practically eliminated. While income maintenance payments were increased to keep pace with inflation during 1976 a reduction in the qualifying age for receipt of the old age pension from 67 to 66 had to be deferred until 1977. Even that apparently minor reform was considered to have been too costly at the time. The 1978 government green paper on the economy, *Development for Full Employment*, illustrates the preoccupation with cutbacks in a period of economic difficulty and high unemployment. In regard to the social welfare system it proposed cutbacks in the children's allowance, smallholder's assistance and emphasised the importance of combatting fraudulent claims.

With reference to social policy in general the green paper states:

> The emphasis of this Green Paper is on economic objectives. It stems from the belief that economic advance carried with it direct social benefits and that substantial social improvements in other areas cannot take place unless there is the necessary economic progress to support and finance them . . . In the present circumstances of our society the elimination of unemployment must be viewed not only as an economic objective but also as a major contribution to social progress . . . Ending unemployment will not of course deal with all problems in the social area, but it is the overriding responsibility of the Government at the present time and must, therefore, command priority. In giving priority to Exchequer expenditures on job creation it will not be possible to allow the simultaneous rapid development of services, no matter how desirable these may be when viewed in isolation.[9]

Policy considerations

Perhaps the most important influence on social provision is the ideological one — the attitudes to social services, the attitudes of society to social needs, and the attitudes to personal responsibility and family responsibility. The government in power is likely to reflect these attitudes in providing for social services. Until recently one of the more noticeable features of Irish society has been the pre-eminence of Catholic social teaching. In the past this emphasised the principle of subsidiarity, i.e. that the state should not undertake functions which could be fulfilled by individuals on their own or by the local community, and that the state function should be to supplement not supplant. The debate over the proposed Mother and Child Scheme in the late 1940s illustrated the importance of this issue (see Chapter 5). More recently, the Catholic Church has, particularly since Vatican Council II (1962-65), been concerning itself increasingly with inadequacies in social policy and social provision. It has been urging the introduction of measures designed not simply to ameliorate the effects of disadvantage and poverty in society but also the removal of the causes of these problems. This renewed emphasis on social issues by the Catholic Church is perhaps best exemplified by the sentiments expressed in the hierarchy's pastoral, *The Work of Justice* (1977).[10] The influence of the Catholic Church (including religious orders) has been very pronounced at all levels of the education system, in the provision of services for the handicapped and the establishment of hospitals.

Party-political ideology is also important in shaping social legislation, but this is likely to vary considerably between countries. The differences in social policy between Labour and Conservatives in Britain appears to be much greater than between Fianna Fáil and Fine Gael in Ireland. This is not to deny that the political parties have, in their policy documents, expressed concern with social issues. But as Coughlan points out, 'the political parties have differed in emphasis on social service policy, not in basic principles.'[11] In the Irish context it may be said that governments have been more influenced by political expediency than social ideology. However, much appears to depend on the strength and personality of individual members of the cabinet and their commitment to social policy. During his short term as Minister for Education (1966-7), Donogh O'Malley made a far greater popular impact (mainly by introducing free post-primary education) than many of his predecessors or successors. A similar impact was made by Frank Cluskey who, as Parliamentary Secretary to the Minister for Health and Social Welfare in the Coalition

Government of 1973-7, had responsibility for the social welfare system. The influence of pressure groups, particularly articulate, well-organised groups may also exert considerable influence. CARE (Campaign for Deprived Children) for instance has, with some effect, been active in pressing for reforms in children's services in Ireland.

These are the main factors which help to explain the level of social provision. It is important to note, however, that the factors are complex and interrelated. The fact that demographic conditions may indicate the need for certain social provision does not necessarily mean that it will be made available. Much depends on the attitude of the government in power, the resources available, the attitude of the community at large and the willingness of groups to campaign for change. At times the government may lead by introducing social legislation, at other times it may merely respond to a growing clamour for reform. It other words, social policies may be the outcome of many different pressures and it is not always possible to single out the most influential of these. As Leaper points out:

> In any reasonably open and democratic society, social legislation if it is to have any lasting effect, has to take account of political conflict, political compromise, of the chance interplay of the right man and the right moment, and of all manner of sequences of administrative draughtmanship.[12]

Social policy developments in Ireland

The foundations of many existing social services in Ireland were laid by British governments before independence had been achieved. Examples of early state intervention in the various social services include primary education (1831), children's services (1908), non-contributory pensions (1908), unemployment and sickness benefits (1911). The influence of the Poor Law, which came into effect in 1838, on the development of Irish social services must also be stressed. It was out of the Poor Law, for example, that the public hospital system developed. The initial central feature of the Poor Law was the workhouse which was designed to cater for the very destitute. The philosophy of the Poor Law was based on the concept of less eligibility i.e. the conditions of persons within the workhouse should be less eligible than those of the lowest paid worker outside. While many of the workhouses, the visible signs and reminders of the mid-nineteenth-century Poor Law, were demolished or remodelled for other purposes after independence, some of the services which the Poor Law spawned remained until the 1970s. These included the dispensary system, replaced by the choice-of-doctor scheme, and home assistance, replaced by the supplementary welfare allowance scheme.

The various social services have developed in a rather haphazard and piecemeal fashion since their establishment. This will be evident in the following chapters which summarise the major developments. Furthermore, developments in social services in general have not, until recently, been accompanied by an ideological debate on the principles underlying these services and any debate which did occur was of a pragmatic nature. The social services have been reformed, improved upon or added to for a variety of reasons. Coughlan has summed up the situation as follows:

> Most people are aware of the ad hoc and fragmentary way in which the social services came into being; they were largely a piecemeal growth, introduced at different times to cover different categories of need and in response to different pressures, the result of a wide variety of motives — humanitarianism, social idealism, political expediency, the desire to damp down social discontent, a response to the spread of democracy and universal suffrage, the need to provide an environment conducive to industrial development. Seldom were they the expression of a coherent philosophical outlook.[13]

Finola Kennedy in *Public Social Expenditure in Ireland*[14] searched in vain for a coherent outlook in Irish policy. In attempting to discover the objectives of social policy in Ireland since World War II she analysed various policy statements and official reports, and distinguished the following three major aims of social policy in post-war Ireland:

1. the relief of poverty and the provision of a minimum standard of living for all;
2. equalisation of opportunity;
3. increased productivity and economic growth.

These aims, she states, might be called the humanitarian, the egalitarian and the economic aims of social policy. These objectives, however, have not been clearly formulated in Ireland and there remains a need to specify clearly what the aims of social policy are and what they ought to be, and to assess achievements in relation to these objectives. In Kennedy's view, this has proved elusive.

In order to define social policy in the Irish context the National Economic and Social Council (NESC) commissioned Professor David Donnison to report on the scope and aims of social policy. In his report Donnison said:

> . . . the social policies of Government are those of their actions which deliberately or accidentally affect the distribution of resources, status, opportunities and life chances among social groups and categories within the country, and thus help to shape the general character and equity of its social relations. Social policies are thus concerned with fairness[15]

According to Donnison there are five main patterns of inequality in Ireland towards which policies should and could be directed.[16] These are:

1. Inequality arising from the life-time cycle, i.e. changes in family income do not correspond to the changes in family need so that, for instance young married couples with families are usually relatively worse off.
2. Inequality related to social class (defined in terms of peoples' income and their position on the labour market). Patterns of life related to social class go far to determine peoples' opportunities for saving, their credit ratings, and hence their opportunity for house purchase, their housing standards and geographic location. These factors then help to shape educational aspirations and opportunities and consequently the skills, earnings and geographical and social mobility of the next generation.

3. Inequality related to urban-rural and inter-regional differences.

4. Inequality related to differences between areas within cities.

5. Inequality arising from discrimination, e.g. against women or against minority groups such as itinerants.

Donnison makes it clear, however, that the uniformity of complete interpersonal equality is not advocated and that plenty of inequality will always remain in any open, evolving society. The equality which should be aspired to, according to Donnison, is:

> . . . a state of affairs in which differences due to taste, talent or luck are as nearly as possible randomly distributed. Then, on average, the poor, the injured, the unemployed or those in trouble with the law would not differ in other respects from the rich, the healthy, the employed or the law-abiding.[17]

This concern with inequalities had also been expressed by The Council for Social Welfare. In its *Statement on Social Policy* (1973) it recommended that the aims of social policy should be:

1. to remove gross inequalities within the community, and
2. to strengthen the bonds of the community itself.

Policy phases
Finola Kennedy identified three distinct policy phases in Ireland from the end of World War II up to 1974.[18] These are closely linked with the prevailing economic environment. The first phase, from 1947 to 1951, she described as expansionary, since public social expenditure doubled (from £31.8 million to £62.5 million) and increased its share of the GNP from 9.6 per cent to 14.9 per cent. Some of the developments in this period included the establishment of separate departments of social welfare and health, extensive hospital construction and an increase in housing output.

The second phase, from 1952 to 1962, was a regressive phase when social expenditure's share of GNP fell from 14.9

per cent to 13.7 per cent. Housing output declined throughout this period but particularly in the late 1950s. There were some minor developments in income maintenance services, for instance contributory old-age pensions were introduced in 1961. Developments were also made in the provision of health services, the most notable being the Health Act, 1953 which extended 'free' hospitalisation to the middle income group, and the establishment of the Voluntary Health Insurance Board in 1957 to enable the higher income group to insure themselves against hospital costs.

The third phase, from 1963 to 1974, was an expansionary phase in the social as well as economic field with development taking place slowly at first and then with increasing momentum. This decade undoubtedly constituted a watershed in the development of the social services; it also witnessed the reversal of the national population decline as increased economic opportunities become available in the country. In each of the social services significant developments occurred during the decade. In education, the scene was set by the publication in 1965 of the *Investment in Education* report, the first major evaluation of the educational institutions and of the educational system generally in Ireland. The introduction of free post-primary education, the establishment of comprehensive and community schools, of regional technical colleges and the introduction of higher education grants, were important innovations. In regard to health services, the period was characterised initially by an analysis, through various reports, of existing services. The white paper of 1966 paved the way for subsequent reform of the administrative framework and of the services themselves. The Health Act, 1970, was the legal embodiment of these changes which included the establishment of regional health boards and provided for the introduction of a choice-of-doctor scheme. In regard to income maintenance, the trend was towards an extension of coverage to groups of people hitherto outside the statutory system, including the introduction of benefits for deserted wives, prisoners' wives and unmarried mothers. In 1974 compulsory social insurance was extended to all employees of insurable age and pay-related benefits were introduced. In housing, output rose steadily from 7,800 in 1963 to 26,300 in 1974. Much of the demand for housing resulted from the increase in numbers marrying which occurred during the 1960s.

It is possible to extend Finola Kennedy's analysis a little further to cover the period from 1975 to the present. This was a period of economic recession, a period when rising unemployment and inflation dominated the economic scene. The average annual number on the live register of unemployed rose from 70,300 in 1974 to 109,000 in 1977. The momentum of social reform of the previous decade declined and many developments which might reasonably have been expected in a more favourable economic climate had to be shelved. Paradoxically, social expenditure increased during this period, owing mainly to inflation. In the case of income maintenance services, for example, the need to maintain the real value of payments to recipients such as old age pensioners, led to increased expenditure as did increases in the number of unemployed. Some services, however, were reduced, e.g. community care services such as the home-help scheme, the number of recipients of the smallholder's assistance scheme (the farmer's dole), and the scheme of general home improvement grants was terminated. Yet a number of developments also occurred, for instance the abolition of home assistance and its replacement by the more equitable supplementary welfare allowance scheme (see Chapter 2). Furthermore, following a change of government in July 1977, several measures (arguably social) were introduced, such as the abolition of rates on private dwellings, of motor taxation on certain types of vehicles, of wealth tax and substantial increases in personal income tax allowances.

Recent interest in social policy
Within the past two decades there has been increased interest in social policy in Ireland. This is reflected in the output of publications dealing with social services and social issues in general. Several of these have helped to create an increased public awareness of social issues. Reference must first be made to an earlier 'pioneering' work however, a paper on 'Social Security' read by Dr Dignan, Bishop of Clonfert and

Chairman of the National Health Insurance Society to the management committee of the Society in 1944. In his paper Dr Dignan outlined what at the time appeared to be radical proposals for a reform of the Irish social security system.[19]

Among the more recent works have been Coughlan's *Aims of Social Policy* (1966), the various publications of Kaim-Caudle in the 1960s and early 1970s, especially *Social Policy in the Irish Republic* (1967),[20] Ó Cinnéide's *A Law for the Poor* (1970)[21] and 'The Extent of Povery in Ireland' (1972)[22] by the same author.

The publications of several agencies and institutions have also contributed to the debate on social services. At one level governments have commissioned reports into various aspects of social services, e.g. *Report of the Commission of Inquiry into Mental Illness* (1966), *Investment in Education* (1965), *Report on the Industrial and Reformatory Schools System* (1970).

At another level various advisory and research agencies have been established and through their publications have contributed to the growing debate on social issues. In 1973 the National Economic and Social Council (NESC) was established, its main task being 'to provide a forum for discussion on the principles relating to the efficient development of the national economy and the achievement of social justice, and to advise the Government on their application.' The reports of NESC, as well as being invaluable sources of information, have raised important social policy issues and have contributed to a continuing debate on social problems and policies. The same could be said of many publications emanating from the Economic and Social Research Institute (ESRI), e.g. the report by Professor Dale Tussing on *Irish Educational Expenditures — Past, Present and Future* (1978).

In 1971 the Catholic hierarchy established the Council for Social Welfare (a committee of the Catholic Bishops' Conference) and one of its aims is 'to promote sensitivity to and action on social need'. It has issued a number of important documents including *A Statement on Social Policy* (1973), *Planning for Social Development* (1976) and it also commissioned a research report on the meaning of poverty which was published in 1974.[23] The establishment in 1971 of the National Social Service Council (see Chapter 6) was another milestone. The functions of the Council are to promote co-operation and co-ordination between local social service agencies and to provide information and advice on the social services, particularly to voluntary organisations.

Periodicals which offer an outlet for discussion and analysis of social issues include *Social Studies* (formerly *Christus Rex*) and to a lesser extent, *Studies.*

Despite the improvement in the provision of statutory social services the role of voluntary organisations in the social service field has not diminished. In fact there has been an up-surge in the activity of such bodies in recent years. New organisations have been established to cater for new needs or needs which are inadequately met by statutory or other agencies. Examples of such new organisations are:

1. *FLAC* (Free Legal Advice Centres), established in Dublin in 1969, provides free legal advice to those unable to pay for the services of solicitors and also campaigns for the introduction of a comprehensive state scheme of legal aid in both criminal and civil matters.

2. *ALLY,* established in 1971, provides a placement service for single mothers.

3. *Simon Community,* Dublin branch established in 1969, meets the needs of the homeless and socially deprived.

4. *Samaritans,* Dublin branch established in 1970, acts as a befriending agency for the lonely, despairing and suicidal.

5. *ALONE,* established in 1977, meets the needs of elderly persons living alone.

These are only some examples of the variety of voluntary, social service organisations established in the past decade.[24]

The growing debate on social policy issues over the past twenty years has been accompanied by an overall growth in the social services and an increase in the social professions, especially social workers. Ireland's entry into the EEC has also served to heighten interest in social matters; comparisons are now more easily made between the type and level of services in each of the member states (see Chapter 7). While it is not the intention of the EEC Commission that uniform social service provision be achieved throughout the community, obvious gaps in social security coverage, for example, may become embarrassingly apparent between nations. The publication in 1978 of a discussion paper on *Social Insurance for the Self-Employed* was certainly influenced by the fact that Ireland is the only EEC country which does not extend social insurance to the self-employed. The EEC has also directly intervened in a number of instances, for example the directive on equal pay for women (1975), and the directive on discrimination against women in social security (1978).

Chapter 2

Income Maintenance

Introduction

There is no universally accepted definition of social security. Kaim-Caudle[1] has pointed out that the meaning attached to the term varies greatly from country to country, and even within a country it often means different things to different people. In most countries, however, it means cash benefits for people in times of sickness, unemployment, retirement, industrial accidents and invalidism against which the individual cannot be expected to protect himself and his family by his own ability or foresight. In some countries the term social security may also include state-financed health services. In this chapter the term income maintenance is used rather than social security and covers the services operated by the Department of Social Welfare and services involving assistance in cash or kind operated by other bodies but subject to the overall control of that Department.

One of the major means by which government can reduce the incidence of poverty, as defined in terms of income levels, is to effect a redistribution of income within society. This is normally achieved in two ways, by subsidies in the form of income maintenance measures to help those on low or negligible incomes and by reducing incomes of others through taxation. There may also be redistribution of income directly through the taxation system, by income tax allowances for dependants or interest on loans.

This latter type of redistribution is only discussed briefly in this book. In addition to ordinary taxation measures, earmarked taxation in the form of social insurance contributions may also be levied. This type of contribution is levied in Ireland and most developed countries from employers and employees. This rather complex system of taxation and social insurance contributions can lead to redistribution of incomes in several ways, for instance from the rich to the poor, from the healthy to the sick, from the employed to the unemployed. The greater the burden of dependency the more difficult it becomes to increase the level of taxation for redistributive purposes among the working population. It has already been noted that Ireland has the highest dependency ratio in the EEC and in recent years there has been growing discontent, particularly among PAYE workers, with the sytem of taxation in Ireland.

In the case of social insurance contributions it is relatively easy to identify the main beneficiaries. But redistribution of income also occurs through state subsidisation of various services such as education, housing, health services, roads and other public services. Who pays and who benefits are interesting though complex questions. Despite the fact that benefits are distributed amongst all income groups there appears to be a general feeling among the middle and upper income groups in Ireland that they pay the taxes which benefit the lower income group almost exclusively. These issues are touched on in the chapters dealing with housing and education.

In most developed countries the emphasis in regard to income maintenance has shifted from social assistance benefits (based on a means test) to flat-rate social insurance benefits (based on contributions) and finally to pay-related social insurance. This trend is also discernible in Ireland. The less prosperous a country is the more it will have to rely on means-tested benefits. In general, benefits based on contributions have normally followed increases in standards of living. Increasingly there has been a growing acceptance in Ireland as in other countries of the need for all working members to contribute to a common fund out of which all members in need may benefit. The first report of the Department of Social Welfare stated:

> ... an insurance or contributory social welfare scheme means that the cost of providing against a risk is spread as widely as possible over the group within which the risk is anticipated.
> ... By paying a contribution to offset this risk, each worker ensures that, if and when in his case the risk materialises there will be a pool of resources from which he can draw to tide him over his difficulty.[2]

A NESC report has estimated that the number of people, including dependants, for whom weekly income maintenance payments were made in 1966, was 536,712 which represented just under 19 per cent of the population; by 1975 these figures had risen to 948,907 and almost 30 per cent of the population (see Table 1 on pages 18-19). The NESC report states that:

> Even allowing for the exceptionally high level of unemployment in 1975 the growth in numbers has been very striking, reflecting the changing structure of population, the extension of coverage of the different services, in particular the reduction of the old age pension age and the introduction of new services. Social welfare payments now determine in whole or in part the incomes of a significant proportion of the population.[3]

Before examining the schemes administered by the Department of Social Welfare, poverty in Irish society is considered briefly.

Poverty
Poverty is not solely associated with income. It would be unfortunate, however, if simply because of the structure of this book, any reference to the recent concern with poverty in Ireland were excluded. It was therefore decided that this chapter was the most appropriate in which to include a brief section dealing with poverty.

There is no universally accepted definition of poverty. Traditionally, definitions of poverty have been based either on nutritional standards, income levels or a combination of both. Definitions of poverty in physiological terms, based on the resources necessary to obtain enough food, clothing and shelter, permit relatively easy translation into cash terms. A poverty line, based on the minimum income necessary to avoid poverty, can therefore be drawn and a quantitative assessment of the problem can be made. Townsend, one of the foremost writers on poverty, defines poverty in relative terms, the poor being those 'individuals and families whose resources, over time, fall seriously short of the resources commanded by the average individual or family in the community in which they live.'[4] Definitions of poverty are continually being developed and there is no absolute definition of poverty based on nutritional standards and necessarily subjective assessments of

Table 1:   Estimated number of recipients of social welfare payments and their dependants (000s) at 31 March 1966 and 31 December 1975.

	1966 Recipients	Dependants Adult	Child	Total
Social Insurance				
Unemployment benefit	33.3	15.3	36.8	85.6
Disability benefit	52.5	22.8	47.5	123
Invalidity pension	—	—	—	—
Old age contributory pension	40.5	15.4	1.3	57.3
Retirement pension	—	—	—	—
Widow's contributory pension	42	—	13.3	55.3
Orphan's contributory allowance	.4	—	—	.4
Deserted wife's benefit	—	—	—	—
Maternity allowance	1.1	—	—	1.1
Total insurance recipients	170.1	53.6	99	322.9
Social Assistance				
Unemployment assistance				
— smallholders	5.6	4.2	11.5	21.4
— others	14.9	6.3	17	38.2
Old age (non-contributory) pension	112.6	9.5[a]	2.1	124.3
Widow's (non-contributory) pension	22.6	—	7.4	29.5
Orphan's (non-contributory) pension	.1	—	—	.1
Total assistance	155.4	20.1	38.2	213.7

[a] No allowance was payable in respect of these dependants until 1974. However, many spouses of pensioners qualify for pensions in their own right and are included under dependants.

Source: NESC Report no. 25, *Towards a Social Report*, Stationery Office, Dublin 1976, Table 8.7.

	1975 Recipients	Dependants Adult	Dependants Child	Total
Social Insurance				
Unemployment benefit	53.9	25.3	58.2	137.5
Disability benefit	67.8	23.9	54.5	146.2
Invalidity pension	9.9	5.1	8.7	23.8
Old age contributory pension	54.7	14.7	2.3	71.8
Retirement pension	21.9	10.2	3.6	35.8
Widow's contributory pension	60.8	—	20.7	81.5
Orphan's contributory allowance	.7	—	—	.7
Deserted wife's benefit	1.4	—	2.7	4.1
Maternity allowance	2.9	—	—	2.9
Total insurance recipients	274.3	79.4	150.9	504.7
Social Assistance				
Unemployment assistance				
— smallholders	29.3	22.3	60	111.6
— others	41.4	20.1	86.5	148.1
Old age (non-contributory) pension	131.4	11.1	5.1	147.7
Widow's (non-contributory) pension	12.6	—	7.3	20
Orphan's (non-contributory) pension	.2	—	—	.2
Deserted wife's allowance	2.9	—	3.5	6.5
Unmarried mother's allowance	2.8	—	3.4	6.3
Single woman's allowance	3.2	—	—	3.2
Prisoners' wife's allowance	.9	—	.2	.3
Total assistance	224.1	53.5	166.4	444.1

what people need or should need. A useful concept in
understanding poverty is that of the poverty cycle (first described and named by Seebohm Rowntree in Britain in 1899),
wherein people tend to experience poverty at different stages of
the family life-cycle such as childhood, early parenthood and
old age. The concept is important in indicating where resources
must be concentrated if poverty is to be eliminated. The cycle
has particular relevance for Ireland with its singular
demographic structure — its high dependency ratio, high proportion of children, large families and high unemployment
rate.

In the 1950s and 1960s several studies appeared which indicated that, despite the increasing affluence following World War II, poverty and inequalities still persisted. This 'rediscovery', as Sinfield[5] describes it, led to poverty becoming a socially acceptable subject for debate and research, to the establishment of pressure groups and eventually to attempts by governments to find a solution to the problem. In Ireland, poverty may be said to have been 'rediscovered' at a conference on poverty organised by the Council for Social Welfare and held in Kilkenny in 1971. The conference sparked off what was to be a growing national debate on how the plight of the underprivileged in the state could be resolved. Several papers were read at the conference including one by Professor James Kavanagh in which he pleaded for a widening of the concept of poverty to include not only bare, subsistence nutritional levels but the ordinary decencies of living including a roof, health, education and participation in decision making at the industrial or community level. He regarded these as basic human rights and stated that 'to be poor is to be helpless, not to have influence, to be a recipient of favours, to be always dependent.'[6] Perhaps the most important paper read at the conference, however, was that on 'The Extent of Poverty in Ireland' by Séamus Ó Cinnéide in which the author estimated the proportion of the population below the poverty line.[7] This line was based on income maintenance rates of payment in Ireland (the Republic and Northern Ireland) in 1971 and on this basis he estimated that at least 24 per cent of the population were living below the poverty line. The social, cultural and educational deprivation associated with poverty were described in other conference papers.[8] It was felt that the causes and effects of poverty in Ireland were not clearly understood and that there was need for further research.

Sheehan,[9] in a study carried out for the Council for Social Welfare, attempts to describe what it means to be poor and has focused on the characteristics and lifestyles of those people in Ireland who live in poor material circumstances. It was hoped, firstly, to create an awareness in the community of what living in poverty means to those who are poor and, secondly, that the data obtained could be helpful in the formulation of social policy. The study was undertaken in an urban area and a rural area and was based on interviews with recipients of home assistance and assistance from the Society of Saint Vincent de Paul. The result is a comprehensive statement of the facts of poverty, the living conditions, the weekly income, the food eaten, the whole way of life as seen by the poor themselves. It also gives a valuable insight into the backgrounds of those on the poverty line, their families and their attitudes to the church, state, social services and their own problems. The areas studied were not the most deprived in the country. There is no reason to suspect, therefore, that the findings are untypical of many areas in Ireland.

National concern for the plight of the poor led the Irish government to seek to have the Social Action Programme of the EEC expanded to include specific policies for the poorest categories of the population. Proposals for the instigation of pilot schemes to test new approaches to anti-poverty policy were put to the European Commission and these were included in the Social Action Programme submitted to the Council of Ministers in December 1973. The EEC Commission recognised that in the generally affluent Community 'there will still remain problems of chronic poverty which are unacceptable in an advanced society... The Commission believes that it can help the member states to identify the problem and methods of solution through pilot studies and experiments involving, among others, social workers, psychiatrists and vocational guidance experts.'[10] In January 1974 the Council accepted the Social Action Programme in full and in the formal resolutions, priority status was accorded to the pilot schemes project.

In May 1974, Frank Cluskey, Parliamentary Secretary to the Minister for Social Welfare, established an advisory committee, the National Committee on Pilot Schemes to Combat Poverty (NCPSCP), to initiate and co-ordinate pilot schemes to combat poverty. NCPSCP has initiated four main pilot schemes, community action research schemes, urban resource schemes, a supplementary welfare allowance project and a social service council scheme. The first three are partially funded by the EEC. Some of the projects are being carried out by NCPSCP staff while others have been contracted out to other organisations.[11] The objectives are to bring about practical intervention in areas of deprivation and to contribute to the evolution of effective long-term policies against poverty. The interim report of NCPSCP stated:

> The Committee appreciates that poverty cannot be eliminated by a small number of experimental pilot schemes. It feels that poverty in Irish Society should be recognised as largely a result of inequality and that its eventual elimination will require quite basic changes. The small programme which is being carried out by the Committee is not intended to bring about such changes. In planning the programme, however, an attempt was made to design projects which will make a very small beginning in initiating a process of social change, and which will, it is hoped, try out new approaches to tackling the problem of poverty...
> The Committee believes that what is learned from the projects by local people and by policy makers will be more important than what the projects themselves achieve during their life-time.[12]

Strategies designed to eliminate poverty will inevitably be influenced by the definition of poverty adopted. A consideration of the various strategies is beyond the scope of this book and, in any case, much has already been written on this subject.[13] Very simply, however, if poverty is defined in terms of low income then solutions to the problem could involve the improvement of levels of benefit under income maintenance schemes or the introduction of a guaranteed minimum income. Alternatively, as is sometimes suggested, it could involve integration of income maintenance and income tax systems and the introduction of a negative income tax system or variants thereof.[14] If poverty is viewed as a multi-faceted problem then no single solution will suffice; it will require a concerted attack from a number of angles. If poverty is viewed in relative terms or as basically arising from inequalities in society then its eventual elimination will require 'a redistribution of resources and power in society which implies basic changes in the social, economic and political systems'.[15] It is highly questionable, however, whether such fundamental changes can be effected in democratic countries. It should be possible at the minimum, however, to ensure that the gap in living standards between those at the bottom and those at the top does not widen further.

Social Insurance

The Department of Social Welfare provides a wide range of cash payments covering contingencies arising from permanent or temporary loss of earnings. These may be divided into three basic schemes, social insurance schemes, social assistance schemes and other schemes.

The essential difference between insurance and assistance schemes is that payments under social insurance are based in part on contributions made by employers and employees whereas payments under social assistance are financed entirely from the exchequer. For this reason the schemes are frequently referred to as contributory and non-contributory respectively. Entitlement to social insurance benefits is conditional on the claimant's having a certain number of contributions paid or credited in each contribution year; the contribution conditions vary according to the different insurance schemes. One of the basic qualifications for social assistance is that the claimant satisfies a means test.[16]

The social insurance schemes operated by the Department of Social Welfare in 1980 include unemployment benefit, disability benefit, maternity benefit, pay-related benefit, invalidity pension, contributory widow's pension, contributory orphan's allowance, deserted wife's benefit, retirement pension, contributory old age pension, death grant, treatment benefit, intermittent unemployment (wet-time) insurance and occupational injuries benefit. The present comprehensive social insurance system has been developed in a piecemeal manner over a period of some sixty-five years. For a chronological development of the major social welfare schemes see Table 2, page 24.

The first social insurance scheme was introduced in 1911 under the National Insurance Act which provided for compulsory *insurance against sickness and unemployment* for certain categories of workers. The necessary funds were derived from contributions by workers, their employers and the state and the

Table 2: Chronological development of main social welfare schemes.

Date	Insurance Schemes	Assistance Schemes	Other Schemes
1838			Poor Law
1908		Old age pension	
1911	Unemployment benefit Sickness benefit		
1920		Blind pension	
1933		Unemployment assistance	
1935	Widow's and orphans' pensions	Widow's and orphans' pensions	
1942	Wet time insurance		Cheap fuel scheme
1944			Children's allowance Cheap footwear
1947	Department of Social Welfare established		
1961	Old age pension		
1966		Smallholder's assistance	
1967	Occupational injuries		Free travel Electricity allowance
1968			Free TV licence
1970	Retirement pension Invalidity pension	Deserted wife's allowance	
1973	Deserted wife's benefit	Unmarried mother's allowance	
1974	Pay-related benefit	Single woman's allowance Prisoner's wife's allowance	
1977			Supplementary welfare allowance

scheme was administered by non-profit making 'approved societies'. By the time the Irish state was founded in 1922, therefore, the foundations of a social insurance system, however inadequate and limited in scope, had been laid. Since then the system has been greatly expanded by the introduction of new benefits to cover other sections of the population, by providing against certain contingencies, by continuing modifications to earlier schemes and by a reform of the administrative machinery.

In 1929 a *marriage benefit* was introduced for insured women; up until then a woman's insurance ceased on marriage and she was not permitted to become a voluntary contributor. State provision for the relief of widows, their children and orphans developed later than other income maintenance measures. The report of the Poor Law Commission, 1927, highlighted the inadequacy of poor relief for widows who were frequently reduced to destitution on the death of their husbands. The Widows' and Orphans' Pension Act, 1935, introduced a contributory *pension for widows and orphans* of wage earners. The Insurance (Intermittent Unemployment) Act, 1942, provided insurance (generally referred to as *wet time insurance*) against loss of income due to bad weather for manual workers in the building, civil engineering and painting trades. A *maternity allowance,* based on a woman's own insurance and payable six weeks before and six weeks after confinement, was introduced in 1953. Contributory *old age pensions* for men and women over 70 were introduced in 1961. Under the *occupational injuries insurance scheme* which came into operation in 1967, benefits are payable to insured persons who are injured in the course of their employment or who contract prescribed occupational diseases. This replaced the workman's compensation scheme which was introduced in 1897 and under which a claimant was compensated either by agreement between him and his employer or by resorting to court action. *Invalidity pension,* payable instead of disability benefit to insured persons who are permanently incapable of work, *retirement pension,* payable to an insured person from the age of 65 onwards, and a *death grant,* payable on the death of an insured person or a dependant of an insured person, were introduced in 1970. The qualifying age for contributory old age pensions was reduced for the first time in 1973 from 70 to 69 years and further reduced in 1974, 1975 and 1977 when the qualifying age became 66 years.

Two important innovations were introduced in 1974. These were the extension of compulsory insurance to all employees of insurable age (16 years and upwards) and the introduction of a limited pay-related insurance scheme. Despite the fact that in 1944, Dr Dignan, chairman of the National Health Insurance Society, had suggested the introduction of pay-related contributions and benefits it was not until thirty years later that partial pay-related contributions and pay-related benefits were introduced for some employees. Pay-related benefit is payable with disability benefit, unemployment benefit and maternity allowance and, in certain circumstances, with injury benefit under the occupational injuries scheme. This marked an important development in Irish income maintenance services; hitherto, contributions were paid at a flat rate irrespective of previous income and benefit only varied with the number of dependants. Under the new scheme which is rather complex and applies to certain categories of workers only, benefits are related to previous earnings up to a certain ceiling. When first introduced, pay-related benefit was to apply for 26 weeks, following which the recipient would go on flat rate, but it has been extended at a progressively reduced rate of benefit for a further 13 weeks on three occasions between 1975 and 1976 to a total of 65 weeks. These extensions were made because of the high level of unemployment.

While the removal of the income limit for social insurance has increased the total number insured by 10 per cent, social insurance is not universal nor are those insured covered for all benefits. By 1978 approximately 982,000 persons were covered by social insurance and of these just over 820,000 were covered for all benefits.[17] About 120,000 persons in the public service are insured only for widows' and orphans' pensions and for occupational injuries. The main group still outside the social insurance system is that of the self-employed which includes farmers and accounts for about one-quarter of the total workforce.

Contribution conditions

Up to 1974 insurance contributions were flat-rate but in that year partial pay-related contributions were introduced for some employees. The flat-rate contribution varied between different categories of employees and thus, women paid less than men and agricultural workers less than non-agricultural workers. In April 1979, however, a comprehensive income-related social insurance scheme was introduced and employees now pay a percentage of their income up to a ceiling. The ceiling was £5,500 in 1979 and this was raised to £7,000 in 1980. The standard rate in respect of employees who are eligible for all social insurance benefits is 12.95 per cent (including 0.5 per cent for redundancy and 0.45 per cent for occupational injuries) of which 9.45 per cent is paid by the employer. For civil servants, the main group with limited social insurance cover, the rate is 2.25 per cent of which 1.75 per cent is paid by the employer.[18] Under the scheme introduced in 1979 the previous distinctions between men and women and between agricultural and non-agricultural employment have been eliminated. The weekly social insurance stamp has also been abolished and contributions are now collected with income tax. The present scheme is more equitable in that contributions are related to income whereas the flat-rate system was regressive.

Recipients of unemployment benefit, maternity benefit, retirement pension, disability benefit and injury benefit, under certain conditions, can have contributions automatically credited to them while they are unable to continue in insurable employment and thus keep their insurance record up to date. While not having the same value as paid contributions, credits are nonetheless important, particularly if the minimum number of paid contributions necessary in order to qualify for benefit have been met.

In the case of 'wet time' insurance, workers and their employers make an extra contribution for a special supplementary insurance stamp which is affixed to a wet time book. The supplementary insurance stamp is a weekly contribution and there are different rates for skilled workers, unskilled workers and young workers under 18 years of age. Rates of benefit are reckoned on an hourly basis and are paid by the employer directly to the insured worker. The employer can subsequently claim a refund from the supplementary unemployment fund into which the contributions have been paid.

Coverage
Since the Department of Social Welfare was established in 1947 there has been a gradual shift in emphasis from assistance to insurance. This is due to the fact that the insurance wing has been strengthened by the introduction of new insurance schemes and by the extension in 1974 of compulsory insurance to all employees of insurable age (16 years and upwards), some of whom had been outside the scope of insurance because of their level of income. This led to an increase of 116,000 in the number insured between March 1974 and March 1975. The total number insured for selected years between 1962 and 1978 and the percentage covered for all benefits is indicated in Table 3 on page 29. Approximately 11 per cent of insured workers are covered only for widows' and orphans' pensions, deserted wife's benefit and occupational injuries benefit because of the special nature of their employment. These include civil servants, teachers and local authority officials.

One of the main gaps in coverage in the Irish social welfare system is the self-employed who are not catered for by social insurance schemes because they cannot pay social insurance contributions to cover themselves against widowhood, disability or old age.[19] Instead, the self-employed must rely on means-tested services where necessary. In 1978 the Department of Social Welfare issued a discussion paper in which the problems and prospects of devising a scheme for the self-employed were highlighted.[20] The objective in publishing the paper was to ensure that the issues involved were raised and debated and that submissions from those likely to be affected would be made before a scheme catering for the self-employed was introduced. The paper indicates the main financial and administrative problems. These include the actual number of self-employed persons, 318,000 in 1971 (over one quarter of the labour force), three-quarters of whom are engaged in farming; it is relatively easy to absorb a small number of self-employed into an existing social insurance scheme but the large number

Table 3: Total number of persons insured under social Welfare Acts and percentage insured for all benefits in March for selected years 1962-1978

Year	Number insured	% insured for all benefits
1962	712,302	89.0
1965	744,032	90.2
1968	781,343	91.4
1971	808,291	90.6
1974	853,492	89.3
1975	969,488	85.8
1978	981,681	83.5

and the diversity within the self-employed category is another matter. A particular problem to which this gives rise is the collection of contributions. This is a demanding task because the majority of farmers are not liable for income tax and some other mechanism would have to be devised for collecting contributions. Another problem is the difficulty of obtaining accurate information on the incomes of self-employed persons and this would be important under the present, income-related contribution scheme. The age-structure of the self-employed population, especially farmers, poses additional problems. In 1971 about three-quarters of farmers were aged 45 or over and if a social insurance scheme were introduced many would not have sufficient contributions paid in order to qualify for the old-age contributory pension at age 66 (approximately ten years' contributions would be necessary). Despite these and other problems, however, there are distinct advantages in including the self-employed in an insurance scheme. It would mean a more equitable distribution of the burden of income maintenance finance between all sections of the community and it could ultimately lead to a phasing out of the means-tested social assistance schemes.

In 1976 the Department of Social Welfare issued a discussion paper entitled *A National Income Related Pension Scheme.*[21] Three options were put forward in the paper for consideration, assessment and discussion. In examining the drawbacks of the present system the paper states that among the major shortcomings is the fact that there is no social insurance pensions cover for the self-employed. In regard to occupational pensions the paper indicates that there is a need for considerable improvement both in terms of the numbers of people catered for and of the levels of pension provided. Other defects in the present arrangements are that the contributory and non-contributory pensions administered by the Department of Social Welfare cannot, in most cases, preserve established living standards in retirement. The paper also refers to the absence of guaranteed protection of pension rights under occupational schemes in the event of, for example mergers or closure. The paper outlined three options as follows:

Scheme A would be a single-tier system of purely earnings-related pensions. This would provide for a guaranteed minimum pension based on existing social insurance pensions, including increases for dependants.

Scheme B would be a two-tier system in which the first tier of flat-rate pensions would be based on the existing social insurance pensions, including increases for dependants. The second tier would consist of earnings-related supplementary pensions.

Scheme C would involve a two-tier system which would provide earnings-related pensions up to a reasonably high level of earnings, leaving the higher levels to be covered by occupational pension schemes.

Social Assistance
The social assistance schemes operated by the Department of Social Welfare in 1980 include unemployment assistance, non-contributory widows' and orphans' pensions, allowance for deserted wives, allowance for prisoners' wives, allowance for

single women aged 58 and over, non-contributory old age pension and blind person's pension. In all these schemes eligibility is determined on the basis of a means test.

Development of Social Assistance
In 1908, following a period of prolonged campaigning by social reformers, statutory provision was made for non-contributory *old age pensions* for persons aged 70 years and over who were in poor circumstances. The 1908 Pension Act was criticised for providing 'a pension which was too low at an age which was too high after a means test which was too severe'.[22] While the provision restricted the classes of persons eligible for pension,[23] at least the principle of state-aided assistance for a certain category of the population had been conceded and it became the first assistance scheme, outside the Poor Law, where benefit was payable without proof of utter destitution. For a considerable time after the pension was introduced, however, the Poor Law still remained the resort of other groups not covered by social insurance. In 1920 the *blind pension* was introduced for people unable to perform any work for which eyesight was essential and who were over 50 years of age. The age limit was reduced to 30 years in 1932, to 21 years in 1948 and to 18 years in 1980.

In 1933 the *Unemployment Assistance Act* was passed. This measure was taken against a background of widespread unemployment not only in Ireland but in most developing countries. The social insurance schemes were designed to tide people over short spells of unemployment between jobs and proved totally inadequate in dealing with the problem of widespread and prolonged unemployment. The scheme introduced in 1933 covered all males whether or not they had been insured against unemployment and was the first measure to make statutory provision outside the Poor Law for the relief of the unemployed, agricultural worker. Applicants had to be capable of, available for and genuinely seeking suitable employment. Persons who wished to receive assistance had first to apply for a qualification certificate. The scheme of unemployment assistance, commonly referred to as the 'dole', is perhaps the most controversial of all income maintenance measures and is frequently the subject of popular criticism. In conjunction with the widows' and orphans' contributory scheme of 1935, a non-contributory scheme was also introduced. In this way, another group hitherto dependent on the Poor Law was statutorily provided for by state aid.

An important extension of unemployment assistance was introduced in 1966, the *smallholder's assistance scheme*. This scheme applied only to landholders in the twelve counties of the western region and was introduced because of growing criticism of unemployment assistance to farmers. It was argued that the receipt of unemployment assistance constituted a disincentive to increase farm output. Under the smallholder's assistance scheme the income of farmers was to be assessed not on the basis of actual farm income but on a notional basis of £20 per £1 land valuation. In effect, therefore, the new scheme allowed farmers to increase their farm income without fear of losing all or part of the 'dole'. The notional income of £20 per £1 land valuation remained unchanged between 1966 and 1976 with the result that each time rates of payment were increased an additional number of farmers became eligible for assistance. Farmers with relatively high valuations and high or potentially high incomes became eligible. Between 1966 and 1975 the average monthly number of claimants of assistance increased from 6,958 to 29,224. Changes in the scheme in 1976, 1977 and 1979 had the effect of reducing the number of recipients from a high point of almost 32,000 in March 1976 to approximately 22,500 in April 1979.

The lowering of the qualifying age for old age contributory pensions which commenced in 1973 also applied to non-contributory pensions and in 1974 an *allowance for an adult dependant* of a non-contributory old age pensioner became payable. During the early 1970s a number of other schemes were introduced to cater for certain groups which had hitherto been obliged to resort to home assistance (replaced by supplementary welfare allowance in 1977), the vestigial remains of the Poor Law. These included the *deserted wife's allowance* (1970), *unmarried mother's allowance* (1973), *prisoner's wife's allowance* (1974) for those women whose husbands are serving a sentence of six months or more, and an *allowance for single women* aged 58 or over (1974). The last scheme was designed to cater essentially for those women who had spent most of their lives looking after an aged parent or parents. Frequently, such women could find themselves without means or entitlement, virtually unemployable and eligible only for home assistance.

The introduction of new assistance schemes has also been accompanied by modifications to existing schemes. Up to 1978, for example, women could not qualify for unemployment assistance on the same basis as men. The restriction was imposed when unemployment assistance was first introduced in 1933, because women who were not wage-earners and not really in the labour market seeking employment, would impose an undue burden on the scheme. In other words the prevailing attitude was that, because women were unlikely to obtain employment or even to be genuinely seeking employment, they were deemed ineligible for unemployment assistance. The different treatment of men and women was highlighted in the *Report of the Commission on the Status of Women*[24] and since its publication in 1972 there have been improvements, for instance the equality of entitlement to unemployment assistance noted above.[25] The main impetus to the removal of remaining inequalities, however, has come from the EEC. In November 1978, an EEC directive on equality of treatment of men and women in matters of social security was issued. Ireland has been granted a period of six years in which to implement the directive.

Means test

Eligibility for all social assistance schemes is determined on the basis of a means test.[26] The amount of means will determine whether a person is entitled to maximum benefit, reduced benefit or is ineligible for any benefit. Means are assessed by officers of the Department of Social Welfare.

In the assessment of means a number of items are taken into account. These include cash income less certain allowances, value of investments, benefit and privilege such as board and lodgings. The last factor is only taken into account for unemployment assistance and the single woman's allowance. Board or lodgings is assessed by taking the net income of the household into account. Against this a number of allowances are made on items such as rent and the interest element of a mortgage. The assessable income is then divided by the number of adults in the household, children over 16 years being regarded as adults and those under 16 years being taken as the equivalent of half an adult. The weekly means thus derived is taken to be the means of the applicant for assistance. The means of an unemployed school leaver, for example, who applies for unemployment assistance are based on those of his parents despite the fact that he or she may not have an independent income.

In the assessment of cash income, supplementary welfare allowance payments, pensions and allowances arising from service in the War of Independence and the first £80 of other pensions or allowances under the Irish Army Pension Act, are disregarded. A portion of earnings is also disregarded in the calculation of means for certain assistance schemes such as blind pension and widow's pension. The income derived from a dwelling through letting, is also taken into account. In relation to farmers, the value of all saleable produce from the farm is taken into account; this includes livestock, poultry, crops and vegetables, and milk yields but deductions are allowed in respect of rent, veterinary surgeons' fees, feeding stuffs, labour and machinery.

Different methods are used for calculating interest from investments (such as bank deposits, stocks and shares) for various social assistance schemes. The schemes are divided into three categories as follows:

1. For unemployment assistance, smallholder's assistance and the allowance for single women, the yearly value of investments is taken to be 5 per cent of the first £400 and 10 per cent of the balance.

2. For old age and blind pensions the first £200 is excluded and the value is taken to be 5 per cent of the next £375 and 10 per cent of the balance. If the weekly value is £1 or more, a further £1 is added.

3. For widow's pension, deserted wife's allowance, prisoner's wife's allowance and the unmarried mother's allowance the first £200 is excluded plus an additional £100 for each depen-

dent child and the yearly value is taken to be 5 per cent of the balance.

The different weekly values arising from the above are best illustrated by example. If it is assumed that all applicants had £1,000 in savings in a bank deposit account then the value of this sum for applicants in (1) above would be £1.55 per week, for those in (2) it would be £2.20 per week and for those in (3) it would be £0.80 per week (£0.70 per week for an unmarried mother with one child).

For some schemes such as unemployment assistance and smallholder's assistance, maximum benefit can only be obtained by those with no means at all. For other schemes, means up to a certain amount per person per week are allowed before entitlement to maximum benefit is affected. In the case of the old age, blind and widow's pensions, deserted wife's, unmarried mother's and prisoner's wife's allowances, the applicant may have means of up to £6 per week (£12 per week for married couples applying for old age or blind pensions) and still qualify for the full pension or allowance. Claimants of the orphan's pension and the single woman's allowance can have weekly means up to £1 and qualify for maximum benefits. Means in excess of the permitted amount will lead to reduced benefits, the maximum cutting off point varying according to the different schemes.

For old age and blind pensions, a married couple may have means of up to twice the personal rate while the number of children will affect the upper limit in the case of the widow's pension, prisoner's wife's, deserted wife's and unmarried mother's allowances. Thus, in 1980 a widow with more than two children can have weekly means in excess of £34 and still qualify for some pension.

It is virtually impossible to give an overall, simplified indication of how means tests operate for social assistance schemes as the applicants' means for various schemes are treated differently. Nevertheless, an attempt is made in Table 4 on page 37 to indicate the major components in the means test.

Modifications to the means test have taken place in recent years. Between 1973 and 1975, for example, the minimum means for pensions increased from 50p to £6 and the maximum means from £5.25 to £14 (personal rate), thus allowing an additional number of persons to qualify for pensions. In 1979 some anomalies were removed, for instance the complex method of assessing investments for some schemes was largely standardised, the exceptions being unemployment assistance and single woman's allowance. Up to 1979 the value of a dwelling house was assessable as means and was calculated on the basis of the rateable valuation less ground rent or mortgage interest. In 1979, stages between rates of benefit for most assistance schemes were reduced from £1.40 to £1.30 for each £1 increase in means. In 1980 the stages were further reduced to £1.20 (see Table 4), page 37.

Despite these and other improvements,[27] however, the present system of means testing is extremely complex and it is difficult for any claimant to be familiar with it. Anomalies still exist and the case for greater rationalisation is overwhelming. In his budget speech, 1979, the then Minister for Finance, George Colley, stated: 'The Government are resolved to remove anomalies in the social welfare means test.'[28]

Other income maintenance schemes
Apart from social insurance and social assistance schemes there are a number of other schemes of an income maintenance nature administered either by the Department of Social Welfare or subject to the control of that Department. These schemes do not fall into either of the two main categories of social insurance or social assistance and while some involve cash payments others involve payment in kind. They include *children's allowance* (the only universal income maintenance scheme), *prescribed relative allowance, free travel, free electricity allowance, free television licence, the cheap fuel scheme, the footwear scheme, school meals* and *supplementary welfare allowance* (formerly home assistance).

Perhaps the most notable of these schemes is the *supplementary welfare allowance* scheme which originated in the Poor Law.[29] The Social Welfare (Supplementary Allowances) Act, 1975, reformed the home assistance scheme. This scheme consisted of payments in cash or kind made to a person who was 'unable either by his own industry or other lawful means, to provide

Table 4: Major components of means test for social assistance schemes, April 1980. (£ per week)

Assistance Scheme	Minimum means allowed before entitlement to full benefit is reduced	Maximum means allowed before entitlement to benefit is removed	Personal income from earnings disregarded
Unemployment Assistance/ Smallholders Assistance	–	17/13.7	–
Single woman's allowance	1	15	–
Old age pension (personal)	6a	23a	–
Blind pension (personal)	6a	23a	6c
Widow's pension (personal)	6	23b	–
Deserted wife's allowance (personal)	6	23b	–
Unmarried mother's allowance (1 child)	6	28b	–
Prisoner's wife's allowance (personal)	6	23b	–

^a This amount is doubled in the case of a married couple.
^b The number of children affects the maximum means, i.e. the more children the higher the maximum means.
^c An additional £4 is disregarded if the blind person is married.

Income disregarded from earnings for each child dependant (£ per week)	Assessment of investments (Yearly value) (£ per week)	Reduction in benefit for every £1 per week increase in mean (£ per week)
—	5% of first £400 and 10% of balance	1
—		1.20
2	Exclude first £200 5% of next £375, 10% of balance[d]	1.20
2		1.20
2	Exclude first £200 5% of balance [d,e]	1.20
2		1.20
2		1.20
2		1.20

[d] If the weekly value of investments if £1 or more another £1 is added.

[e] A further £100 is excluded in respect of each dependent child.

the necessaries of life for himself or his dependants', and was available to those living at home as distinct from an institution. The scheme was administered by health boards and in some cases by local authorities subject to the general direction and control of the Minister for Social Welfare.

Home assistance was the only statutory form of assistance, other than institutional assistance, provided for persons in need until the beginning of the century. The overall need for the service declined as state social insurance and assistance schemes were introduced to cover specific groups and contingencies over a number of decades. Consequently the numbers in receipt of home assistance fell from 75,443 in 1946 to 30,156 in 1975. Increasingly it became a support service of last resort, a residual service catering for those not covered at all by any of the state insurance or assistance schemes or acting as a supplement to other cash payment schemes such as old age pension or disability benefit. In practice there were no detailed regulations determining the class or classes of persons who should receive assistance, nor how means were to be assessed, nor were there any fixed or uniform scales of assistance. The philosophy underlying home assistance, the discretionary nature of allowances, the variation in allowances between areas, the characteristics of recipients and other aspects of the service have been highlighted by Ó Cinnéide.[30]

In June 1975, the Social Welfare (Supplementary Welfare Allowances) Bill was introduced in the Dáil and passed in December 1975. For all practical purposes the Act repealed the Public Assistance Act, 1939, which modified previous legislation governing the Poor Law and thus removed from social welfare legislation the last vestiges of the Poor Law. In introducing the second stage of the Bill in 1975, Frank Cluskey, Parliamentary Secretary to the Minister for Health and Social Welfare, referred to the Poor Law as 'the legal embodiment of the attitudes of the last century, harsh and unfeeling attitudes which should have no place in the society of today.'[31]

The 1975 Act grants a supplementary allowance to any person whose means fall below a certain limit. The most significant advancements are the statutory rights to an allowance and to appeal against a refusal of the allowance. The Acts previously governing the home assistance service did not confer a right to assistance and there was no appeal machinery; home assistance officers used informal guidelines in deciding how much assistance to give in particular cases but these guidelines had no legal force. The effect of the 1975 Act was to establish uniform minimum guidelines. Some categories are excluded from the allowance, full-time students, those on strike and people in full-time employment. The scheme is administered by health boards under the direction of the Minister for Social Welfare and the cost is met from local taxation and the exchequer. The supplementary welfare allowance scheme became operative on 1 July 1977.

Children's allowance is another scheme which is neither an insurance nor an assistance scheme. In fact it is the only universal income maintenance scheme in Ireland and applies to all people with dependent children irrespective of their means. Children's allowance was first introduced in Ireland in 1944, an allowance of 12½p per week being payable on the third and subsequent children under the age of 16 years. Farley states that 'the average family at that time comprised two children and the purpose, primarily economic, was to assist families where the numbers of children exceeded the average'.[32] In 1952 the system of weekly payments of allowances was replaced by monthly payments, allowances were extended to the second child and the rate of payment was increased. In 1963, allowances were extended to the first child and rates of payments again increased, the changes being designed to offset the increased cost of commodities resulting from the introduction of turnover tax in that year.

While rates of payments for social insurance and social assistance benefits are normally increased annually, rates of the children's allowance have only been increased periodically. From 1963 to 1969 there was no change in the rates of 50p (first child), 75½p (second child), £1.32½p (third and subsequent children). In 1969 rates for the second child were increased to £1.50 and to £2 for the third and subsequent children. In 1970 the third child allowance was increased to £2.25p and there was no increase again until 1973. In that year the first child allowance increased from 50p to £2, the second child allowance from £1.50 to £3 and the third and subsequent children's allowances from £2.25 to £3.75. By 1980 the rates were as follows: £4.50 (first child), £7 (second and subsequent children).

In 1974 the definition of a qualified child was extended to include those between 16 and 18 years undergoing full-time education, serving an apprenticeship or incapacitated and likely to remain so for a prolonged period. In the same year another change in the scheme was introduced when title to children's allowance was put in the mother's name instead of the father's.

It is important to note that there is also an income tax allowance for children. Between 1969 and 1974 the income tax allowance varied with income so that in effect increases in the children's allowance were offset by a reduction in income tax allowance. This meant that only families in greatest need benefited from the increases. In 1974, however, a uniform tax allowance was introduced which applied irrespective of income. The net result of the 1974 income tax simplification was that the people with the highest taxable income benefited more than people with lower taxable income while those not paying tax, that is the unemployed, did not benefit from the tax concession at all. In 1979 the income tax 'clawback' was reintroduced and was continued in 1980.

An increase in the number of qualified children together with increases in rates of payment has meant a sharp increase in total expenditure on the scheme. The number of children eligible for allowance increased from 924,292 in 1965-6 to 1,196,567 in 1978. Over the same period, total expenditure on the scheme rose from £10.2 million to £50.9 million.

The growing awareness of the existence of poverty in the community and the necessity to provide a minimum standard of living for all, especially in a period of economic entrenchment, has highlighted the need to evaluate the effectiveness of existing measures. The children's allowance scheme seems an obvious instance where expenditure might be used more effectively and Kennedy[33] calls for greater selectivity in the scheme as an immediate means of effecting a redistribution in favour of poorer families. In the government green paper *Development for Full Employment* (1978), it was suggested that an element

of selectivity in the children's allowance scheme could be introduced by treating the allowance as taxable income.[34] A number
of submissions from various organisations such as NESC,
NSSC, the Council for Social Welfare and the Irish Congress
of Trade Unions opposed such a measure. The subsequent
government white paper *Programme for National Development
1978-81* (1979) stated that since there was no indication that
treating children's allowance as taxable income would, in fact,
be regarded as an appropriate means of channelling funds to
those in greatest need, the government did not propose to
proceed with this particular suggestion.[35]

A number of other services, existing mainly for pensioners or
persons of pensionable age, are operated by the Department of
Social Welfare in conjunction with other state or state-
sponsored bodies. These include *free travel*, introduced in 1967,
on public transport and on the services of certain private bus
operators for all persons of pensionable age (66 at present),
irrespective of whether they are in receipt of a pension or not
and blind pensioners. Since its introduction in 1967, free travel
has been extended to other groups. By 1980 these included all
blind persons aged 21 years or over, blind persons aged 18 to
21 years in attendance at a special workshop or training school,
recipients of a invalidity pension or the disabled person's
maintenance allowance, and the spouses of eligible pensioners
(regardless of age) when accompanying the pensioner. The
scheme is operated in conjunction with Córas Iompair
Éireann.

A free *electricity allowance* is also available to recipients of an
old age pension, blind pension, contributory widow's pension,
invalidity or retirement pension or deserted wife's benefit and a
number of other specified groups. This service also came into
operation in 1967, is operated in conjunction with the Electricity Supply Board and the eligible person must be living alone or
with specified dependants. People entitled to a free electricity
allowance have been automatically eligible for a *free television
licence* (monochrome set only) since 1968.

The *prescribed relative allowance* was introduced in 1969 and
provides for an allowance to old age or blind pensioners receiving full-time care and attention from a prescribed relative. The

eligibility conditions attached to receipt of this allowance are particularly restrictive. Apart from the prescribed relative, for example, the pensioner must be living only with children under 18 years or persons who are mentally or physically handicapped.

A further set of services for people in need is operated by local authorities under the direction of the Department of Social Welfare. These services are financed out of local taxation, a proportion of the expenditure being recouped from the exchequer. In certain circumstances *school meals,* consisting of milk/cocoa, bread and butter, may be provided by county borough councils, urban district councils and town commissioners for children attending national schools. This service began in 1914 and in 1978 meals were provided in 370 schools, the average daily number receiving meals was 80,723 and the average cost per meal was 4.7p. In 1930 the service was extended to Gaeltacht or Irish-speaking districts and in 1978 meals were provided in 150 national schools in these areas, the average number receiving meals being 8,592 and the average cost per meal was 2.6p. In 1978 approximately 16 per cent of all national schools were providing meals and a similar proportion of pupils in such schools were benefiting. It is the headmaster who decides which pupils may be eligible for these meals.

Certain local authorities also operate a *cheap fuel scheme* for specified groups. The scheme originated in 1942 when fuel supplies were restricted owing to the war and it was to ensure that the needy people would receive fuel at relatively low cost. The scheme was confined to non-turf areas of the country and is still confined to seventeen urban areas mainly in the east and southeast. From October to April a weekly amount of 1 cwt of fuel, usually turf, could be obtained by persons covered by the scheme. Recipients of supplementary welfare allowance (formerly home assistance) obtained the allowance without payment while old age (non-contributory) pensioners, blind pensioners and widows in receipt of pensions paid a contribution of 2½p and persons on unemployment assistance with dependants paid 5p. Other families on low incomes could also receive 1 cwt fuel for 10p. This scheme came in for much criticism in recent years mainly from a group called Cold Comfort Campaign which highlighted deficiencies in the scheme. From October 1979 a more flexible scheme was introduced. Eligible persons are now issued with weekly cash vouchers (valued at £1.50 in 1979-80) which can be used to buy any kind of fuel — electricity, gas, coal or turf. The nominal contributions from eligible persons remain. The net cost of the scheme, less contributions from recipients, local administration costs and the cost of fuel to recipients of supplementary welfare allowance is recouped by the local authorities from the state. Most health boards now operate a somewhat similar fuel scheme.

Under a *cheap footwear scheme,* introduced in 1944, boots and shoes are provided free of charge to children up to the age of 16 whose parents or guardians are in receipt of supplementary welfare allowance. Footwear is obtainable at retail shops in exchange for vouchers and other necessitous persons may be eligible for the service subject to a charge. The scheme is administered by health boards and in some cases by local authorities; the state meets up to 50 per cent of expenditure. In 1978 a total of 43,536 footwear vouchers were issued as compared with 46,622 in 1961-2.

Prior to 1974, cash payments from the Department of Social Welfare ceased to be payable on the death of the recipient. Under a scheme introduced that year, however, dependants of such a person continue to receive payments for six weeks following his/her death. This allows dependants the opportunity to apply for and receive benefits to which they may be entitled in their own right and the scheme was designed to ensure against loss of income for dependants during the time lag between application for and receipt of benefits.

The Department of Health also administers a number of income maintenance schemes through the regional health boards. These include disabled person's maintenance allowance, infectious diseases maintenance allowance and a domiciliary allowance for handicapped children.

Redundancy payments
The Redundancy Payments Acts, 1967, 1969 and 1979 provide

yet another income maintenance service for those suffering loss of earnings through unemployment. Under the redundancy payments scheme administered by the Department of Labour (in conjunction with the Department of Social Welfare) and introduced in 1967, a redundant worker who satisfied certain conditions was entitled to compensation in the form of a lump-sum payment and, if he or she remained unemployed, weekly redundancy payments. The lump-sum payment was related to years of service and subject to an earnings ceiling. Similarly the amount of the weekly payments was related to the worker's income at the time of redundancy and to the length of service. The employer normally paid the lump sum and got a partial rebate from the Redundancy Fund which was financed by employers' and workers' contributions.

Following the Redundancy Payments Act, 1979, some changes were made in the redundancy payments scheme. The principal changes are that weekly redundancy payments have been abolished and workers' contributions to the Redundancy Fund have also ceased. The earnings ceiling for calculating the lump sum has also been increased from £2,500 to £5,000. There is an Employment Appeals Tribunal for aggrieved workers.[36]

Administration

Prior to the National Insurance Act, 1911, a number of societies provided schemes for sickness benefit. Following the Act, sickness and unemployment benefit schemes continued to be operated mainly by these existing societies under the general supervision of the Irish Insurance Commissioners. A statutory condition of admittance to the scheme was that a society be non-profit making. Commercial insurance companies which formed separate non-profit making branches also became engaged in the scheme. By 1933 the number of insured persons in the state was about 474,000 and these were catered for by sixty-five approved societies with membership ranging from fifty-five in a small mutual benefit society up to over 100,000 in a central society covering the whole country.[37] Societies had considerable freedom in selecting workers to be admitted to

membership and some societies were relatively more prosperous than others. The latter, by accumulating reserves,
were able to increase the statutory cash benefits while at the
other end of the scale some small societies had difficulty even in
meeting the statutory benefits. Apart from these differences
between societies, the administrative costs of the scheme were
also relatively high. The National Health Insurance Act, 1933,
made provision for the amalgamation of all societies into a
single society to be known as the National Health Insurance
Society. In 1947 the Department of Social Welfare was
established and all social insurance and assistance functions
previously performed by the Department of Local Government
and Public Health (e.g. old age pensions, widows' and orphans' pensions) and Industry and Commerce (e.g. unemployment assistance, children's allowance, wet-time insurance)
were transferred to the new department. The National Health
Insurance Society was dissolved in 1950 and its functions taken
over by the Minister for Social Welfare. The Social Welfare
Act, 1952, established a unified social insurance scheme,
replacing the separate schemes for unemployment, national
health and widows' and orphans' pensions. The net effect of
these changes was not only to simplify administrative procedure and reduce costs but also to ensure that one government
minister would be responsible for the overall direction of all
social insurance and assistance schemes.

Reference has already been made to the role of local
authorities in administering some schemes such as cheap
footwear and cheap fuel. A number of other government
departments also co-operate with the Department of Social
Welfare in administering social insurance and assistance
schemes. The Department of Posts and Telegraphs provides, at
the post offices under its control, outlets for the payment of
children's allowances, pensions and, in some cases, unemployment benefit and assistance. The Department of Justice
through the Garda Síochána also assists by certifying evidence
of unemployment for claimants who live more than six miles
from a local social welfare office. The Revenue Commissioners
provide the necessary information for calculation of the amount
of pay-related benefit due and also collect the pay-related contribution.

What has evolved over the years is, from a legislative viewpoint, a complex system of income maintenance. There are approximately sixty social welfare acts and over 350 regulations governing the administration of these acts. Many of these regulations have been replaced by later ones. The Council for Social Welfare in its *Statement on Social Policy* (1972) stated that:

The present legislation on social services is too diffuse. Not only is it divided between too many Acts of the Oireachtas (and of the Westminster Parliament) but the legislation itself is almost impossible to read .... The net result of this is that few people can understand the legislation. In order to ameliorate this situation consolidation of the Social Welfare Acts and of other relevant legislation should be undertaken.[38]

The Social Welfare (Consolidation) Bill, 1976, was designed to consolidate all previous legislation governing social welfare schemes but by 1979 the bill had not been passed. Such a composite act would benefit administrators, social workers and politicians, who sometimes find it extremely difficult to relate to the principal act of 1952 and all the subsequent updating amendments. A consolidation of the Department's regulations is also envisaged.

The services provided by the government and public agencies have been increasing in complexity as well as in quantity, in particular the schemes operated by the Department of Social Welfare. Ironically, an increase in the number of laws, regulations and schemes designed to benefit the population or sections of it, results in a more complicated system where claimants have greater difficulty in interpreting the schemes which exist for their benefit. Furthermore, those most in need of income maintenance are frequently the people who are most disadvantaged in terms of education and knowledge and thus, in gaining access to information concerning benefits available to them. In this context it should be noted that the Department of Social Welfare has improved its information services in recent years with an increase in staff at central offices and the appointment of additional information officers at various centres throughout the country. The Department now operates over twenty information offices outside Dublin. It also publishes annually a booklet entitled *Summary of Social Insurance and Assistance Services*. This is normally available shortly before increases in contributions, rates of payment or other changes become operable. An important innovation during 1976, designed to help claimants in seeking entitlements, was the simplification of terminology used in leaflets and application forms issued by the Department. Community information centres, under the aegis of the National Social Service Council, have been established in recent years, the first twenty-five being registered in July 1975. Such centres, manned by trained voluntary workers, provide information on a wide range of services and their establishment marks an important development in the provision of an essential community service. By 1978 there were seventy-three community information centres throughout the country and in the year ended May 1978 a total of 24,807 queries were dealt with, 45 per cent of these relating to services of the Department of Social Welfare.[39]

An important part of the administration of income maintenance schemes is the appeals system. This system is designed to safeguard the rights of those who apply unsuccessfully for insurance or assistance payments. A claimant who is refused payment or, in the case of the means-tested assistance schemes, feels he or she is entitled to higher rates of payment, can have the whole case reviewed by appealing against the decision. Appeals are dealt with by appeals officers and the case may be decided summarily (especially those dealing with contribution records) or orally (normally in cases involving unemployment benefit or assistance, disability benefit, occupational injuries and questions of insurability). In the period 1962-3 to 1978 the number of appeals received annually has fluctuated between 9,029 in 1963-4 and 19,554 in 1977. Approximately one-third of appeals result in a more favourable decision for the applicant[40] and Table 5 on page 49 indicates that in 1978 the three largest categories of applicants concerned (1) unemployment benefit, (2) old age and blind pensions, and (3) qualification certificates for unemployment assistance, in that order.

Table 5: Number and percentage of appeals by category, received by the Department of Social Welfare in 1978

Category	Number	%
Insurability	203	1.3
Unemployment benefit	6,096	38.3
Disability, maternity and marriage benefit	1,331	8.4
Wet time insurance	17	0.1
Widow's and orphan's pensions (contributory and non-contributory)	323	2.0
Children's allowance	83	0.5
Old age and blind pensions	4,449	28.0
Qualification certificates	2,182	13.7
Old age (care) allowance	—	—
Unemployment assistance	461	2.9
Appeals under Section 15 (a) Health Act, 1953	—	—
Old age (contributory) pension	43	0.3
Retirement pension	46	0.3
Occupational injuries benefit	410	2.6
Deserted wife's allowance	90	0.5
Social assistance allowance	33	0.2
Single women's allowance	145	0.9
Prisoner's wife's allowance	3	0.0
Total	15,915	100.0

Source: *Report of the Department of Social Welfare* 1976-78

Since annual statistics relating to appeals were first publish-ed in 1953-4 the percentage of appeals concerning old age and blind pensions has been relatively high, the range being from 43.9 per cent in 1966-7 to 18.1 per cent in 1976 (the figure fell below 30 per cent for the first time in 1975). Up to 1972 old age and blind pension appeals accounted for the largest percentage of annual appeals by category. This suggested to Kennedy, 'that there are many elderly persons living in the shadows of poverty, but who are excluded by existing schemes and the prescribed criteria used in the administration of the schemes'.[41] With the easement of the means assessable in recent years this may no longer be as valid as formerly. Furthermore, the relatively high proportion of appeals concerning old age pensions may also be related to a feature of the social welfare system which is peculiar to the old age pension alone — the pension committee. The Old Age Pension Act, 1908, provided for the establishment of pension committees in each borough and urban district with a population of 10,000 or over and in each county. Members of pension committees are appointed by the local authority. The committee's function is to consider and determine, subject to a right of appeal, all claims to a pension and all questions as to continued entitlement to a pension. The social welfare officer's assessment containing a recommendation for full, partial or no pension is forwarded to the local pension committee. Where a committee subsequently recommends a higher pension than the social welfare officer, the latter must appeal against the decision. Where the committee recommends a lower rate than the social welfare officer the claimant is informed by the clerk of the committee of his or her right to appeal within twenty-one days. This procedure inevitably contributes to the relatively high number of appeals concerning old age pensions and since no similar procedure applies to other assistance schemes it is questionable whether pension committees should continue to perform functions delegated to them at the beginning of the century.[42]

Finance

Total expenditure on income maintenance has risen sharply in recent years owing partly to the increase in scope and range of social insurance and assistance schemes. In 1965-6 the total expenditure amounted to £55.8 million, in 1968-9 to £113.7 million, in 1972-3 to £151.2 million and in 1978 to £582.1 million.

The cost of social assistance falls wholly on the exchequer and is met from general taxation. The cost of social insurance, on the other hand, falls on the social insurance fund which is financed by contributions from employers, employees and the exchequer. In recent times the exchequer contribution has begun to decline proportionately: in 1957 the exchequer grant accounted for 38.2 per cent of the social insurance fund; by 1978 this had fallen to 20 per cent while employers' and employees' contributions accounted for 53.1 per cent and 26.6 per cent respectively; income from investments and other receipts accounted for 0.3 per cent. These figures relate to insurance only. It is appreciated therefore, that the burden on the state is much greater when insurance is combined with assistance. The net effect is to increase the state's contribution dramatically.

The income of the Department of Social Welfare is derived from state funds, contributions by employers, contributions from employees, investment and other receipts and local authorities. The state's contribution to the department's income has been falling in recent years and there has been a corresponding increase in the contributions by employers and employees (see Table 6, page 52). Nevertheless, by comparison with other EEC countries, the state's share is relatively high (see Table 43, page   ). In his budget speech of 1975, Richie Ryan, Minister for Finance, stated:

> The Government have decided in principle to transfer the Exchequer contribution towards the cost of social insurance to the other contributors to the Social Insurance Fund over a period of six years or so. This will have the effect of bringing the Exchequer's overall share of income maintenance expenditure more in line with practice in other EEC countries, and of making the Social Insurance Fund more self-financing.[43]

Since the Social Welfare Act, 1952, which marked a shift from assistance to insurance services, the proportion of total expenditure devoted to assistance schemes has been falling. In 1947, assistance payments comprised 77 per cent of total income maintenance payments compared with 48.5 per cent in 1965-6 and 41.8 per cent in 1978 (Table 7, page 53). Administration, including the cost of services rendered by other government

departments, remained at around 6 per cent for several years
and has been less than 5 per cent in the past decade.

Table 6:   Percentage distribution of income of Department
             of Social Welfare by source of income for selected
             years, 1965/66-1978

Source	1965/66	1968/69	1972/73	1978[a]
Contribution by employers	14.6	19.5	19.9	30.5
Contribution by employees	13.9	15.5	17.1	14.8
Investment and other receipts	1.3	2.1	1.4	0.4
Local authorities	0.6	0.5	0.3	0.1
State	69.6	62.4	61.3	54.2
Total	100.0	100.0	100.0	100.0

[a]Provisional

Source: *Reports of Department of Social Welfare* 1963-66,
          1967-71, 1972-5 and 1976-8

In 1978 the main categories of expenditure on social insurance services were: disability benefit (23.6 per cent), old age
contributory pensions (21.2 per cent), widow's contributory
pension (17.4 per cent) and unemployment benefit (14.6 per
cent). In relation to social assistance and other schemes in the
same year the main categories were old age and blind pensions
(38.4 per cent), unemployment assistance (26 per cent) and
children's allowance (20.9 per cent).

The main categories accounting for all expenditure (both insurance and assistance) in 1978 were old age and retirement
pensions (33.8 per cent), unemployment benefit and assistance
(19.4 per cent), disability, maternity and treatment benefits
(14.3 per cent), widow's and orphan's pensions (11.2 per cent)
and children's allowance (9.1 per cent).

Rates of payment
Simply to analyse increases in benefits for various schemes over
time is meaningless because account would have to be taken of

the falling value of money and, therefore, only real increases would have any meaning. It is also possible to relate benefits to average wages in the country and compare trends in this way. But here again some difficulties arise, and questions such as what proportion of average wages should benefits constitute, arise. The question also arises was any meaningful relationship between benefits and wages worked out when benefits were introduced in the first instance. It can be stated with certainty, however, that benefits have not been officially related to wage levels nor have increases been index-related (though in recent years the government has ensured that the effects of inflation would not erode the value of welfare recipients' payments). In other words, increases have been, in the main, decided arbitrarily. It cannot be said that increases in payment have been consistently related to any specific index or indexes.

In the white paper, *A National Partnership* (1974), the government stated its belief 'that those who are dependent on social welfare payments should be cushioned against price rises and should be assured of at least an adequate maintenance of their position vis-à-vis other sections of the community'.[44] This commitment led the government to introduce increases in April and October 1975. This was the first time that welfare payments were increased twice in the one year. The 1976

Table 7: Percentage distribution of expenditure of Department of Social Welfare for selected years, 1965/66-1978

Source	1965/66	1968/69	1972/73	1978[a]
Social Insurance services	45.9	50.3	52.6	53.7
Social assistance and other services	48.5	44.8	42.8	41.8
Administration	5.6	4.9	4.6	4.5
Total	100.0	100.0		100.0

[a]Provisional

Source: *Reports of Department of Social Welfare* 1963-66, 1967-71, 1976-78

budget contained no such commitment and only provided for increases in April. Following a brief period of campaigning, mainly by the Irish Congress of Trade Unions, further increases for recipients of long-term benefits such as pensions were granted in October of that year. The budget of 1977 provided for increases in all social welfare payments in both April and October.

In its election manifesto prior to the general election of June 1977, the Fianna Fáil party declared its intention to 'maintain the living standards of social welfare recipients by regular adjustments of the level of payments at least in line with the cost of living'.[45] In his budget statement of 1978 the Minister for Finance, George Colley, stated that 'the Government are satisfied that social welfare recipients should participate in the prospective growth in the wealth of the community generally'.[46] As part of the National Understanding for Economic and Social Development agreed between government, employers and trade unions in 1979 there were increases in social welfare payments in October of that year in addition to the increases of the previous April.

The recent commitment by successive governments to at least maintain the real value of social welfare payments represents an important advance. But there still exists a need to establish the adequacy of existing levels of payments under various schemes and once realistic levels are established to relate them to some established index such as increases in the average industrial wage. In reference to old age pensions and other social welfare payments, a report of NESC stated:

> The adequacy of social welfare benefits and pensions should be assessed regularly by calculating what goods and services the pension can buy, and by surveying what goods and services are actually bought. This survey would show what the problems of living on a pension are, and whether they are best met by diet education, by rent supplementation, or by increasing the pension. The present Government policy of maintaining the real value of social welfare payments and calculating increases in benefits on an across-the-board percentage increase involves no fundamental assessment of

the basic adequacy of the benefits. Progress is at present assessed by the increase in the level of expenditure on social welfare, not on whether the benefits provide adequately for the recipients.[47]

A somewhat similar criticism was voiced by the Council for Social Welfare in its *Statement on Social Policy* (1972) which recommended that 'the principle of a guaranteed minimum income, related to the cost of living index, for each household, whatever the circumstances, ought to be accepted'.[48]

It is reasonable to expect that insurance benefits should be considerably higher than assistance benefits since the insured person contributes towards those benefits by weekly contributions. In fact the difference between them is not so great and in some cases the gap has been narrowing. An indication of the difference between the maximum personal rate for a number of assistance payments, expressed as a percentage of the personal rate for the corresponding contributory rate during March for a few selected years from 1965 to 1980, is given in Table 8 on page 56. In the case of unemployment the gap has been narrowing between the maximum personal rate and the contributory flat rate. This does not include the pay-related element introduced in 1974. If this were included the gap would be larger. In the case of both widows' and old age pensions a more gradual narrowing of the differential is discernible. In particular, the difference between the maximum personal rate for the widow's non-contributory pension and the personal rate for the contributory pension is very slight and in April 1980 the actual difference was £1.50 (£22.50 *v.* £21.00). In view of these considerations, therefore, it is questionable whether insurance contributors are now getting value for money on a purely insurance basis. Across-the-board percentage increases, initiated in 1974, have ensured that the proportionate differences between various assistance and insurance schemes have been maintained since that year.

Fraud
There is frequent popular criticism of income maintenance schemes, especially those for the unemployed. Such criticism is

Table 8:   Assistance rates (maximum personal rate) as percentage of corresponding contributory rate in March for selected years, 1965-1980

	1965	1968	1971	1974	1977	1980
Unemployment	68.2	76.5	80.0	81.7	81.9	83.0
Widow's pension	84.7	97.4	94.4	93.2	93.3	93.3
Old age pension	75.0	88.5	85.0	85.4	84.5	85.7

likely to grow during a period of high and continuing unemployment. Criticism may take various forms, for example that people are working while claiming state benefits for being officially unemployed or that levels of compensation are too high, amounting to a disincentive to seek employment.

It is possible for unemployed persons to work either part-time or full-time while receiving unemployment benefit or assistance; in this instance neither the employer nor the employee report the employment of the supposedly 'unemployed' person. The advantages to the employee are obvious while the employer also has the advantage of being able to employ relatively cheap labour and does not have to pay a social insurance contribution. The real extent of this type of fraud is not known. Where employers fail to pay insurance contributions at the proper time, civil proceedings may be instituted for the amount due. In this context an annual average of 169 cases were heard in the period 1968-78. Employers who persistently fail to pay contributions are liable for prosecution. In the period 1968-78 an annual average of 162 employers had fines imposed while the Probation of Offenders Act was applied in the case of an annual average of sixteen employers. People making false statements or concealing material facts for the purpose of receiving payment under social insurance or assistance schemes are also liable for prosecution. The most common type of fraud relates to claiming unemployment benefit or assistance (Table 9, page 57). The only other prosecutions made in the period 1968-78 were in respect of children's allowances (a total of four) and injury benefit (a total of one).

Table 9:   Number of prosecutions for offences related to social welfare benefits for selected years 1968/69 to 1978

	1968/69	1972/73	1975	1978
Insurance Schemes				
Disability benefit	13	11	4	48
Unemployment benefit	55	92	12	23
Assistance Schemes				
Children's allowance	-	1	-	—
Unemployment assistance	23	12	2	9
Total	91	116	18	80

Source: *Reports of Department of Social Welfare* 1963-66, 1967-71, 1972-75

The number of prosecutions in respect of unemployment benefit and disability benefit are seen in proper perspective when related either to the total number of persons insured for or in receipt of those benefits. The total number of persons insured for all benefits (including unemployment and disability) increased from 688,410 in 1965-6 to 832,042 in 1978. The number of recipients of disability benefit increased from 166,848 in 1968-9 to 341,846 in 1978, the annual average being 229,915. Over the same period the weekly average number of claimants for unemployment benefit was 44,584 and the weekly average number of applications for unemployment assistance was 33,251. By comparison with these figures, therefore, the number of prosecutions was minimal.

In 1976 new legislation to provide for increased penalties for offences under the social welfare code was introduced. This was introduced partly in response to public opinion concerning the real or imagined growth in the level of fraud. In introducing the Bill in the Dáil, Frank Cluskey, Parliamentary Secretary to the Minister for Health and Social Welfare, stated that there was no sudden upsurge in abuses of the various social welfare schemes though there was evidence that the incidence of failure by employers to pay contributions for their employees was on the increase.

Reference has already been made to the fact that resentment against welfare payments for the unemployed is likely to grow during a period of high and continuing unemployment. This occurred in Ireland during 1975 and 1976[49] when real or imagined abuses of certain income maintenance schemes, such as pay-related benefit and the smallholder's assistance, were singled out for special attention. Much of the criticism, however, was misguided owing to an ignorance of the operation of these schemes.

In the case of pay-related benefit it was contended that in a large number of cases the payment of such benefit resulted in the recipients' having larger incomes when unemployed or ill than when working.[50] There was no ground, however, for sustaining the argument that invariably, unemployment resulted in an improved financial position.[51] The Redundancy Payments (Weekly Payments) Order, 1976, provided that an unemployed person's income from all available benefits and concessions would not exceed 85 per cent of net (or after tax) income or £50, whichever is the lesser, prior to unemployment. Another change made in 1976 was that an unemployed person's benefit would be counted in full in the calculation of differential rent if he lived in a rented local authority dwelling. Previously only half such benefit was taken into account. In 1979, for recipients of unemployment benefit who were wholly unemployed, the combined total of flat-rate benefit, pay-related benefit and income tax rebate could not exceed 85 per cent of the average weekly earnings after deduction of income tax and social insurance contribution. The Finance Act, 1979, also provided for the taxation of short-term social welfare benefits such as unemployment or disability benefit but this measure was not introduced.

Criticism of the smallholder's assistance also led to changes in that scheme in 1976, 1977 and 1979. As already mentioned the smallholder's scheme is a unique assistance scheme in that entitlement to benefit is based on a notional income rather than an assessment of actual income. The notional income of £20 per £1 land valuation remained unchanged between 1966 (the year the scheme was introduced) and 1976 while rates of payment were increased annually and on two occasions in 1975. The combined result was that each year an additional number of farmers became eligible for assistance and the average annual number of claimants increased from 6,958 in 1966 to 29,224 in 1975. Over the same period expenditure on the scheme increased from less than £1 million to almost £16 million.[52]

It is sometimes contended that welfare payments to the unemployed have a demoralising effect, destroy initiative and make recipients unwilling to work. Unfortunately no research has been undertaken in Ireland which would justify this belief[53] and it would constitute a very difficult research task. Of interest in this context, however, are the reports of the Department of Social Welfare which indicate the incidence of people who, while claiming disability benefit, are capable of work. Of the number of cases referred to medical referees for a second medical opinion each year in the period 1968-78, proportions varying from 13.1 per cent to 27.9 per cent of those examined were reported as being capable of work.[54]

While allegations of abuse of income maintenance schemes almost invariably centre on schemes for the unemployed and while the reported incidence of fraud tends to justify the selection of these schemes for special attention, it is well to bear in mind that the largest single category of beneficiaries are in fact, old age pensioners and that in 1975 there were more people dependent on home assistance than there were in receipt of pay-related benefits. A certain amount of abuse of the income maintenance system is to be expected as the complete eradication of abuse would involve an unacceptably high level of vigilance on the part of administrators thus diverting resources from their primary function, i.e. the relief of need in the community. In this context it should be noted that a feature of the income maintenance system is the small proportion of expenditure devoted to administration.

Chapter 3

Housing

why Housing policy at all

Introduction

The question is sometimes raised, though infrequently in Ireland, why should it be the responsibility of government to intervene in the area of housing; in other words why not leave the provision of housing to market forces, to the influences of supply and demand? In the first instance certain housing conditions such as homelessness, over-crowding and slums are aspects of poverty. Most democratic governments have as their basic social objective the elimination of poverty. Secondly, housing is but one element in the total physical environment and thus not only is the individual or family affected by housing but the entire community. From a national viewpoint it is therefore necessary to ensure that certain basic standards in regard to design and planning are met.

The market system is the main mechanism for allocating housing in Ireland. In 1978, for example, three-quarters of dwellings built were in the private sector, the remainder being supplied by local authorities. Yet even in the private sector the state intervenes by the provision of subsidies whether direct or indirect. In the white paper, *Housing in the Seventies,* it is stated that: 'The basic objective of Government is to ensure that, as far as the resources of the economy permit every family can obtain a house of good standard at a price or rent they can afford.'[1] In order to meet this objective government intervention is necessary because of shortcomings in the market system. The major shortcomings relate to income and access to housing. Because housing is an expensive commodity very few people are in a position to purchase a dwelling outright. Instead they borrow money from lending agencies and incur payments over a considerable period of time. The state intervenes in this instance by, for example, the provision of

60

grants and income tax relief on the interest element of mortgages. Some people, however, are unable because of low incomes to meet the requirements for obtaining loans and in such cases the state also intervenes to provide subsidised dwellings, through local authorities, mainly for renting but also for purchase.

State intervention in various forms has been the accepted policy of successive governments in Ireland and owner-occupation is widely encouraged. What is important, however, is whether state subsidies operate in such a way as to equalise opportunities in regard to housing to the greatest extent possible between all sectors of the community. Questions must be raised as to whether the system operates in such a way as to give occupiers in some sectors an unfair advantage over others or whether state resources could be distributed more equitably to ensure that 'every family can obtain a house of good standard'. These issues are considered towards the end of this chapter.

Administration

The Department of the Environment (formerly the Department of Local Government), established in 1924, is the central authority responsible for national housing policy. It exercises a general supervision over the social, financial and technical aspects of local authority and private housing and is responsible for the distribution of most of the capital and subsidies for housing provided by the state. The Department also promotes legislation on housing, co-ordinates the activities of local authorities and is responsible for legislation on building standards.

The National Building Agency, established in 1960, is a state agency which operates under the general control of the Department of the Environment and has as its primary function the building of houses for new or expanding industries. The Agency is also responsible for the provision, on behalf of local authorities, of approximately one-third of the national public housing output.

There are eighty-seven local authorities engaged in the provision of public housing — four county borough councils, twenty-seven county councils[2] and fifty-six urban district councils.

A number of other government departments are concerned with housing, though this is only a minor element of their work. These include:

1. Roinn na Gaeltachta which pays grants for the building and improvement of dwellings in Gaeltacht areas.

2. The Department of Industry, Commerce and Tourism which pays grants for the provision of houses by the Shannon Free Airport Development Company for persons working on the industrial estate at Shannon.

3. The Department of Agriculture which engages in housing work in connection with land division and resettlement and provides loans for farmers towards house purchase and improvement.

4. The Department of Justice also has certain functions in regard to rent-control and ground rents.

Major trends in housing output

In this section the major trends in housing development are divided into two periods, prior to 1921 and 1921 to the present.[3]

Housing prior to 1921

Urban Housing. The first series of legislative enactments dealing with housing was passed in the 1850s and 1860s. While these and other Acts passed in the 1870s provided a strong legislative basis for a housing drive, little was accomplished under these Acts except in Dublin city. The Housing of the Working Classes Act, 1890, was a more comprehensive measure which repealed practically all the preceding Acts and made a serious effort to deal with the problems of urban housing and slum clearance. The next important piece of legislation dealing with urban housing was the Housing of the Working Classes (Ireland) Act, 1908. This Act set up the first subsidy system for urban housing. The Irish Housing Fund was established, a sum of £180,000 invested and the income directed towards the cost of dwellings erected after the 1908 Act. By 1919 only 8,700 houses had been provided under the Housing of the Working Classes Act.

In 1921 the problem of urban housing still remained unsolved. A survey of housing needs in municipal areas carried out in 1919 estimated that 46,416 houses were required, one-third of them to replace inhabited houses unfit and incapable of being made fit for human habitation.

Rural Housing. The first attempts to improve rural housing in Ireland were aimed at getting landlords to take the initiative in building cottages for their own tenants. The Dwellings for Labouring Classes (Ireland) Act, 1860, enabled landlords to obtain loans for the provision of cottages.

The Census of 1881 indicated that there were 215,000 cottiers and the majority of dwellings in which they lived were single-room cabins with mud walls and thatched roofs. Under the Labourers (Ireland) Act, 1883, housing operations were to be carried out locally by the rural sanitary authorities, the Boards of Guardians, under the general supervision of the Local Government Board for Ireland. The provision of cottages was no longer left to the initiative of individual landlords or famers. By 1921 approximately 48,000 cottages had been erected.

Private Housing. The demand for private dwellings was stimulated by the Small Dwellings Acquisition Act, 1899, which enabled local authorities to advance loans for the purchase of existing houses. Another source providing finance for house purchase was the building societies and the main Act governing these societies was passed in 1874. Banks and insurance companies also provided finance in this period. The total number of owner-occupiers at the time, however, was small and most of the houses were purchased by investors and let to tenants. A significant development was the introduction, under the Housing Act, 1919, of a scheme of grants for persons who constructed houses in accordance with prescribed conditions. The political conditions of the time prevented the extensive use of the scheme. Nevertheless, the scheme marks one of the first steps in direct state aid to the house purchaser, a policy which has since been sustained and which accounts, in part, for the relatively high proportion of owner occupied dwellings in Ireland at present.

Housing in the 1920s

The first real attempt to provide houses on a large scale was made by the Free State government which initiated what is referred to as the 'Million Pound Scheme'. Under this scheme local authorities were required to provide £125,000 from rates (local taxation) and raise a further sum of £375,000 by way of short-term loans from banks, giving a total of £½ million. This was matched by £1 million in state aid and enabled 2,000 houses to be built at the average total cost of £750 per house.

Under the Housing Act, 1924, grants were again made available to people constructing their own dwellings. This Act also empowered local authorities to supplement the state grants by further grants or loans and also free or cheap sites for development work and provided for the partial remission of rates over nineteen years on grant-aided houses. Reconstruction grants were also made available under the 1924 Act.

The housing problem of urban areas, however, remained to be tackled in earnest. A survey carried out by urban authorities in 1929 indicated that almost 44,000 houses were needed and highlighted the need for slum clearance.

Housing in the 1930s

The main drive against slums was begun in the 1930s. The Housing Acts, 1931 and 1932, were particularly important, giving effect to the recommendations of previous commissions of enquiry on slum clearance and compulsory acquisition of land and providing greater financial assistance to local authorities for re-housing displaced families.

The output of housing rose steadily during the 1930s reaching a peak of 17,000 in the year ended 31 March 1939. Between 1932 and 1942 a total of 82,000 dwellings were built. During the same period over 11,000 condemned houses were demolished by local authorities as well as an unknown number by private people. This period was one of the most productive ever in the building of Corporation houses in Dublin. The estates of the south-west, centring on Crumlin, which constitute the largest concentration of municipal housing in Dublin, were built at this time.

Housing in the post-war period
During the wartime period, the rate of new housing sank to a low level and only 1,300 dwellings were built in 1946.

In 1948 a white paper was issued containing an estimate of the number of houses needed. Despite pre-war accomplishments it was estimated that 61,000 dwellings were required, 44,500 in urban areas and the remainder in rural areas. The major problem was in Dublin where an estimated 23,500 dwellings (approximately 40 per cent of the national need) were required.

The Housing (Amendment) Acts, 1948 to 1952, provided among other things for more generous grants for private dwellings particularly for people building dwellings for their own occupation, for higher loans to house purchasers and for the strengthening of local authority powers to deal with special housing problems. These measures had a stimulating effect on the housing programme and in the early 1950s an annual average of 14,500 dwellings were erected.

By the late 1950s, however, a downward trend was again evident. This was partly due to the belief (later found to be erroneous) that sufficient progress had been made with the satisfaction of housing needs throughout the country. It was also due to cutbacks in local authority capital expenditure on housing. In 1959 the report, *Economic Development,* stated:

> Private housing needs have been largely met, while local authority housing programmes have already been completed in a number of areas and are expected to be completed in all areas outside Dublin within three or four years.[4]

Between 1956 and 1958 capital expenditure on housing by public authorities was halved from £14.3 million to £7.6 million[5]. In the late 1950s the population of the Republic was falling by about 10,000 per annum, emigration was running at over 40,000 annually and some local authority housing estates were reporting vacancies. There was a dramatic rise in the number of vacancies in Dublin Corporation estates from 1954 onwards which reached a peak of well over 1,200 per annum between 1958 and 1961 and rapidly declined again later in the 1960s. Output of local authority housing in Dublin declined from a high point of 2,600 in 1951 to 279 in 1961.

In the 1960s economic growth was accelerated and led to an upsurge in social spending. Furthermore, significant demographic changes occurred giving rise to an increased demand for housing particularly in urban areas.

In 1964 a white paper, *Housing: Progress and Prospects,* estimated that 50,000 dwellings were required to cater for existing needs and 8,000 for future needs. In the following year Dublin Corporation initiated the Ballymun scheme, one of the largest single housing projects in Europe at the time. The construction of over 3,000 dwellings was a formidable achievement and undoubtedly helped to alleviate housing needs in the Dublin area.

In 1969 the government issued another white paper, *Housing in the Seventies,* which estimated that the number of dwellings required to cater for accumulated needs was 59,000 while the annual prospective need was 9,000 for the period 1966-71 and 11,500 for the mid 1970s.

During the 1960s output of housing increased steadily and in the early 1970s increased dramatically, reaching a record peak of almost 27,000 in 1975. The number of dwellings completed in each of the nine most recent calendar years is set out in Table 10 on page 66.

Table 10: Number of dwellings completed annually, 1971-1979

Year	Number	Year	Number
1971	15,380	1975	26,892
1972	21,572	1976	24,000
1973	24,660	1977	24,548
1974	26,256	1978	25,444
		1979	26,544

Future housing requirements

The increase in population experienced by the Republic since the 1960s is expected to continue into the 1980s and has implications for future housing requirements. A report by the National Economic and Social Council (NESC) in 1976 estimated that between 314,000 and 372,000 new dwellings need to be built in the fifteen years 1971 to 1986 if adequate housing is to be provided for the projected population at the latter date.[6] These housing projections take account not only of population growth over the period but also of the need to eliminate overcrowding and to replace existing dwellings which are unfit for use.

Factors in planning housing needs

A consideration of the principal factors affecting housing needs is a matter of concern for each local authority and for the state in general. The Housing Act, 1966, makes it the duty of every housing authority to ascertain the extent of the need for dwellings in its area at least once every five years and to assess the adequacy of the supply and prospective demand for housing. In general, two kinds of housing needs may be recognised, accumulated or existing needs and prospective needs.

Accumulated need refers to the existing replacement requirements arising from the necessity: (1) to replace unfit dwellings, (2) to relieve overcrowding, and (3) to provide housing for certain categories of people on medical, compassionate or other similar grounds.

An estimate of unfit dwellings may be derived by taking age of dwellings into account. The Census of Population of 1971 indicated that 315,800 dwellings or 45 per cent of the national housing stock were built prior to 1919. Since statistical information is not available on the materials used in the construction of these dwellings and since it is not possible to generalise on the standard of maintenance, only detailed local surveys can identify the real number of unfit dwellings.

Overcrowding arises when families have to live involuntarily with other families or when the ratio of people per room is high. In the absence of local surveys it may be difficult to distinguish between voluntary and involuntary sharing in multi-family households, the number of which was 25,200 in 1971. Two or more persons per room is normally taken to be a measure of overcrowding. In 1971 the number of overcrowded households was 54,400 or 7.5 per cent of the national housing stock. Almost one-fifth of these contained multi-family households.

Prospective need refers to future need which can arise from (1) replacements, (2) increase in households, or (3) internal migration.

Apart from existing replacement requirements owing to unfitness it is inevitable that other dwellings will either become unfit for habitation with the passage of time or will fall out of use or be lost through obsolescence, conversion, demolition or other factors.

One of the more important factors affecting housing needs is demographic change and, in particular, changes in the household-forming age groups. During the 1960s there were significant increases in the young adult age groups (20- 29) and in the number of married couples. Migration within a country is a source of demand for housing though it may overlap with other housing needs. The pattern in Ireland, as indeed in most countries, has been one of a proportionate increase in urban and decline in rural population. The concentration of industrial development and other employment opportunities in relatively large urban centres has obvious implications for housing needs.

Apart from the demand for housing occasioned by the foregoing factors there may be a certain saving in housing requirements owing to vacancies and the essential repairs scheme. Under this latter scheme, introduced in 1962, which applies only in rural areas, a certain number of substandard dwellings which would normally have to be replaced may be repaired by local authorities. This scheme is particularly suitable for elderly persons living in remote rural areas where a continuing need for new dwellings is not anticipated following the death of the occupiers.

A certain amount of duplication may occur in household numbers and those arising from migration. Different emphasis may be required over time owing to changes in particular needs and housing policy must be responsive to these changes at national and local level. In addition to the demand factors, other considerations such as capital available for housing investment will have a considerable influence on housing output.

For local authorities a primary consideration in planning dwellings is the availability and price of building land. Local authorities must compete with commercial interests in their quest for land and this has led to inflated prices particularly in the large urban centres. In 1971 the government established a committee to examine the means by which the price of building land could be controlled. The committee's report was published in 1974 and is usually referred to as the Kenny Report, after the committee chairman, Justice J. Kenny.[7] The majority recommendation, which the government then accepted in principle but which demands comprehensive legislation, was that certain areas would be designated as areas of potential building land. A new jurisdiction would be conferred on the High Court to designate areas where, in the opinion of the Court, the land should be used for the next ten years for the purpose of providing sites for houses or factories. The local authority would have the power to acquire all or any part of the land within the area for the ten years after its being so designated, at its existing use value plus one quarter and compensation for reasonable costs of removal, but without regard to its development potential. The report is still under consideration by the government.

Local authority housing
Local authorities provide some dwellings for sale but are mainly concerned with renting to people living in unfit and overcrowded conditions, to people whose income does not allow them to provide adequate accommodation for themselves, and for special categories such as the aged, disabled persons and newly-weds. The types of dwellings provided include houses, flats, demountable dwellings and special dwellings for the elderly and disabled.

In the seven-year period 1971-78 a total of 51,972 local authority dwellings has been completed, the annual output ranging from 4,789 in 1971 to 8,794 in 1975. As a proportion of total dwellings completed, the local authority output has also fluctuated, the range being from 25 per cent in 1973 to 33 per cent in 1975.

Financing of local authority housing
The capital costs of local authority housing is met by borrowing, usually from the state. Since economic rents would prove prohibitive to many tenants the state and local authorities give subsidies in order to reduce rents to a level that tenants can afford. Subsidy is paid by the state towards the current costs of local authority dwellings to enable local authorities to let their dwellings at reasonable rents without undue loss. The subsidy takes the form of a contribution towards the loan charges payable by the authorities on the capital borrowed by them for the construction of their dwellings. Where necessary a further contribution is made by the local authority from rates (local taxation) to bridge the gap between what the tenant can afford and the total current cost of the dwelling. Since 1973 the rates contribution to housing has been transferred to the central exchequer on a phased basis and by 1977 it ceased to be an element of local taxation.

In 1976, the latest year for which provisional statistics are available, approximately one-third of the total current outgoings of local authorities was met by tenants and the sale of dwellings and two-thirds was met by subsidies from central and local taxation (Table 11, page 71).

Rents
Local authority dwellings are let either at *fixed rents* or *differential rents*. The letting of dwellings at fixed rents was a feature of local authority housing in the past. In general, the tenant's capacity to pay was not considered, irrespective of changes in household income. In 1934 income-related rents were introduced in Cork city, the rent being based on one-sixth of family income less certain deductions and subject to review with changes in that income. Since 1967, however, all new local authority dwellings are let on differential or income-related schemes. This ensures that the subsidies are distributed

Table 11: Local authority housing current receipts and expenditure 1976[a]

Receipts	£ million	Expenditure	£ million
Rents	8.8	Loan charges	29.76
Net proceeds of sales	6.4	Maintenance	9.92
		Other	7.57
Subsidies			
from State	29.6		
from rates	1.5		
Miscellaneous	.95		
Totals	47.25		47.25

[a] Provisional

Source: *Quarterly Bulletin of Housing Statistics* Stationery Office, Dublin

equitably on the basis of need and that no one is refused housing because of inability to pay rent. Under the differential rent system, rent increases with household income and if income is reduced rent is also reduced.

For each type of local authority dwelling minimum and maximum rents are fixed and within these limits the tenant pays a proportion of his income in basic rent. The minimum rent may range from 12½p to 50p per week. The maximum rent is based on the full cost of providing and maintaining the dwelling together with administration costs.

Prior to 1973 differential rent schemes varied from one local authority to another, principally in regard to allowances deductable from household income. In 1973, however, following a prolonged strike by the National Association of Tenants Organisations, a new national differential rent scheme was introduced. In the assessment of income for rent purposes the total household income (less certain allowances) is taken into account and not merely the income of the head of the household. A rather complex method is used in calculating assessable income which is then divided by a certain fraction in order to arrive at the tenant's rent. The lower the assessable income the lower the fraction, for instance where the assessable income is less than £19 the fraction is one-twelfth and where assessable income is over £39 the fraction is one-seventh. A revised scheme was introduced in 1978 and another in 1979. Full details of the 1979 differential scheme are contained in an Appendix on page 91.

Table 12: Number and proportion of local authority dwellings let on fixed and differential rents for selected years 1966/67 to 1978.

Year	Fixed Rents	Differential Rents	Total
1966/67	57,929	49,642	107,571
%	53.9	46.1	100.0
1971/72	35,108	71,642	106,750
%	32.8	67.2	100.0
1973/74	31,856	77,357	108,943
%	29.0	71.0	100.0
1978	13.984	87,212	101,196
%	13.8	86.2	100.0

Source: *Quarterly Bulletin of Housing Statistics,* Stationery Office, Dublin.

In 1978 over four-fifths (86.2 per cent) of local authority dwellings were let on differential rents. This proportion has increased steadily over the past decade as Table 12 on page 72 indicates. While the average weekly rents (exclusive of rates) of local authority dwellings has been increasing in recent years (see Table 13, page 73) the level of these rents is still low in relation to average earnings and to the value of accommodation as measured either by the resale value or the cost of providing

Table 13: Rents of local authority dwellings 1971/72 to 1978

Financial Year	Estimated number of rented dwellings at mid-year	Annual rental income (£m)	Average weekly rent (£)
1971/72	106,000	6.27	1.14
1972/73	106,000	7.89	1.43
1973/74	107,000	8.46	1.52
1974 (April - December)	108,000	6.32	1.50
1975	105,000	8.67	1.59
1976	101,000	9.86	1.88
1977	99,000	12.26	2.39
1978	100,000	13.88	2.67

Source: *Quarterly Bulletin of Housing Statistics,* Stationery Office, Dublin.

it. This low level, £2.67 in 1978, is mainly due to the sizeable proportion of dwellings still let on fixed rents and those let initially to persons with low incomes at uneconomic rents which have not since been changed. If fixed rents were excluded then average rents would be considerably higher.

Purchase schemes
Most local authorities operate purchase schemes for tenants. The terms of most purchase schemes (which are subject to the sanction of the Department of the Environment) permit a discount from the market or replacement value of a house. In urban areas the discount is approximately 2 per cent per annum for each year after the fifth year of occupation up to a maximum of 30 per cent. In rural areas discount figures are 3 per cent and 45 per cent respectively. In the four-year period 1975-9 over 29,000 local authority dwellings were sold. It has been pointed out in a NESC report, however, that the sale of

local authority dwellings reduces the number of dwellings available for meeting the principal aims of local authority housing, which are to provide dwellings for persons living in unfit and overcrowded conditions and those unable to provide adequate accommodation for themselves. 'There is thus a danger', according to the report, 'that, if sales continue at this rate, the local authorities will be left managing the most unattractive portion of the dwelling stock'.[8] It is estimated that to date over 120,000 local authority dwellings have been sold, leased or vested.

Low-rise Mortgage Scheme
In 1976 a low-rise mortgage scheme was introduced. The aim of the scheme is to assist local authority tenants or persons on local authority housing lists to purchase reasonably priced private houses. Under the scheme, thirty-year loans of up to 98 per cent of the cost of a house purchased by eligible applicants, subject to a maximum loan of £12,000 (in 1980) are advanced at the interest rates currently applicable to local authority house purchase loans. Mortgage repayments are subsidised on a diminishing scale over a nine-year period by the exchequer, and by local authorities to a similar amount at their discretion.[9] In 1977-9 the number of loans provided for the purchase of non-local authority dwellings was 1,728.

Priority in letting of dwellings
A scheme of priority in the letting of dwellings operates so that families or persons most in need of housing receive prompt attention. Overall priority is given to:
1.   Families living in dangerous premises.
2.   Families which become homeless through emergency situations such as fire or flood.
3.   Families in which a member or members suffer from infectious tuberculosis and live in overcrowded conditions.
4.   Families evicted through no fault of their own.
5.   Families displaced from areas required for redevelopment.
   Some local authorities may operate a points system in order to establish priority. In practice, this would only occur in the

large urban areas.[10] The highest number of points are generally allocated to families living in unfit or overcrowded dwellings. The report of the chief medical officer is also important and may determine which of two families, in otherwise similar circumstances, receives priority on medical grounds. Apart from these instances one-tenth of new dwellings may be allocated to elderly persons and some local authorities allot a certain number to newly married couples.

Over the past decade approximately half of new dwellings let by local authorities annually were to families living in overcrowded conditions (see Table 14, page 76). In September 1977, there were 25,575 applicants on the waiting list for local authority dwellings and one-third of these were in the Dublin area (Dublin County, Dublin County Borough and Dun Laoghaire Borough).[11] The following is a breakdown of the applicants by number of people in the family: one and two people, 33 per cent; three and four people, 49 per cent; five and six people, 13 per cent; seven or more people, 5 per cent.

National Building Agency

In the context of local authority housing it is appropriate to refer to the role of the National Building Agency (NBA) which was established in 1960 as a private company under the Companies Act. Its main objectives are (1) to ensure that appropriate housing is available to personnel recruited in centres for industrial development and (2) to act as agent for departments of state in meeting the housing needs of employees.

In 1965 its functions were extended to enable it to engage in such activities as may be assigned to it by the Minister for Local Government (now Minister for the Environment). At the request of the Minister the NBA undertakes the provision of dwellings for local authorities on an agency basis.

The building activities of the NBA range from the construction of individual dwellings for persons employed in industry, through special schemes for the housing of Garda and Army personnel, co-operative schemes for private groups and special projects for industrial workers generally, to major schemes for local authorities.

Table 14: Number and proportion of lettings of new local
authority dwellings by category of person/family
in selected years 1966/67 to 1978.

Dwellings let to	Year			
	1966/67	1971/72	1973/74	1978
Families living in	1,325	1,606	1,754	1,724
unfit dwellings	(36.3)	(32.9)	(30.0)	(29.1)
Families living in overcrowded conditions	1,821 (49.9)	2,786 (57.0)	3,000 (51.2)	2,936 (49.6)
Elderly persons	8 (0.3)	218 (4.5)	125 (2.1)	398 (6.7)
Other families in need of housing	492 (13.5)	275 (5.6)	981 (16.7)	864 (14.6)
Total	3,646 (100.0)	4,885 (100.0)	5,860 (100.0)	5,920 (100.0)

Source: *Quarterly Bulletin of Housing Statistics,* Stationery
Office, Dublin.

In the case of houses provided for industrial workers the
NBA is empowered to advance loans out of money lent by the
exchequer. Such advances are reckoned as part of the state's
capital allocation for housing. At the end of 1977 there were
1,240 Agency loans outstanding, representing a capital sum of
£6,288 million. Between 1961 and 1978 the NBA provided
21,448 dwellings, the breakdown being shown in Table 15 on
page 77.

Private Housing
By comparison with other European countries Ireland has a
relatively high proportion of owner-occupiers. The most recent
comparative figures refer to 1970 and indicate that of the nine

Table 15: Dwellings provided by the National Building Agency, 1961-1978

	Number	%
Local authority housing	18,093	84.4
Industrial housing	2,195	10.2
Private housing	615	2.9
Housing for state employees	545	2.5
Total	21,448	100.0

Source: *National Building Agency,* Annual Report and Accounts, 1978

members of the European Economic Community, Ireland with 69 per cent had the highest proportion of owner-occupied dwellings followed by Belgium with 55 per cent, while Germany had the lowest proportion, 34 per cent.[12] This figure includes former local authority tenants who have purchased or are in the process of purchasing their dwellings. The relative importance of owner-occupation in Ireland is due to a number of factors. Chief among these are historical and cultural factors and the schemes of state aid to the owner-occupier.

The Irish economy is predominantly agrarian in nature with approximately one-quarter of the labour force engaged in agriculture, the highest proportion in Europe, and Irish farmers are owners of their land rather than tenants. This situation is the result of the land agitation and consequent Land Acts of the later nineteenth century and early decades of the present century and in itself accounts for a considerable proportion of owner-occupation in Ireland. But it is the legacy of the land reform measures which has influenced the pattern of owner-occupation. Pfretzschner summed it up as follows:

The typical Irishman prefers not to live in a flat but in a house... and if the opportunity can be had, he prefers the option of owning the land to renting it. In this history-minded country, the past centuries of eviction and forced emigration have left their mark on the housing system. Furthermore Ireland did not experience any large-scale industrialisation with its consequent rapid growth of urban areas where rented accommodation had to be provided for workers. The absence of the excessive problems of urbanisation allied with the predominantly rural-based population have been important influences on the housing system, making ownership rather than tenancy the norm.[13]

The state has also contributed to Ireland's relatively high proportion of owner-occupiers by a system of financial aid, part of which originated in the latter part of the nineteenth century. This system includes grants, loans provided by local authorities, rates remission (until 1978) and income tax relief on the interest element of mortgages.

Grants
Since the introduction of grants for the provision of new dwellings in 1919 the grant levels have been increased on several occasions and the system has been altered to answer the needs of particular sections of the community. In July 1977 all previous grant schemes (state and local authority) were rescinded and a new £1,000 grant for first-time owner-occupiers of new houses was introduced. The grant is payable subject to certain conditions, e.g. the dwelling must be built to a standard laid down by the Department of the Environment, and where the dwelling is being purchased the builder must obtain a certificate of reasonable value from the Department.[14]

The provision of grants for new dwellings has undoubtedly helped people to meet the cost of buying or providing a house and has also provided a stimulus to the production of houses. In recent years, however, grant levels have not been raised sufficiently to keep pace with inflation and hence their significance has diminished considerably. For example, between the quarter July-September 1977, when the £1,000 grant was introduced, and July-September 1979, the average price of new houses for which all lending agencies gave loans increased by 56 per cent (from £15,307 to £23,816), while the grant itself remained unchanged. On the merit side, however, it may be said that the linking of the grant system to reasonable standards of construction has ensured that grant-aided houses do not fall below a minimum structural standard. Since the inception of the grant system in 1919 grants have been paid on 285,000 private houses, 50 per cent of the present privately-built, housing stock.[15]

Grants have also been provided by the state for the reconstruction and improvement of existing houses. Of the total number of housing units in the state in 1971, 45 per cent were at least fifty years old. It is reasonable to conclude that practically all dwellings of that age are defective or fall below current minimum standards in one or more respects. Under a scheme introduced in December 1977, the maximum grant for reconstruction work was £600 or two-thirds of the estimated cost. This scheme of home improvement grants was terminated in January 1980 but grants are still available for handicapped persons and local authority loans for home improvement are also available subject to a means test.[16]

Grants are also available for the installation of private water and sewerage facilities, the grants being two-thirds of the estimated cost up to a maximum of £200 and £150 respectively. In the case of group schemes the maximum grants are £300 for water supply and £250 for sewerage installation.

The essential repairs scheme, already referred to, is of particular importance in rural areas. Between 1967 and 1975 a total of 6,331 essential repair grants were paid, 60 per cent being in the province of Connacht.[17] Between 1971 and 1979 inclusive, the number of improvement grants paid was 120,205 and the number of water and/or sewerage grants paid was 122,347.

Loans
Apart from commercial organisations local authorities also provide house purchase loans but at fixed rates of interest. Loans are subject to an income limit and in the case of farmers a valuation limit of £44. Between 1973 and 1977 the income limit was £2,350 per annum and the maximum loan £4,500. Despite inflationary trends these limits were not revised during

Table 16: Number and value of local authority housing loans
paid, 1972-1979.

Year	Number	Value (£000s)
1972	3,781	11,007
1973	5,152	16,288
1974	9,636	38,682
1975	10,001	42,058
1976	6,732	25,327
1977[a]	5,021	18,767
1978[a]	5,697	32,413
1979[a]	6,943	36,443

[a] Includes loans prescribed under low-rise mortgage scheme.

Source: *Quarterly Bulletin of Housing Statistics,* Stationery
Office, Dublin.

that period. This made it increasingly difficult for low-income
earners to obtain houses. The number and value of local
authority loans fell sharply after 1976 as Table 16 on page 80
indicates. In 1977 new income and loan limits were introduced,
the income limit being raised to £3,500 and the loan limit to
£7,000. In 1978 the loan limit was raised to £9,000 and the
income limit to £4,000. In 1980 the limits were raised to
£12,000 and £5,500 respectively.

Rates Remission
Up to 1978 remission of rates over a nine-year period was
available on new grant-aided dwellings and other new houses
of less than 116 square metres. As such it constituted an
important indirect subsidy, particularly in the private sector.
In 1978, however, rates on all private dwellings were
abolished.

Income tax relief
The interest element of a mortgage is tax deductible. People
borrowing from a life assurance company receive income tax
relief not only on the amount of interest paid on the loan but

also on the premiums paid towards the life assurance policy. Income tax concessions to house purchases are a consequence of the income tax code and were not intended as specific housing subsidies. Yet they operate as such and are of most benefit to persons with the highest taxable incomes. The actual saving in tax remission will depend on the marginal rate at which the person pays tax. Thus, for example, where the interest element of a mortgage amounts to £1,000 per annum, a person with a marginal tax rate of 60 per cent would only pay a net figure of £400 per annum whereas a person with a marginal tax rate of 35 per cent would pay a net sum of £650 per annum. The Finance Act, 1974, stipulated that the total amount of personal interest (including house-mortgage interest) liable for income tax relief would be limited to £2,000 per annum. This figure was raised to £2,400 in 1979.

Other aids

Apart from the major aids outlined above a number of other aids are designed to encourage owner-occupation.

There is no stamp duty payable on a new house for which a state grant is payable or on houses of less than 116 square metres. On other dwellings a graded scale applies according to the price of the dwelling, e.g. 2 per cent on houses costing between £7,500 and £10,000, 3 per cent on houses costing between £10,000 and £20,000.[18]

Local authorities are empowered to provide developed sites for private, modestly-priced houses. The local authority may dispose of such sites at a price related to the cost to them of acquisition and development (including their administrative costs) less the equivalent of a state subsidy, which is up to £300 per site. These sites are disposed of to small builders, to people vacating local authority houses and to a few other special categories of people. The object of this subsidy, like the object of grants, is to assist people to obtain their own houses by controlling the cost of the sites.

Financing of private housing

Apart from state and local authority investment in housing a number of other agencies are involved in the provision of house purchase loans. Up to recently the two main agencies were building societies and assurance companies. In the supplementary budget of 1975, however, the Minister for Finance directed the associated banks to provide house purchase loans totalling £40 million over the following two years. The directive was intended to provide a stimulus to the construction industry during a difficult period as well as providing an additional source of loans to the house purchaser. It also brought banks into an area which they have traditionally avoided because of the short-term nature of their deposits. The banks, while exceeding the figure stipulated by the Minister, have continued to provide loans beyond this period.

The amount paid out in house purchase loans by the various agencies has increased substantially over the past decade or so, but the distribution of loans between agencies has also changed considerably (see Table 17, page 83). In 1966-7, for example, assurance companies and local authorities paid out roughly similar amounts while the building societies contributed the largest share, accounting for just over two-fifths (42 per cent) of the total value of loans. By the mid 1970s, however, the local authorities' share had increased to over one-third while the assurance companies' share had fallen to 7.5 per cent. With the entry of the associated banks coupled with the effects of a real decline in the number and value of local authority loans, the situation changed further. By 1977 the associated banks' share of the total value of loans exceeded that of local authorities and assurance companies combined. In the same year, however, the number of loans provided by the banks was about half that provided by local authorities and assurance companies. This is explained not only by the fact that the price of houses for which bank loans were provided was considerably higher, but also by the limit placed on local authority loans.

The building societies have a long tradition of involvement in the provision of house purchase loans. They obtain funds in the open competitive market and in order to do so they must offer an attractive rate of interest to depositors. Consequently their rates must be higher than other institutions such as banks. Between May 1973 and the end of 1975 the government subsidised building societies in order that they could compete with

Table 17: Number, value (£000s) and percentage distribution of house purchase loans paid for new and other houses by major agencies for selected years, 1966/67 to 1979

Year	Building Societies	Assurance Companies	Local Authorities	Associated Banks	Total
1967-68					
Number	n.a.	n.a..	n.a.	—	n.a.
%	—	—	—	—	—
Value	6,683	4,265	4,969	—	15,917
%	42.0	26.8	31.2	—	100.00
1971					
Number	6,665	1,850	3,213	—	11,728
%	56.8	15.8	27.4	—	100.00
Value	27,867	7,896	8,118	—	43,881
%	63.5	18.0	18.5	—	100.00
1975					
Number	9,943	1,259	10,001	38	21,241
%	46.8	5.9	47.1	0.2	100.00
Value	65,086	8,716	42,058	378	116,238
%	56.0	7.5	36.2	0.3	100.00
1979					
Number	14,783	522	6,943[a]	2,494	24,742
%	59.7	2.1	28.1	10.1	100.00
Value	200,192	5,913	50,372	36,443	292,920
%	68.4	2.0	17.2	12.4	100.00

[a] Includes loans provided under low-rise mortgage scheme.

Source: *Quarterly Bulletin of Housing Statistics*, Stationery Office, Dublin.

the relatively high rates of interest obtainable during that period in the banks. Since building societies depend heavily on short-term borrowing they usually retain the right to vary interest rates during the currency of the loan. Interest rates are therefore subject to change.

Unlike building societies, the provision of house purchase loans is only one of the activities engaged in by assurance companies. Consequently, they may either reduce or withdraw their commitment to housing loans if more attractive investment opportunities arise elsewhere. In recent years their relative importance in housing finance has declined sharply.

Private Rented Sector

There is less information (on rents, type of dwelling, type of tenancy) and considerably less discussion relating to the private rented sector than to owner-occupiers or local authority tenants.

From the Census of Population it is possible to distinguish between private furnished and private unfurnished lettings. Between 1961 and 1971 there was an overall decline of 19,500 such lettings (see Table 18, page 84). Over that period, however, unfurnished lettings declined by 35,500 while furnished lettings increased by 16,000. In 1961, furnished and unfurnished private lettings accounted for 17.2 per cent of total housing stock in Ireland. By 1971 this figure had fallen to 13.4 per cent. In 1971, over half (56 per cent) of furnished dwellings and one-third of unfurnished dwellings were located in the Dublin area.

Table 18: Furnished and unfurnished dwellings rented privately (i.e. other than from local authority) in 1961 and 1971.

| | Number of Dwellings | | % Change | % of total housing stock | |
	1961	1971	1961-1971	1961	1971
Unfurnished	100,495	65,048	- 35.3	14.9	9.0
Furnished	15,806	31,836	+101.4	2.3	4.4
Total	116,301	96,884	-16.7	17.2	13.4

Source: *Census of Population, 1961,* Vol. VI; *1971,* Vol. VI.

In this private rented sector a further important distinction can be made between those dwellings whose rents are controlled (restricted) and those whose rents are uncontrolled (unrestricted). While the rents of tenants in uncontrolled dwellings are largely determined by market forces, rents are controlled for certain dwellings under the Rent Restrictions Acts, 1960 and 1967. The categories of dwellings excluded from rent control are complex but, for example, all furnished lettings and dwellings built since 1941 are excluded.[19] In practice most unfurnished dwellings are subject to rent control and, as can be seen in Table 18, about two-thirds of all private lettings in 1971 were unfurnished. The Department of the Environment estimates that the number of rent-controlled lettings is between 45,000 and 50,000.

While rent control has been a controversial topic for many years in Britain, Irish housing rent controls have not received the same degree of discussion. On the one hand, rent controls have been unfair on landlords who have often received only a nominal income from their property and have consequently been unable to maintain it in reasonable repair. On the other hand, the sudden ending of control could mean that some tenants would be faced with rent increases well beyond their means.

The rent control system encourages landlords to let their property deteriorate through lack of maintenance because the returns on expenditure are negligible. When the opportunity arises, therefore, landlords will rid themselves of tenants and make the property they hold, particularly where this is near urban centres, available for office or other development. In parts of Britain this has been a factor in the depopulation of centre city areas. Another obvious effect on the withdrawal of private capital investment has been that local authorities have been forced to become increasingly involved in the provision of accommodation. The decline in unfurnished lettings in Ireland is an indication of the unattractive nature of rented accommodation (controlled) for investment purposes.

Level of Subsidy by Tenure Group
Housing subsidies, according to Kaim-Caudle, 'enable people

to occupy dwellings superior to those they would wish to have if they had to pay the proper unsubsidised price'.[20] While such subsidies are quantitatively very important in Irish housing it is difficult in practice to quantify accurately the relative value of subsidies, whether direct or indirect, to the various tenure groups. Such an attempt was made, however, in NESC Report No 23 which estimated that in 1975 the total state subsidisation of housing came to £96 million as compared with £38.6 in 1971-72.[21] The report estimated that in 1975, owner-occupiers received nearly £15 million in direct subsidies from the state and a further £30.5 million in implicit subsidies, mostly in the form of income tax relief on loan interest. Thus, the total subsidy to this group was £45.3 million and it was estimated that 175,000 owner-occupied households benefited. Approximately 10,000 local authority tenants who purchased their dwellings received £21 million point of sale subsidies, making them the most heavily subsidised of all groups on a per household basis (see Table 19, page 86). The 110,000 local authority

Table 19 Value of housing subsidies by tenure group 1975.

	Value (£ millions)	Number	Per household subsidy (£)
Owner occupiers	45.3	175,000	259
Local authority tenants who purchased their dwellings	21.0	10,000	2,100
Local authority tenants	26.2	110,000	238
Tenants in rent-controlled dwellings	3.5	50,000	70
Tenants in uncontrolled dwellings	Nil	47,000	

Source: NESC Report No. 23, *Report on Housing Subsidies,* Stationery Office, Dublin 1976.

tenants received rent subsidies of £26.2 million in 1975, the subsidy here being measured as the difference between the economic rent (the cost to the local authority of debt service maintenance and management of dwellings) less the actual rent paid by tenants. The remaining tenure group are tenants renting privately-owned accommodation. In 1971 they numbered 97,000 and just over half were in rent-controlled accommodation. In the case of rent-controlled dwellings there is, according to the NESC report, an unusual subsidy from the state in that if the dwellings were not controlled the income of the landlords would be higher and the state would consequently benefit from higher income tax receipts. The tax foregone is estimated to be £3.5 million at most. There are no subsidies, direct or indirect, for those in the uncontrolled private rental sector.

Baker and O'Brien[22] present an excellent over-view of the housing system in Ireland with reference to efficiency and equity. They argue that while the system is tolerably efficient at providing accommodation it is also seriously unfair to the extent that it favours those who already own or rent houses at the expense of young married couples and others seeking houses. The authors state:

> It is the interaction between the financial requirements for entering the owner-occupier sector, the social criteria for becoming a local Authority Tenant and the cost of private renting which creates the greatest inequity in the housing system.[23]

In their general assessment the authors refer to the wide variations in the quality of dwellings and housing costs within each tenure group as well as between them.

Among the main recommendations in the report by Baker and O'Brien are the provision of local authority housing to individuals as well as families, the phasing out of rent-control and an end to discrimination in favour of new houses over old ones. The report also suggests that as much as £20 million in public funds could be released if maximum rents on older local authority houses were raised substantially, if purchase prices to tenants were set more realistically and if time and amount limitations were placed on mortgage tax relief in the case of private houses. These funds could be used to encourage more owner-occupation, improve the differential rent scheme and provide subsidies, with certain safeguards, for low-income tenants in the private rented sector. The case for diverting some public subsidy from other sectors into the private rented sector is, according to the authors, 'overwhelming'.

Housing Conditions
Housing quality is an indication of social conditions in a community. In general, the quality of housing may be measured by reference to the age of dwellings, the degree of overcrowding and the presence or absence of such amenities as piped water, electricity and sanitary facilities.

Age of dwellings
The latest available information on the age of dwellings in Ireland is contained in the 1971 census of population. At that time the total number of housing units was 705,180. Of these, 45 per cent were built prior to 1919, 20 per cent between 1919 and 1940, 20 per cent between 1941 and 1960 and 15 per cent between 1961 and 1971. By comparison with other European countries the proportion of Irish housing stock built since World War II is relatively small (see Chapter 7). This is due in part to the absence of extensive war damage, and to a declining population up to the 1960s.

Within Ireland, a considerable disparity exists between urban areas (towns with 1,500 or more inhabitants) and rural areas, with 58 per cent of dwellings in rural areas having been built prior to 1919 compared with less than one-third (31 per cent) in urban areas.

Degree of overcrowding
Two or more people per room is generally deemed overcrowding. By this standard the proportion of overcrowded dwellings has fallen considerably since the foundation of the state. In 1926 the proportion of people in private households having two or more people per room was 37.1 per cent. By 1971 this

figure had fallen to 14.8 per cent. While there was little difference in the proportion living in overcrowded dwellings in urban and rural areas in 1971, it should be stressed that over-crowding in high density urban areas is more often associated with serious social problems than it is in rural areas.

Amenities

As in the case of overcrowded dwellings, there has been a considerable improvement in the standards of living accommodation, measured by the presence of certain basic household amenities. In the decade 1961-71 the proportion of dwellings lacking piped water supply and sanitary facilities declined sharply (see Table 20, page 89). Despite the commendable achievements, however, one in every five dwellings still lacked piped water and sanitary facilities in 1971. The majority of such dwellings were located in rural areas where approximately two-fifths of dwellings lacked such amenities. Part of the reason for such a disparity lies in the fact that it is much more difficult and costly to provide such facilities in areas of scattered settlement than it is in high density urban areas.

Table 20: Percentage of dwellings lacking piped water supply, electricity and sanitary facilities, 1961 and 1971

	1961	1971
Piped water supply	43.0	21.0
Electricity	17.0	5.3
Sanitary facilities	35.0	19.0

Source: *Census of Population 1971*, Vol. VI.

Since 1971 there has undoubtedly been a continuing improvement in housing conditions in rural areas. In the absence of a comprehensive census however, the exact extent of this improvement will not be clear for a considerable time. While the census of 1971 indicated that approximately 154,000 dwellings, nearly all of them in rural areas, had no piped water, the Department of the Environment estimates that the figure had been reduced to approximately 60,000 dwellings by the end of 1978.[24]

Community Facilities

Housing policy in Ireland has tended to emphasise the number of units built rather than the types of neighbourhood created. A preoccupation with quantity of housing units has meant that ancillary community facilities have often been neglected or that there is a considerable time lag between the completion of housing estates and the provision of community services. This is particularly true of the fast-growing fringes of urban areas. The problem is seen in perspective when it is remembered that many suburban areas in Dublin, for example, compare unfavourably with small urban centres throughout the country in the range of services they possess, despite the fact that they contain a much higher population.

The Ballymun complex with its high-rise flats illustrates the point clearly. While the construction of this complex undoubtedly alleviated housing problems in the Dublin area it also posed serious social problems for the residents; with a population of approximately 16,000 it lacks safe play areas for children, a cinema, community centre, sports complex or library. A survey carried out among residents in Ballymun by the Department of Sociology, Trinity College, in 1974 indicated a high level of dissatisfaction.[25] The findings indicate that while 70 per cent of residents felt that their accommodation was superior to their previous home, over half intended to leave. Of those who wanted to leave, half were already on the housing list. As the survey report stated, '...a quarter of the people in Ballymun are waiting for the Corporation that moved them into Ballymun to move them out again'. In short, Ballymun may be described as a community lacking the necessary community facilities which are so essential to creating a sense of identity.

The largest housing scheme in Dublin since Ballymun is at Darndale in north county Dublin. Eventually, Darndale will constitute a new town of 4,000 dwellings with a population of more than 20,000. In many ways Darndale is designed to avoid the problems associated with Ballymun, and above all is intended to encourage a community atmosphere. Unlike Ballymun it is a low-rise, high density scheme incorporating the principle of the segregation of vehicular and pedestrian traffic.

Perhaps one of the disagreeable features of Darndale is the monotony of design. This is true of many suburban housing estates and particularly of local authority schemes. On this topic Pfretzschner comments:

A great deal of the housing built since the creation of the Republic is evidence of the dire necessity to erect shelter for human beings as quickly and often as cheaply as possible. Whether constructed for private or public owner-ship, the resulting neighbourhoods are nearly all char-acterised by repetitive motifs, undeviating habit in the use of materials, and a lack of spaciousness in a nation with the lowest population density of any in Europe.[26]

In practice, it is sometimes very difficult to resolve the dilemma which arises between housing needs and the con-straints of capital resources on the one hand, and varied design of housing estates and provision of community facilities on the other.

APPENDIX: Differential Rent Scheme (applicable from 1 March 1979)

Assessable income
Income for the purpose of rent assessment is the weekly basic income of the principal earner (the member of the household whose weekly income is greatest) after deduction of income tax and social welfare contributions. Income from the following sources is assessed in full for rent purposes:
1. Basic income
2. Income from position as a self-employed person
3. Unemployment, pay-related and disability benefits in respect of new claims for these benefits received after 17 September 1976

4.   Income from pensions other than social welfare pensions. Fifty per cent of the income from the following sources is assessed for rent purposes:
1.   Social welfare pensions
2.   Social assistance payments
3.   AnCO training allowances
4.   Unemployment, pay-related and disability benefits in respect of persons in receipt of these benefits on 17 September 1976, and continually after that date
5.   Redundancy weekly payments in respect of new claims received after 17 September 1976
Income from the following sources is disregarded:
1.   Children's allowances payable under the Social Welfare (Children's Allowance) Acts.
2.   Scholarships
3.   Allowances payable under the Boarding Out of Children Regulations, 1954
4.   Disabled person's maintenance allowance, and domiciliary care allowance for handicapped children under the Health Act, 1970, infectious diseases maintenance allowance under the Health Act, 1947
5.   Supplementary welfare allowances
6.   Allowances or assistance received from any charitable organisation
7.   Income from redundancy weekly payments in respect of person in receipt of these payments on 17 September 1976 and continually after that date
8.   Lump sum compensation payments

Allowance for children
There is an allowance of £1.30 per week for every child of 16 years or under or those under 21 years attending a full-time course in education and who are wholly or mainly maintained by the tenant.

Calculation of Rent
The rents of dwellings let on differential rent are calculated on the basis of the following scale:

Assessable income of principal earner	Principal earner's allowance	Allowance for children	Rent fraction
Up to £19	£10	£1.30 per child	1/12
Over £19 up to £24	8	"	1/10
Over £24 up to £28	6	"	1/9
Over £28 up to £39	5	"	1/8
Over £39	2	"	1/7

In the application of this scale, it will be open to local authorities to make appropriate rent adjustments at the marginal points of the scale.

Subsidiary Earners
After the rent payable in respect of the principal earner has been assessed, 1/7 of the basic income or social welfare payment of each subsidiary earner which exceeds £14 and does not exceed £24.50 per week should be added. The maximum weekly amount of rent attributable to each subsidiary earner is £1.50.

Chapter 4

Education

Introduction

As in the case of housing, it is generally accepted in Ireland and most other democratic countries that there is a need for some government intervention in education. If education was left exclusively to the market, for example, then access would be largely determined by household income. The government's objectives in relation to education are to provide economic benefits for the community in general and equality of opportunity.

Education provides an economic benefit to the state in that it trains individuals in certain skills for participation in the future labour force. It is generally recognised that expenditure on education will inevitably lead to increased productivity of the labour force and hence to national economic growth. Thus, expenditure on education may be viewed as an investment for the future. Indeed the major report on the Irish education system viewed education primarily in this light, as its title *Investment in Education* suggests.

Access to education has, increasingly, become regarded as a basic right, that is, there should be equality of educational opportunity for all, irrespective of household income. In the preface to a booklet entitled *All Our Children,* issued by the Department of Education in 1969, the then Minister for Education, Brian Lenihan, referred to equal opportunity in education as 'our most urgent social and educational objective'.

The extent to which the above objectives are realised is related to the method of allocating resources in education. If education is viewed as a right of all citizens then the question arises, do people in reality, have equality of opportunity and are national resources distributed in such a way as to achieve this objective? If education is viewed as a means of attaining national economic objectives then the question must also be raised, is state expenditure being utilised to the best advantage? Does the allocation of resources, for example, favour the pursuit of academic subjects to the detriment of technical subjects or the over-production of certain types of skills and the under-production of others? In this context a conflict may arise between individual and family aspirations and the more general needs of the economy.

While it is not intended to deal with the above and related policy issues in depth they are considered briefly in this chapter.

The system of education in Ireland is highly complex. Education is carried out at three levels and considerable variation exists not only between these levels but within them. The management and financing of first and second level schools are different and at first level, there are different kinds of primary schools while at second level there are four distinct subsections. Despite the fact that there is substantial state support at all levels, there are few state schools in the accepted sense. The influence of the churches (especially Catholic) on the development of the system is profound at all levels.

The present system represents a curious mixture of state and church interests particularly at first level and in some parts of the second level. Secondary schools, for example, are in receipt of various state subsidies yet are privately owned and managed. Apart from the churches there are various other interest groups such as the teachers' unions and, more recently, parents' organisations. The presence of these groups coupled with the fact that there is little legislative basis for education means that it is often difficult to obtain agreement on policy changes. The following pages will illustrate this.

Since the mid 1960s some important changes have occurred in the educational system. These include the introduction of free post-primary education and the establishment of new institutions such as comprehensive and community schools at second level and regional technical colleges at third level. These innovations have been accompanied by an increase in the population and increased participation rates at all levels. All this has involved greater public expenditure and almost inevitably, owing to budgetary constraints in recent years, questions have been raised about the appropriate allocation of resources at the various levels of education.

First Level Education

Origins of present system[1]
Many basic features of modern Irish primary or first level education can be traced back to the National Board of Education, established in 1831. Prior to 1831 there was no uniform system of primary education and while some areas were well served by schools others had only rudimentary forms of schooling.[2] A number of organisations promoted first level education in the early decades of the nineteenth century, for example the Kildare Place Society and Catholic religious orders.

In 1831 the British House of Commons voted a sum of £30,000 towards primary education in Ireland. This money was to be administered by a Board which consisted of seven Commissioners representing the main religious denominations. The Board was given power to contribute to the cost of building schools, pay inspection costs, contribute to teachers' salaries, establish model schools and provide school books. The system was to provide for 'combined moral, literary and separate religious education'. It was decided that schools run by religious orders were to be given the same assistance as other schools provided they complied with the rules of the Board.

The Board's early success was hindered by opposition and lack of co-operation. In 1837, for example, the Irish Christian Brothers withdrew their schools from connection with the Board. Four years later, however, Pope Gregory XVI encouraged Catholics to support the national schools. While some of the Catholic hierarchy welcomed the new system others, notably Dr John MacHale, Archbishop of Tuam, were less enthusiastic and forbade their clergy to co-operate with the Board.

The training of teachers for the national schools proved to be another contentious issue. In 1837, the Board established a training school and three model schools at Marlborough Street,

Dublin. Teachers were to be trained on the principle of the 'mixed system', the teaching of children of all denominations where religious and secular instruction would not be separate. The Catholic hierarchy forbade their clerical managers to appoint teachers trained in the model schools to schools under their control. In 1883 the Board decided to recognise denominational training colleges and two Catholic colleges (St Patrick's, Drumcondra, for men and Our Lady of Mercy, Blackrock, for women) were established in Dublin. A Church of Ireland training college for men and women was affiliated to the Board in the following year. Three other training colleges, at Waterford (1891), Belfast (1900) and Limerick (1907), were established.

Notwithstanding its limitations and somewhat tempestuous history the national system could, by 1922 when the Commissioners of the National Board of Education were replaced by a branch of the newly-founded Department of Education under an Irish Minister for Education, claim credit for considerable achievements since its foundation.[3] Perhaps the most important consequence of the national system was that it was the chief means by which the country was transformed from one in which illiteracy predominated into one in which most people could read and write: in 1841 over half (53 per cent) the population aged five years and over could neither read nor write, and by 1901 this proportion had declined to 14 per cent. In the eradication of mass illiteracy, therefore, credit must be given to the national system. The system also ensured that in all parts of the country national schools were established. The number of schools increased from just over 1,000 in 1834 to almost 8,000 in 1921 and the school-going population increased from 107,000 in 1833 to 685,000 in 1891. This occurred despite a decline of over 50 per cent in the total population from 1841 to 1921.

One of the main objectives of the National Board of Education, the establishment of non-denominational schools, was not achieved. The state system of non-denominational education established in 1831 had become, by the time the Irish state was founded, a system of denominational education and has remained so ever since. In fact, as stated in the *Rules of*

National Schools under the Department of Education, the state gives explicit recognition to the denominational character of these schools.

Compulsory schooling

Under the Irish Education Act, 1892, attendance on at least seventy-five days in each half year was made compulsory for children between the ages of six and fourteen. A number of acceptable excuses for non-attendance were specified by the Act, e.g. sickness, harvesting operations, fishing, any other unavoidable cause or that the child was already receiving suitable elementary education. Initially the application of the Act was limited to municipal boroughs and towns but in 1898 it was extended to all parts of the country. The enforcement of the Act was particularly difficult in rural areas. School attendance committees set up by local authorities helped to enforce the law but not all local authorities set up such committees.

While the Act may not have had the desired effect, it nevertheless brought about a change in school attendance. By 1902 the average yearly attendance was 63 per cent and this increased to 76 per cent by 1908.

The School Attendance Act, 1926, made further provisions for the enforcement of compulsory schooling and remains the main statute governing school attendance. In county boroughs, school attendance committees containing members of the local authority and educational interests were established. These committees employ school attendance officers; in other areas members of the Garda Síochána are appointed as school attendance officers. The Act proved far more effective than the earlier one of 1892 and the average daily attendance figure continued to rise in the following years — 73.5 per cent in 1926, 88.1 per cent in 1963 and 90.5 per cent in 1978. The Act of 1926 provides for the issue of a warning notice to parents who fail to send a child to school and the fining of parents who fail to comply with such a warning. It also provides that 'the Court, if it thinks fit, may order the child to be sent to a certified industrial school'.[4]

Two amendments have been made to the Act of 1926. The

first provided for the delivery of 'warnings' by registered letter instead of in person. The second was of far greater significance. It raised the school-leaving age to fifteen years and came into effect in 1972.

Management and finance
Initially, the National Board of Education was willing to give special consideration to any joint applications for aid from members of different religious denominations within a parish. What happened in practice was that where there were sufficient numbers of children of different denominations then the Catholic or non-Catholic clergy or members of religious orders applied for separate aid in building a school. The pupils, therefore, were concentrated in separate schools under local clerical or religious order management. This was the beginning of the managerial system which survived up to 1975.

Ironically, while the direct government of primary schools and the appointment and dismissal of teachers has remained in the hands of local managers, the state has always paid a large share of the cost of building schools and pays the teachers' salaries in full. The non-state character of the school has been preserved by the provision of a site from local funds together with a local contribution (maximum 15 per cent) towards the cost of building the school. The state also contributes towards the maintenance of schools (approximately two-thirds up to 1975). In the case of schools run by religious orders the non-state costs are met by the order involved. There are approximately 100 private primary schools in the country and these schools receive no state subsidy and are totally financed by parents' fees.

In 1977 the estimated total amount of capital expenditure on primary schools was £15 million, of which the local or non-state contribution accounted for £1.8 million or 12 per cent.[5]

In practice a distinction can be made between primary schools. The majority are referred to as ordinary national schools and are mainly under either Roman Catholic or Protestant clerical patronage.

Schools run by religious orders are referred to as Roman Catholic monastery (male orders) or convent (female orders)

Table 21: Number and type of first and second level educational institutions

Type	Number (1976/77)	Management	Finance
First Level Private schools	108	Single managers	No state assistance, financed by fees.
Ordinary national schools	2,795	Management committees consisting of representatives of patron, parents and teachers	Parish provides school site plus up to 15% building costs. Current cost met by state grant of £10 per pupil and local contribution of £2.50 per pupil.[a]
Roman Catholic convent	405	Management committees as above, but with religious order's representatives instead of patron's representatives	As for ordinary national schools, except that non-state capital funds are met by the religious order.
Roman Catholic monastery	140	Management committees similar to convent schools	As for convent schools.
Special national schools (for physically and mentally handicapped children)	96	Management committees mainly, some founding committees	As for ordinary national schools.
Model national schools	14	Joint management between Department of Education and Office of Public Works	Financed by Office of Public Works.

Special Irish national schools	18	Management committees	As for ordinary national schools, but local contribution may come from parents' committee.
Second Level Secondary schools	532	Single managers, normally members of religious orders	School management provides site. State provides grant of 80% of approved building costs. Current costs are paid by (1) capitation grants (2) free education scheme grants.[b] Schools not in the free scheme charge fees and are paid capitation grants only.
Vocational schools	245	Nine-member board of management representative of VEC parents and teachers	Financed by local rates levy but the main contribution comes from the state.
Comprehensive schools	15	Three member board of management – chief executive officer of VEC plus representative of Department of Education and local Catholic or non-Catholic Bishop	Total costs met by State.
Community schools	24	Normally a six-member board of management with two VEC representatives, two representatives of religious orders and two parents	Capital costs met by state (90%) and merged schools (10%). Current costs met fully by state.

[a] These capitation grants are those for 1979/80.
[b] For 1979-80, thecapitation grants were £38 per senior pupil, £28 for the first hundred junior pupils and £26 for the remaining junior pupils. The value of free education scheme grants (or supplemental grant) in 1979-80 was £70 per pupil.

schools. In addition there are special schools for physically and mentally handicapped children and schools in which the curriculum is taught wholly or mainly through the medium of Irish. There are also a number of model national schools directly under the control of the Department of Education. For a list of these schools and their distinguishing characteristics see Table 21 on pages 100 and 101.

In recent years the management of primary schools has been the subject of debate. In 1969 the Catholic hierarchy suggested that parents become involved in the management of schools and, addressing a meeting of the Catholic Primary School Managers Association in Athlone in June 1973, the Secretary of the Department of Education, Sean O'Connor, suggested that the managers examine the possibility of involving parents and teachers formally in school management. A subsequent attempt to introduce joint management committees as pilot projects in the Dublin area was hindered by the lack of cooperation of the Irish National Teachers Organisation (INTO) which was not opposed to parental involvement per se but was justifiably anxious that the functions of the proposed committees be clearly defined first.

The oil crisis of 1973-74 presented an unexpected opportunity of establishing joint management committees. The soaring cost of heating oil meant that the state would have to substantially increase its maintenance subsidy to primary schools, otherwise the burden would fall on the local community. In October 1974, the Minister for Education, Richard Burke, announced a new scheme of state aid towards the maintenance costs of primary schools. Instead of paying schools a proportion of the maintenance costs, a grant of £6 per pupil (to be matched by £1.50 per pupil collected locally) would be given only to those schools which had set up joint management committees by October 1975, composed of four nominees of the patron and two parents. The Minister subsequently indicated that teachers should also be represented on these committees. Schools which had not set up the committees would have to accept a lower subsidy from the Department of Education towards the upkeep of their schools. From a financial viewpoint therefore, it was in the manager's interest to establish committees. The scheme has been aptly described as a form of 'gentle blackmail'.[6] It also illustrates the difficulty of making policy changes in the Irish education system. In the absence of a legislative basis, change is introduced by agreement among the various interests involved rather than by legislation. In this instance, a financial carrot achieved in one year something which in all probability would have taken several years to achieve.

At a special congress of INTO in 1975, delegates voted overwhelmingly in favour of the principle of parent representation on management committees. INTO entered into negotiation with the Catholic hierarchy, the Catholic Primary School Managers Association and the Department of Education in order to ensure that the rights and entitlements of national teachers would be safeguarded in the new system. Committees were established by October 1975, in order to avail of the new grant from the Department of Education. Nevertheless, there followed a prolonged period of negotiation between the parties involved (except parents) about the exact functions of the boards of management and the composition of the boards. It was not until November 1976 that the constitution and rules of procedure for the management boards were published and issued to the chairmen of the school boards. The composition of the boards varied according to the number of teachers in the school as shown in Table 22 on page 103.

Table 22: Composition of school management boards.

Schools with 6 teachers or less	Schools with 7 teachers or more
a) 4 nominees of patron	6 nominees of patron
b) 2 parents elected by other parents	2 parents elected by other parents
c) Principal teacher	Principal teacher
d) —	One other teacher elected by teaching staff
Total 7 members	10 members

The patron of the school appoints the chairman of the board. For Catholic national schools the bishop or archbishop is normally the patron, for example, the Archbishop of Dublin is patron of 541 schools and the Bishop of Cork is patron of 206 schools. In all, Catholic bishops are patrons of 3,333 schools while the Church of Ireland bishops are patrons of 202 schools.[7] The boards are concerned with the general management of the schools but have little effective power. The patron, for example, must approve of the appointment of the principal teacher and each assistant teacher.[8] The management boards are responsible for the collection of the local contribution (which must not be a levy on parents), and the maintenance of the school. By 1979 the Department of Education grant per pupil was £10 and the local contribution £2.50.

When the boards were first established in 1975 a commitment was given to INTO that a review of the scheme would be conducted at the end of the first three-year period of operation. When the new boards were established in October 1978 INTO refused to participate until a review was undertaken. INTO's dissatisfaction with the scheme arose for several reasons, for instance teachers and elected parents were in the minority on boards; a review of the system of appointing teachers was needed; machinery for resolving disputes arising between teachers and management boards. Subsequent meetings between all the parties concerned endeavoured to amend the scheme but by early 1980 the issues had not been resolved.

Rationalisation
A relatively high density of population in the mid-nineteenth century combined with the fact that education was based on the parish encouraged the building of small primary schools serving a rather limited catchment area. As population declined throughout the latter part of the nineteenth and first half of the present century, however, many schools, particularly those in rural areas, became vulnerable to closure. Since its establishment the Department of Education has sought to amalgamate those schools with the smallest number of pupils. In many areas there has been considerable opposition to school closures, reflecting the value of the school as a focal point in the local community.

The *Investment in Education* report (1965) indicated that on a cost-effective basis the one-teacher and two-teacher primary schools were inefficient, for example in the range of subjects taught and in the rate of progress through school.[9] This report influenced subsequent policy towards small schools and an intensive programme of primary school rationalisation was embarked upon. Between 1966 and 1977, 542 one-teacher and 1,263 two-teacher schools were closed or amalgamated. During the same period the total number of primary schools fell from 4,324 to 3,372.[10] In 1966, one-teacher and two-teacher schools accounted for almost three-quarters (71 per cent) of all primary schools. By 1977, however, the proportion had fallen to less than two-fifths (37.5 per cent).

Apart from declining population, two further factors aided the process of rationalisation, the introduction of the free school transport service in 1967-8 and the introduction of the new curriculum in 1970-71. By 1977 approximately 13 per cent of pupils in primary schools were availing of the free transport system.

The free transport scheme facilitated the transference of pupils from small schools to larger units. Under the new curriculum, which followed the abolition of the primary certificate, the emphasis has been on a child-centred rather than a subject-centred approach. This approach necessitated the introduction of such facilities as audio-visual aids, and the development of new activities in arts and crafts, environmental studies and physical education. These could not be provided satisfactorily in small one-teacher and two-teacher schools and hence the necessity for the creation of larger schools and the pursuance of the policy of amalgamating small schools.

A NESC report published in 1976 questioned the efficacy of closing small rural schools and referred to the trend in Scandinavian countries, especially Norway, where the process of rationalisation had been reversed.[11] The NESC report stated:

In view of the evidence of population renewal in some rural areas perhaps it is opportune to re-examine the policy of rationalisation of small rural primary schools. Furthermore, the cost of transporting pupils to larger schools has undoubtedly risen considerably since the introduction of free transport in 1967. In rural areas which have begun to exemplify population stability or growth the cost of maintaining existing schools may be offset to some extent by a saving in transport costs consequent on the closure of such schools.

The Minister for Education, Richard Burke, issued a statement the day after the NESC report was published in which he said that from evidence based on experience and from expert advice recently offered to him, he considered that the educational advantages offered by a large school over those available in a small school had been greatly overrated. The statement added that the economic benefits to the community at large arising out of school amalgamations had also been exaggerated.[12]

In February 1977, the Minister for Education, Peter Barry, in his first major policy statement since taking office two months previously, made an announcement that the Department of Education would no longer force the amalgamation of small schools into larger units.[13] The Minister stated that the educational and economic arguments on which the policy was based were either unproven or no longer applied. He also stated that the economic advantages of the centralised system had been eroded by the oil crisis which had resulted in a substantial increase in transport costs. 'It may cost marginally more to keep the small schools open, but I think the social arguments outweigh the economic considerations', said the Minister; 'the small school is an important part of the social fabric of rural areas and I believe we are beginning to see signs of a shift away from built-up areas to a more rural environment'. Nevertheless he made it clear that if in future any rural community wished to close down the remaining small schools and to centralise them in, say, a village unit, his Department would actively encourage the move.

In July 1977, the Department of Education issued a circular to all small schools authorising 'necessary improvements' in school facilities such as electricity and sanitary facilities. Previously, some schools, earmarked for closure, had been refused grants for these purposes.

Enrolment and Class Size

In the decade from 1967-68 to 1977-78 enrolment in ordinary national schools increased from 479,047 to 531,612, an increase of 11 per cent. Over the same period the teaching force (excluding temporary, unqualified teachers) in these schools increased from 14,794 to 17,595. The increase in enrolments therefore has been offset by an increase in the number of teachers and on the basis of the above figures this has resulted in a fall in the pupil/teacher ratio from 32.4 to 30.2. These ratios, however, are national averages and, as such, conceal the wide disparity which exists between schools.

A more realistic indication of overcrowding is the proportion of pupils in classes of various sizes. Since 1967-68, the proportion of pupils in classes of forty-five and over has continued to decline (see Table 23 page 107). Over the same period the proportion in classes of between fifteen and twenty-nine pupils has also fallen. The net result has been that the proportion in classes of between thirty and forty-four has continued to increase and classes of this size now account for almost three-quarters of pupils. Overcrowded classrooms are likely to be

Table 23: Percentage distribution of national school pupils by class size, 1967-68,[a] 1970-71, 1973-74 and 1976-77.

| Year | Class Size | | | |
	0-14	15-29	30-44	45+
1967-68	1.8	25.1	41.2	31.9	100.0
1970-71	1.3	23.4	46.5	28.8	100.0
1973-74	1.1	22.3	62.9	13.7	100.0
1976-77	0.7	20.1	70.6	8.6	100.0

[a] Comparative figures are not available prior to 1967-68.

Source: *Department of Education Statistical Reports.*

found in the large urban areas and very often in areas which tend to be disadvantaged in several other respects such as poor housing conditions and high levels of unemployment.

Denominationalism and Primary Schools
It has already been noted that despite the intentions of the National Board of Education to establish a non-denominational school structure, what emerged was a system of denominational schools. The preface to the *Rules for National Schools under the Department of Education* gives recognition to such schools:

> ... the State provides for free primary education for children in national schools, and gives explicit recognition to the denominational character of these schools.[14]

State support for the denominational system has come under scrutiny in recent years. Surveys carried out in Dalkey, Marley Grange and Firhouse (Tallaght), all in the Dublin area, in 1975 and 1976 indicated that a majority of parents in these areas would prefer an interdenominational or multi-denominational national school. In the Dalkey area which already has a Church of Ireland national school the Dalkey School Project (DSP) was established in 1975. The DSP opened a multi-denominational school in temporary premises in 1978 and in its first year had about ninety pupils.

Second Level Education
Second level education is conducted in four distinct types of schools, secondary, vocational, comprehensive and community. Since the financing, ownership and management structure of these schools differ, each will be examined separately in this section. Some regional technical colleges provide second level courses but since these institutions cater mainly for third level education it is more appropriate that they be discussed later in the context of that sector.

Secondary Schools
While state aid was made available for primary education in 1831 it was not made available for secondary education until 1878 and even then the level of aid was comparatively small.

Origins of present system. It was not until the passing of the *Intermediate Education Act,* 1878 that the secondary school education system in its present form took shape. The Act established the Intermediate Education Board with seven commissioners, to administer funds for examination purposes. The word 'intermediate' was taken to imply a system of education between elementary or primary instruction and higher education. Junior, middle and senior grade examinations were established under the Act and results fees were paid to the managers of schools in which candidates passed the examinations. The principal means of obtaining state aid, therefore, was through success in examinations. On the credit side the new system imposed a uniform curriculum on secondary schools where variety had predominated. Since aid available from the state was limited, however, schools relied heavily on students' fees to meet capital and current costs. Unlike the primary school system whereby schools could be established in practically every area with state support the distribution of secondary schools was mainly confined to urban areas. Consequently many areas of the country lacked secondary schools, the greatest concentration being in the Dublin area and along the east coast generally, while few existed in the province of Connacht.

In 1922 the Intermediate Education Board was dissolved and in 1925 its functions were taken over by the Department of Education. Under the Intermediate Education (Amendment) Act, 1924, the system of paying grants to schools on the results of public examinations was discontinued. Instead, capitation grants were paid to schools for pupils over twelve years of age who followed prescribed courses and who made a certain number of attendances (130 days during the school year). The initial grant was £7 per junior pupil and £10 per senior pupil.

In 1924 the junior, middle and senior grade examinations were replaced by the intermediate and leaving certificate examinations. In 1925, the first year of the new examination system, 2,903 pupils sat for the intermediate certificate examination and 995 for the leaving certificate. By 1978 these numbers had increased to 49,423 and 35,804 respectively.

In 1925, incremental salaries for recognised secondary

teachers were introduced in schools which fulfilled certain conditions regarding size and staffing ratio. Recognition of schools
was conditional on the employment of a certain number of
recognised teachers each of whom (if not a member of a
religious order) would have a contract of employment and
would be entitled to a certain minimum basic salary to be paid
by the manager of the school. At present the basic salary is
£400 for male and female teachers.

Finance. The government of the Free State recognised the
private ownership of all secondary schools and decided to give
neither building nor maintenance grants but to help them indirectly by means of capitation grants. An opportunity was
therefore lost of redressing the serious imbalance in the
distribution of secondary schools. It was not until 1965 that
state capital grants were made available for secondary schools.
Under this scheme, capital grants of 70 per cent of the cost of
building the school or an extension were made available and
the present level is 80 per cent. Where a loan is borrowed from
a source other than the Department of Education, 80 per cent
of the annual repayments (capital and interest) are paid by the
Department. Alternatively, the Department may pay the total
cost of the building, 20 per cent being repayable by the school
authorities over a fifteen-year period.

Current expenditure of secondary schools is subsidised in
two ways:

1. By means of capitation grants. For 1979-80 the maximum
rates are £36 for each senior pupil, £28 for each of the first 100
junior pupils and £26 per head on the remaining number of
junior pupils. The rates are based on attendance of pupils in
the previous school year and a sliding scale is operated — the
lower the attendance, the lower the rate of payment. The maximum rate of £36 is payable on senior pupils who have attended
on 145 days or more whereas only £30 is payable on those who
attended on 120 to 140 days and so on.

2. By means of a supplemental grant to schools which are participating in the free post-primary education scheme launched
in 1967. In 1979-80 this grant was a flat rate of £70 per pupil.
Those schools outside the scheme receive capitation grants and
charge fees.

Separate funds are available to secondary schools for science and other equipment for practical rooms.

The subsidy for Protestant secondary education is organised on a different basis. Apart from capitation grants the Department of Education pays a lump sum roughly equal to £70 for every Protestant child of post-primary age to the Secondary Education Committee which distributes it, in accordance with a means test, to Protestant parents in order to subsidise their children's attendance at Protestant schools.

Management. Secondary schools are privately owned and managed, the majority by Catholic religious orders and a minority by Catholic or Protestant laymen or foundations. As already stated, the regulations of the Department of Education require that schools in receipt of state grants employ a certain minimum number of registered teachers and pay each of these teachers, if a lay teacher, a fixed minimum basic salary of £400. In addition to the basic salary an incremental salary is paid by the Department of Education to a recognised teacher.

Free post-primary education scheme. One of the more significant findings of the *Investment in Education* report was that there were serious inequalities in the numbers from different socio-economic groups in post-primary schools; in particular, the report showed that only 29.1 were the children of semi-skilled and unskilled workers while 70.2 were the children of professionals, employers, managers and senior salaried employees.[15]

The introduction of the free post-primary education scheme in 1967-8 by the then Minister for Education, Donogh O'Malley, was an attempt to ensure equality of opportunity for all seeking education beyond first level. Prior to this entrance to secondary schools, in general, depended as much on ability to pay fees as intellectual capacity. It must also be stressed, however, that while all secondary schools charged fees prior to the introduction of the scheme, ability to pay fees was not a condition of entry to schools managed by some religious orders. In effect, they operated a free scheme for necessitous pupils long before the Department of Education took the initiative.

Under the scheme, secondary schools which opted to discontinue charging school fees for pupils would be paid a supplemental grant per pupil equal to the fee charged in the school year 1966-7, subject to a minimum grant of £15 per pupil per annum and a maximum of £25. In 1969-70 a flat rate grant was introduced and by 1979-80 this grant was £70 per pupil. In 1978-9 there were 532 secondary schools and of these, 461 (or 87 per cent) were in the free education scheme. Of the 71 schools not participating in the scheme, 41 were in Dublin.[16]

The free post-primary education scheme also provided for grants towards free school books and accessories for necessitous day pupils. In 1977 over one-quarter of pupils in secondary schools and two-fifths of pupils in community and comprehensive schools were receiving free school books. Under the scheme free transport was also provided for pupils living more than three miles from a school in which free education was available. Pupils living outside the range of the transport services may be given allowances in aid of their maintenance at low fee, boarding schools or for lodging expenses if they attend a day school and stay in lodgings nearby. By 1977 almost one-third of all pupils in second level education were being conveyed to post-primary schools under the free transport scheme.

The numbers participating in second level education have risen dramatically since the introduction of the free post-primary education scheme,[17] but whether this is due entirely to the availability of free education is open to question. During the 1960s there was an increase in the number of young persons aged 10 to 19, many of whom in all probability would have pursued their education beyond first level in any case. The introduction of the scheme also coincided with a period when the country was experiencing substantial economic growth and job opportunities were being created on a hitherto unprecedented scale; education was seen as a means of attaining occupations with relatively high incomes in a growing labour market. The free transport service introduced as part of the scheme has undoubtedly led to increased participation in rural areas. The scheme also altered the composition of those entering the labour force, with older and more educated persons seeking first jobs.[18]

The rising cost of the school transport system (for first and second level pupils) led the government in 1976 to commission a study of the service. The study was carried out by Hyland Associates Limited, management consultants, and was published in 1979.[19] The consultants were asked to assess the organisation of the system, to evaluate its cost-effectiveness and the possibility of introducing a subsidised rather than a totally free system. The report indicated that between 1968 and 1979 the cost of the service had increased from £1.7 million to £14.5 million. By 1979, more than 160,000 pupils were being catered for at an average cost of £84 per annum. The report recommended that an annual charge of £21 per pupil be levied for use of school buses. It appears, however, that the government have rejected the notion of a levy on the grounds that it would interfere with equality of opportunity.[20]

From primary to post-primary. The primary and post-primary sections are two parts of the educational system which should work in harmony but, more often, seem to be at cross purposes. The lack of communication between these two sectors is exacerbated by different administrative structures and different curricula. Pupils move from a child-centred curriculum in primary schools to a subject and examination centred system in post-primary schools.

Another problem is that while both sectors provide free education it is ironic that no pupil has the right to attend any secondary school. In the large urban areas, entrance examinations are used by many secondary schools to select the better pupils. This practice runs counter to the concept of the new curriculum in primary schools. The 'creaming off' of the better pupils also accentuates the traditional distinctions between secondary and vocational schools. Since secondary schools are privately owned they have the right to accept or reject any particular pupil. Despite the fact that these schools are in receipt of substantial state subsidies there is no statutory means by which the Department of Education, however much it may deprecate the practice of holding entrance examinations, can exercise control over the enrolment of pupils.

Vocational schools
There was little emphasis in Ireland on technical education prior to the early decades of the present century. The Vocational Education Act, 1930, remains the basic statute governing vocational and technical education and has provided the framework for development in this area. The subsequent development of vocational schools helped to redress partially the regional imbalance of secondary schools. The important provisions in the Act covered administration and financial arrangements.

Administration. The administration of the Act is in the hands of local, elected committees, subject to the general control of the Minister for Education. Each committee has a minimum of fourteen members selected by the local rating authority and holds office for the same period as the authority. Not more than eight of the members may be members of the rating authority. Membership must be representative of educational, cultural, industrial and commercial interests in the area. Each vocational education committee (VEC) has, as its secretary/accountant, a chief executive officer, who is responsible for the organisation and administration of the schools under its control. There are thirty-eight VECs; one each for the county boroughs (Dublin, Cork, Limerick and Waterford) and seven for urban areas (Bray, Drogheda, Dun Laoghaire, Galway, Sligo, Tralee and Wexford) and one for each administrative county.

The functions of a committee are to provide, or assist in the provision of, a system of continuation education and a system of technical education in its area. In the discharge of these functions it may establish schools, employ staff and generally perform all the functions of an education authority, within the general powers conferred by the Act. A committee's programme is subject to the approval of the Minister for Education, but generally once the basic educational and financial schemes have been approved a considerable degee of flexibility and discretion is allowed in regard to the actual organisation of courses. Committees can initiate action on matters relating to continuation and technical education in their areas and are thus in a position to be responsive to local needs.

In May 1974, the Minister for Education, Richard Burke, requested all VECs to establish boards of management in each of their schools by 31 October 1974. Each management board was to include a minimum of two VEC representatives and two parents. The Minister indicated that these boards 'should ensure that the school facilities are adequate to meet the needs of the community and report any deficiencies to the parent VEC for remedy'. By 1979 boards of management had been established by twenty-five VECs and normally consist of six VEC members, two parents and a teacher.[21] These boards are sub-committees of the local VEC.

Finance. The financial arrangements of the Act provided for a local rate contribution and corresponding grant from the state. In the first year, 1931-2, the total contribution from the rates was £99,059 and the state contributed a further £204,338. In 1977, total current receipts of all VECs amounted to £42.9 million, of which 90 per cent came by way of grants from the Department of Education, 4.5 per cent from local rates and the remainder from such miscellaneous sources as tuition fees for evening classes, sales of books and bank interest.

'Continuation' and 'Technical' education. The 1930 Act uses the word 'vocational' to cover both 'continuation' education and 'technical' education. Continuation education is defined as 'education to continue and supplement education provided in elementary schools and includes general and practical training in preparation for employment'. The system of continuation education has been built up since 1930.

'Technical' education is defined as 'education in or pertaining to trades, manufactures, commerce and other industrial pursuits', and includes science, art and domestic subjects. Under this heading full courses for apprentices, whole-time day courses leading to professional qualifications, whole-time and part-time technical training, special training courses in connection with new industrial development and evening courses whether of a professional, technical, general or leisure type are provided. Outside the boroughs of Dublin, Waterford, Cork and Limerick facilities for technical education are limited.

Apart from administrative and financing differences between secondary and vocational schools a number of other important differences are discernible. From the outset vocational schools have been inter-denominational and co-educational whereas secondary schools are mainly denominational and single sex. By 1978-9, nine out of ten vocational schools but only four out of ten secondary schools were co-educational.[22]

While vocational schools have been under the control of local authorities the Church has nevertheless had some influence on the development of the system. At the time of the passing of the Vocational Education Act the Catholic hierarchy was given an assurance by the then Minister for Education that the vocational system would not impinge upon the field covered by the denominationally controlled secondary schools.[23] Clergymen of various denominations are represented on each of the thirty-eight VECs and in 1980 the chairmanship was held by a clergyman in eleven cases.[24]

Only in recent years with the introduction of Intermediate and Leaving Certificate courses in vocational schools have the social and educational barriers between the two systems begun to be slowly removed. The vocational system with its emphasis on technical subjects was popularly regarded as a type of educational cul-de-sac where qualifications led to low paid occupations; the secondary schools, on the other hand, with their emphasis on academic subjects were regarded as having higher social status, their qualifications being passports to third level academic education and more remunerative occupations. The demand for skilled technicians in the economy, the expansion of the vocational schools' curriculum and the development of third level technical education, together with the shortage of job opportunities for academically qualified school leavers, has tended to leaven the distinction between the two systems.

In 1978-9, there were 246 vocational schools providing continuation education.

Comprehensive Schools
Apart from inequalities based on social groups the *Investment in Education* report also indicated that there were inequalities based on geographical location in the participation of children in

post-primary education.[25] The reasons for this have already been outlined in the foregoing sections. An attempt to remedy this deficiency was the establishment of comprehensive schools, plans for which were first announced in 1963 by the Minister for Education, Dr Patrick Hillery. In his policy statement, the Minister referred to

> ... areas where the population is so scattered as to make the establishment of a secondary or a vocational school a most unlikely event. Even if it were at all possible through private enterprise to establish a school of the kind required, its smallness would decree that even the best of its pupils would have little choice of subjects in the minimal programme which it could offer. We have ... reached the point where in these particular regions some new kind of approach is needed in post-primary education.[26]

What the Minister envisaged was the establishment, in areas where post-primary education was inadequate or non-existent, of schools which would be completely financed by the state. The first four comprehensive schools were to be established at Cootehill (County Cavan), Carraroe (County Galway), Shannon (County Clare) and Glenties (County Donegal). Each of these schools were sited in rural areas and were open to all children within a radius of ten miles.

The comprehensive school also represented an attempt to rectify the division of interest between secondary and vocational schools by combining academic and practical subjects in one broad curriculum. In this way pupils would be offered an education structured to their needs, abilities and interests. Unlike secondary schools, there is no entry test.

Protestant Comprehensives. Because of the absence of any Protestant equivalent of the Catholic religious orders which have reinvested members' salaries in the establishment and maintenance of their schools, the cost to Protestants of providing their own secondary schools has been relatively high. The introduction of the concept of a comprehensive school where capital and current costs are met fully by the state presented an opportunity to establish Protestant schools without the burden of heavy costs. Three Protestant comprehensives have been established, two in Dublin and one in Cork, but the intake of pupils in these schools is not exclusively Protestant.

Management and finance. Comprehensive schools are managed by a three-member board of management normally consisting of the chief executive officer of the local VEC, a representative of the Department of Education and a representative of either the Catholic or Protestant hierarchy. Both capital and current costs are met in full by the Department of Education. By 1978-9, there were fifteen comprehensive schools; fourteen of these were established in the period 1966-73.

Community Schools

Another important finding of the *Investment in Education* report was that there were gaps in the efficiency of the educational system in the use of existing educational resources. In particular, the report referred to duplication of resources and staff in secondary and vocational schools. In a statement to the authorities of secondary and vocational schools in 1966, the Minister for Education, George Colley, indicated that the two rigidly separated, post-primary systems could no longer be maintained, although their distinctive character should be retained. He urged:

> ... That there should be a pooling of forces, so that the short comings of one will be met from the resources of the other, thus making available to the student in either school the post primary education best suited to him. For example, the vocational school could afford facilities for the teaching of woodwork to pupils of the secondary school while that school would give facilities for the teaching of science to the pupils of the vocational school ...[27]

He recommended that in each locality the authorities of the secondary and vocational schools should confer and formulate proposals on the use of existing accommodation or facilities and, where necessary, the provision of additional facilities. The Minister's recommendations, however, had little effect.

In 1970, Patrick Faulkner, Minister for Education, announced plans for community schools to be created by agreement rather than legislation. In a circular on community schools (see appendix page 139) the Minister indicated that in some areas community schools would result from the amalgamation of existing secondary and vocational schools or in growing suburban areas from the development of separate secondary and vocational schools. The community schools were to be co-educational, and non-fee-paying with enrolments of 400 up to 1,000.

The community schools concept seemed a logical development and would help to eliminate many of the obvious deficiencies in the educational system. An added attraction was that the capital costs would be covered mainly by the state and, in a period of rising costs, this would be an incentive to religious orders to participate in community schools. Another dimension to the community school concept was the involvement of the community. The community schools were to be focal points in the locality, their facilities being made available outside school hours to the community in general.

The announcement of plans for community schools gave rise to a considerable controversy. In the debate which followed opposition was expressed towards the merging of two distinct educational systems. Much of this was undoubtedly influenced by the higher prestige accorded to secondary schools. While the basic concept of community schools as outlined in the original proposals in 1970 represented an admirable and practical step forward, the ideal has, in general, not been implemented.

More recently controversy has centred on the deeds of trust and by 1979, seven years after the establishment of the first community school, the issue was finally resolved. The deeds of trust are legal documents to be signed by the main parties — the VEC, religious orders and the Minister for Education. There is no legislation governing community schools and the deed of trust is the document which will give them a legal base. The two lay teachers' unions concerned (the Teachers' Union of Ireland representing teachers in vocational schools and the

Association of Secondary Teachers of Ireland) objected to the deeds' being signed not in principle but because of certain clauses in them, principally the one relating to reserved teaching posts for members of religious orders. In 1979 the unions withdrew their objections.

Management and finance. Community schools are normally controlled by a six-member board of management composed of two representatives of secondary schools (usually one boys' school and one girls' school both run by religious orders), two representatives of the VEC and two elected parents. There may be considerable local variations in this pattern.

Current expenditure in community schools is borne entirely by the state as are at least 90 per cent of capital costs, the remainder being met by the religious orders and the VEC whose schools are being merged in the new foundation.

By 1978-9 there were twenty-six community schools, one-third of them in the expanding suburbs of Dublin where traditionally, separate secondary and vocational schools would have been established.

Third Level Education
Third level education in Ireland may be broadly divided into two sectors, university and non-university.

Non-University Sector
The regional technical colleges, the colleges of the Dublin Institute of Technology and a number of other institutions providing courses in areas such as domestic science, commerce, retail distribution and management studies, provide most further education in Ireland. It is a small but rapidly growing sector.

The idea of the regional technical colleges was first mentioned in a policy statement on post-primary education in 1963 by the Minister for Education, Dr Patrick Hillery.[28] It was his intention to arrange for the provision of, among other things, a limited number of technological colleges with regional status. The colleges were to work towards a projected Technical Leaving Certificate. The idea was taken further in

1969 by a steering committee on technical education set up in 1966 by Donogh O'Malley, then Minister for Education. This steering committee still saw the colleges as, for the most part, second-level institutions but suggested that some of them might also provide post-leaving certificate full-time or equivalent part-time courses over one or two years leading to higher technician courses.[29] Both the report of the steering committee and the *Investment in Education* report stressed the need in Ireland for high-level technicians to service our growing industrial sector.

The regional technical colleges opened in the period 1970-72 at Athlone, Carlow, Dundalk, Galway, Sligo, Letterkenny and Waterford. Others were subsequently established in Cork and Tralee. While they were originally intended to reinforce the technical dimension of the second-level system they quickly found themselves called upon to cater increasingly for third-level demand. In this dual capacity they were to some extent a new departure and so carried the seeds of innovation. Some of the colleges have Leaving Certificate courses while at third level all colleges offer two-year certificate courses in business studies/secretarial science, in engineering and in science. A variety of other certificate courses is available, e.g. architecture, electronics, plastics technology, hotel management, social science, but not in all colleges.

Each regional technical college is administered by a seven-member board of management which operates as a sub-committee of the local VEC. The board is comprised of one representative each of agricultural, employer and trade union interests; one representative of the Department of Education; one representative of the local VEC; the chief executive officer of the VEC and the college principal. All finance (capital and current) for regional technical colleges is from the Department of Education via the VEC.

Another recent development in the non-university sector is the National Institute for Higher Education (NIHE) at Limerick. The idea of the Institute was first put forward by the Higher Education Authority (HEA) in 1969. The Institute began functioning in 1972 and offers degree and diploma courses with a strong bias towards technology and European studies. The board of the Institute has representatives from staff, students, regional technical college principals, business and trade union interests. Sharing the Plassey campus with the NIHE is Thomond College (the National College of Physical Education) which opened in 1972. Both the Institute and the College are financed by the Department of Education and student fees.

In 1975 the National Institute for Higher Education, Dublin, was established. The Institute will discharge a national and local role in the operation of programmes leading to certificate, diploma, degree, profession and post-graduate awards through full-time and part-time study. In addition it will provide a wide range of other courses not necessarily leading to a particular qualification, for instance for industry, the public service, commerce and the professions. The first students will be enrolled on courses in 1980.

Following proposals made to the Minister for Education by the steering committee on technical education in 1969, and the recommendations of the Higher Education Authority in 1969, the National Council for Educational Awards (NCEA) was set up by the Government in April 1972 on an ad hoc basis, pending the passing of legislation to establish it on a statutory basis.

The NCEA is an independent self-governing body, whose primary function is to award national qualifications at technological levels. It is also responsible for the promotion, co-ordination and development of technological education at third level.

University Sector

The two universities in the Republic are: (1) Dublin University with one college, Trinity College (TCD), and (2) The National University of Ireland (NUI) with three colleges at Dublin (UCD), Cork (UCC) and Galway (UCG).

St Patrick's College, Maynooth, the national Catholic seminary, is recognised by the National University of Ireland for degree-awarding purposes. There is also an independent medical school, the Royal College of Surgeons in Ireland, founded in 1784.

Trinity College. Dublin University received its charter from Elizabeth I in 1591. From the beginning it was identified with English rule and the governing class in Ireland. For much of its history, according to F.S.L. Lyons,[30] Trinity was 'intensely conscious of its position as a bastion of the Ascendancy in general and of Anglicanism in particular'. In 1793 Catholics were admitted to degrees in Trinity College and by the mid-nineteenth century they constituted about 10 per cent of the undergraduate body.

The Queen's College, 1845. In 1845 Sir Robert Peel introduced a Bill providing for the establishment of three 'Queen's Colleges' in Ireland. The colleges were to be established at Belfast, Galway and Cork. There would be no interference with religious convictions, but the establishment, by private endowment, of a theological school within the colleges was permissible. Opposition to the Bill was considerable, particularly from some members of the Irish Catholic hierarchy who feared that lectures in philosophy, history and science were bound to reflect contemporary thought on these subjects. At the Synod of Thurles the hierarchy condemned the Queen's Colleges, and exhorted laymen to avoid them as students or teachers on the grounds that they were dangerous to faith and morals. A minority of bishops unsuccessfully appealed against these decisions. Despite ecclesiastical opposition, the three colleges were established.

The Royal University 1879. The University Education (Ireland) Act, 1879, provided for the formation of a new university (the Royal University) and for the dissolution of the Queen's University. The Royal University was modelled on the University of London, which at the time was purely an examining body. Authority was granted to confer degrees on all students irrespective of where they had studied. The religious difficulty was overcome and Catholics and Protestants presented themselves for examination.

The Catholic University 1854. At the Synod of Thurles a section of the Catholic hierarchy favoured the establishment of a

Catholic University styled on that of Louvain which had been founded with Papal approval in 1834. Dr John Henry Newman, a distinguished Oxford convert, was invited to become rector of the new university. An application by the hierarchy for a charter for the University was unsuccessful as was an application for state funds. Newman left Ireland in 1858 and the University declined. In 1890 it was placed in the charge of the Jesuits who administered its affairs until the establishment of the National University in 1908.

The National University of Ireland 1908. The National University of Ireland was established by the Irish Universities Act, 1908. In the following year the Royal University was formally dissolved. The Act provided for the establishment of two new universities, one in Dublin and one in Belfast. The one in Belfast was to become the Queen's University replacing the former college of that name. The new National University of Ireland, centred in Dublin, was to take over the Queen's Colleges in Cork and Galway as constituent colleges as well as the new college founded in Dublin to replace the Catholic University. It was further allowed to affiliate 'such institutions as have a standard deemed satisfactory by the University', an arrangement which allowed the subsequent entry of Maynooth. No test whatever of religious belief was to be permitted for any appointment in either of the universities, thus denying the denominational university which the Catholic hierarchy had long demanded.

St Patrick's College, Maynooth. St Patrick's was founded in 1795 as a seminary for the training of the Catholic clergy. It was the only Catholic educational institution to receive state aid at the time. In 1910, under the provisions of the Irish Universities Act, 1908, the College was recognised by the Senate of the National University as a recognised College of the University in certain faculties. A decision by the hierarchy to admit lay students to courses at Maynooth in 1966-7 led to the wider use of an institution which had hitherto been confined to the training of priests. Since then the number of clerical students has declined while the number of lay students has increased steadily.

Trinity College in the Twentieth Century. The future status of Trinity College became a leading question during the early years of the present century. A Royal Commission of 1907 recommended that Dublin University should be enlarged to include the Queen's Colleges, and that a new college acceptable to the Catholic authorities be founded in Dublin. Opposition to this proposal, however, ensured that Trinity maintained its independence when the National University was established in 1908.

At the National Synod of Maynooth in 1875 the Catholic hierarchy had coupled Trinity College with the Queen's College as places forbidden to Catholic students. Yet for many years the bishops took no active steps towards implementing this decision apart from periodical instructions to priests to refrain from advising parents to send their children to Trinity College. After 1944, the Archbishop of Dublin began issuing annual condemnations of the attendance of Catholics at Trinity, in his lenten pastorals. Such attendance would, he affirmed, be permissible only 'for grave and valid reasons'. The consequence was not only to limit the entry of Catholic students, but that of students from the lower income groups as well. Local authorities proved unwilling to oppose the hierarchy's position by offering scholarships under the 1908 Act to Trinity College, though some were prepared to award them in special circumstances to Protestant candidates alone. The most commonly accepted 'grave and valid reason' was an inability to take the compulsory matriculation qualification in Irish which was required by the National University. Perhaps the most significant barriers created by the ban were not so much religious as social and served to isolate Trinity from the life of the vast majority of the Irish people.

The regulations of the Catholic hierarchy in regard to the attendance of Catholics at Trinity College are outlined in the report of the Commission on Higher Education.[31] In the same report the Rev Dr Philbin (presently Bishop of Down and Connor) referred to the colleges of the National University as substantially satisfying Catholic requirements whereas Trinity College was seen as having a neutral and secularist character.[32]

One effect of the ban was to lead to an influx of non-Irish

undergraduates. In 1965-6, 27 per cent of Trinity's students were from the United Kingdom (excluding Northern Ireland) and a further 9 per cent were from other foreign countries. In the same year Catholics accounted for 20 per cent of the total number of students. In 1967 the Board of Trinity College decided to limit the entry of non-Irish students, up to a maximum of 10 per cent, to those who had associations with Ireland or those who belonged to educationally-developing countries. This measure partly paved the way for the removal of the ban which occurred in 1970. By 1975-6, 3 per cent of Trinity's students were from the United Kingdom (excluding Northern Ireland) and 6 per cent were from other foreign countries. In the same year Catholics accounted for 65 per cent of students at the college.

Recent attempts at reorganisation of universities. The findings of the *Commission on Higher Education* (1967) recommended 'far-reaching changes' to provide for 'continually increasing numbers'. Trinity College should keep its independence intact, while co-operating with University College, Dublin, in the sharing of facilities and staff; the National University, organised more as 'a loose aggregation of colleges than as an integrated system', should be broken up into three viable universities at Dublin, Cork and Galway.

Shortly after the publication of the report the Minister for Education, Donogh O'Malley, announced in April 1967 that he intended to reorganise Trinity College and University College, Dublin, within a common University of Dublin. In his statement the Minister referred to

> ... two separate and very differently constituted university institutions, each endowed in major part by the State, but each ploughing its own furrow with virtually no provision, formal or even informal, for co-ordination of their efforts or the sharing by them of what must always be scarce but very valuable national resources.[33]

As a follow-up to the Minister's announcement of his proposal and the lack of agreement by the two Colleges as to how the proposal might be effected, the government issued in July 1968 its plan for a single University in Dublin, declaring at the same time its intention to reconstitute the Cork and Galway Colleges as universities. In accordance with the recommendations of the Commission on Higher Education the government also decided to set up a permanent authority to deal with the financial and organisational problems of higher education.

In July 1972 the Higher Education Authority, which had been established in 1968, issued a *Report on University Re-Organisation*. In broad terms the HEA accepted a compromise agreement worked out by the authorities of the two Dublin colleges in 1970 in response to the government's proposals.

In December 1974 yet another statement was issued, this time by Richard Burke, Minister for Education. The Minister's proposals envisaged that TCD would continue as an independent university, UCD would become an independent university, UCG and UCC would remain as constituent colleges of the NUI, Maynooth would have the option of becoming a constituent college of any one of the three universities and the NCEA would be abolished. These proposals gave rise to considerable controversy.

In July 1976, in what can only be described as a complete turnabout in policy, Richard Burke stated that there were to be five universities in the state, in other words that UCC, UCG and Maynooth would be independent as well as Trinity and UCD. Following the change in government in July 1977, the new Minister for Education, John Wilson, decreed that the NCEA would have its degree-awarding functions restored. A bill giving statutory recognition to the NCEA and outlining its functions was published towards the end of 1978.

As a result of a national referendum on the seventh amendment of the Constitution held in July 1979 it is now possible for the government to introduce legislation providing for the abolition of the NUI and the establishment of independent universities at UCD, UCC and UCG.

Higher Education Grants

The report of the *Commission on Higher Education* contained surveys carried out by the Investment in Education team and by Monica Nevin which indicated that children of manual workers comprised less than one-tenth of university students, farmers' children not more than two-tenths, with the children of non-manual workers accounting for the remainder.[34] Consequently, the Commission felt that while scholarships would assist students of limited means but with special abilities,and loans would remove immediate barriers to higher education for the qualified student, there was need for additional assistance available only to students from the lower-income groups. This assistance, the Commission envisaged, would take the form of a grant and would further remove financial barriers, and by providing a special incentive might also help to remove psychological barriers. The Local Authority (Higher Education Grant) Act, 1968, provided for such a scheme, grants being payable to students reaching a required standard in the Leaving Certificate examination and subject to a means test. The grant is administered by local authorities and is operated on a sliding scale related to parental income and number of children in the family. It also distinguishes between students living within commuting distances of university centres and others (see appendix on pages 143 and 144). Approximately one-quarter of university students are in receipt of higher education grants.

Higher Education Authority
The Higher Education Authority was established in 1968 on the recommendation of the Commission of Higher Education but it was not until 1972 that it became a statutory body following the passing of the Higher Education Act, 1971. The Higher Education Authority has two main functions:
1. As an advisory body it must monitor, review, advise and play its part generally in furthering the development of higher education and in the co-ordination of state investment therein.
2. Its central statutory power and function as an executive body is to assess in relation to annual or other periods the financial requirements of the institutions of which it is the founding agency; to recommend for state grants the capital and current amounts so assessed and to allocate to the institutions concerned the state funds provided.

Finance

The two main sources of recurrent funds for third level institutions are state grants, the most significant source, and student fees. In 1978-9, the state grant accounted for 83 per cent of the total income of third level institutions funded by the HEA.[35] The HEA believed, however, that in the same year, the state grant represented more than 83 per cent of total income in many other third level institutions.[36] In the 1978 green paper, *Development for Full Employment,* the government argued that since the high level of benefits accrued, in large part, 'to a small and privileged section of the community', it seemed more equitable to increase student fees. In order to minimise the impact on students from low-income backgrounds the government envisaged improvements in the level of higher education grants and the possibility of introducing a loan scheme. In the 1979 white paper, *Programme for Development 1978-81,* the government felt that third level institutions should be endeavouring to collect a greater proportion of their income in fees and that this should be accompanied by improvements in the grants scheme for students.[37]

In February 1978, the Minister for Education, John Wilson, announced that for 1979-80 university entrance fees would be increased by 25 per cent and by 10 per cent for those already attending university. At the same time he also announced improvements in the higher education grant scheme.

The issue of fees/state subsidies at third level, while important in itself, cannot be divorced from the level of subsidy at other levels. The final section of this chapter will deal with this and other related issues.

Enrolment at Third Level

Many of the developments which occurred at second level, e.g. the free post-primary education scheme, together with the introduction of higher education grants and the expansion of the non-university sector, has inevitably meant an increase in the numbers attending third level institutions since the mid 1960s. Between 1966-7 and 1976-7 the total number increased by two-thirds, from 19,304 to 32,387 (see Table 24, page 130). The largest proportionate increase occurred in institutions

Table 24: Number of students in third level institutions
1966/67 and 1976/77

	1966/67	1976/77	% increase
Universities	15,845	21,921	38.3
Teacher training colleges	1,466	2,542	73.4
Other	1,993	7,924	297.6
Total	19,304	32,387	67.7

Source:　O'Callaghan, D.F. 'Manpower Training for Regional Needs' Paper read at conference on *Regional Planning Policy — An Appraisal* Regional Studies Association, Dublin 1978, p.7.

outside of universities and teacher training colleges and this is largely accounted for by the establishment of regional technical colleges. The increase in teacher training colleges was also relatively high. The main impetus here arose from an increase in the youth population in the late 1960s and early 1970s and the consequent need for more teachers at first level.

Sheehan[38] has indicated that in 1976 about 17 per cent of students in the senior cycle of second level schools could be expected to obtain places in third-level institutions. He estimated that in order to keep participation rates at this level would mean an additional 14,000 third-level places by 1991. If participation rates already achieved in other EEC countries were to be reached, however, an additional 33,000 places would be required by 1991.

Adult Education
With the introduction of important developments in the Irish educational system at all levels during the 1960s and early 1970s it was inevitable that attention would be focused on adult education and, more specifically, on those who for whatever reason had terminated their education at an early age.

The census of 1971 indicated, for example, that 43.1 per cent of males and 36.6 per cent of females in the 20-24 age group had not progressed beyond first level education. As might be expected, these percentages increased with age. The census also revealed that while 75 per cent of all fifteen-year-olds were receiving full-time education, this figure had fallen to 26 per cent for eighteen-year-olds.

At present, adult education is the responsibility of many different groups and organisations. At one level it is the responsibility of Vocational Education Committees which provide adult education classes in many of the schools under their control. At another it is promoted by the extra-mural departments of the university colleges in Cork, Dublin and Galway. Finally, it is provided in many areas by voluntary agencies.

In May 1969, the then Minister for Education, Brian Lenihan, announced the appointment of a committee under the chairmanship of Con Murphy, 'to carry out a survey of the needs of the community in the matter of adult education and to indicate the type of permanent organisation to be set up in order to serve those needs'. The committee published an interim report in April 1970 and in November 1973 the final report, *Adult Education in Ireland,* was published.

The interim report estimated that 10 per cent of the total adult population engages in adult education annually. The report concluded that informal adult education should be provided first for the functional illiterates. Functional illiteracy was defined as 'the inability to cope with the ordinary functions of living which require a knowledge of reading and writing; it is manifested by an inability to read advertisements, warning signs, notices, or to write letters and complete forms'.[39] The report further states that:

> There is no inexpensive way of finding out the extent of functional illiteracy in our society but through submissions, especially from some Trade Unions, we conclude that the situation is a good deal worse than is generally believed. It has been submitted to us that the level of literacy and numeracy is so low amongst many of the working population that promotion, even to minor supervisory grades or further training that is not strictly manipulative is virtually impossible for many. We have also been urged to take

account of a similar type of functional illiteracy amongst many farmers and farm workers, although the evidence is that no such problem exists among adult females in the rural community.[40]

The final report (commonly referred to as the Murphy Report) broadly defines adult education as 'the provision and utilisation of facilities whereby those who are no longer participants in the full-time school system may learn whatever they need to learn at any period of their lives'.[41] In this definition no distinction is made between formal and informal education.

On the question of early school leavers the report states that. 'despite the availability of free post-primary education, the raising of the school leaving age to 15 and the changing attitudes of parents to education, there will be for many years to come a great number of persons who have prematurely dropped out of the educational system'.[42] Between 1967 and 1970, approximately 19,800 persons aged 14 or less dropped out of full-time education, according to the report.

While accurate figures on the number of adults in Ireland who participate in adult education are not available, the report estimates that 10 per cent of the adult population participates in adult training, in-service and retraining programmes. The report listed the characteristics of participants in adult education as: (1) persons in the 21-45 age group; (2) persons with at least two years post-primary education; and (3) members of upper socio-economic groups.

The report estimated that in 1972-3 the total expenditure from central and local government on adult education was £2.5 million. Such a figure was deemed inadequate to meet even existing needs. The committee therefore recommended that a separate budgetary provision be made in the Department of Education for (1) the general improvement and extension of the existing service, and (2) the implementation of the main recommendations of the report. The main recommendations of the report included the creation of county education committees, the establishment of regional education committees, the creation in third level institutions of departments of adult education and community development, training of adult educators, research in adult education, grants to organisations engaged in adult education, and the establishment of resident-ial centres of adult education.

While there was no positive reaction from the government at the time to the recommendations of the Murphy report some developments have taken place in recent years. Aontas, the national association for adult education, established in 1969, has been prominent in publicising the various courses and activities of the numerous agencies that are affiliated to it. It represents voluntary agencies, statutory bodies and individuals involved in adult education and provides a national focal point for discussion, co-ordination and development. Aontas has been actively seeking the implementation of the Murphy report recommendations.

In 1978 the NCEA published a discussion document on an award structure for recurrent education.[43] Its main recom-mendation was that a new award, the Foundation Certificate, be instituted, providing a 'second chance' for those whose early education was curtailed. The new qualification would indicate that the holder had reached a level of educational achievement enabling him or her to benefit from third-level education. The other major suggestions were that work experience be evaluated under such a course and that part-time courses be integrated with a comprehensive awards system which would cater for all levels of recurrent education.

In February 1979, the Minister for Education, John Wilson, announced that fifty adult education officers were to be recruited and that these would work mainly in the vocational sector. He expressed the hope that all schools, including secondary schools, would become involved in the adult education field.

Equality of opportunity in education

It was only in the nineteenth century that the notion that children should have the opportunity of being educated emerged. Since then and particularly in the last few decades the achievement of equality of opportunity in education has become one of the main prongs in the social policies of developed nations. With this in mind, efforts have been concentrated on ensuring that all children have equal opportunity to participate in education at all levels. Efforts were initially concentrated on first level education, subsequently on second level and more recently on third level. Free education schemes and grant schemes were introduced to ensure that children from lower income families would not be excluded because of lack of finance. Poorer children were thus given access to education in theory at least. In practice, however, free education does not ensure against poor parents being unable to do without the income they forego by allowing their children to attend school instead of taking up a job.

The attempt to achieve equality of opportunity has not been as successful as might be imagined. A survey carried out by McGréil in 1972-73 indicated the great disparity in standards of education achieved in various districts of Dublin.[44] Thus, the percentage of the population with first level education only ranged from 85.5 per cent in Ballyfermot to 24.4 per cent in Killiney/Kill o' the Grange. In commenting on these differences the survey report stated:

> In modern society there is a direct correlation between education and occupational status. Therefore those districts with lowest educational qualifications are inevitably the districts whose citizens have the least opportunity of achieving the better occupations.[45]

It could be argued that the survey results could not possibly reflect the change in participation rates which followed the introduction of the free post-primary education scheme in 1966-67 since many of those interviewed would have left school before the introduction of the scheme. The overall pattern of educational standards between districts, however, is unlikely to have changed substantially as a result of free post-primary education.

It is at third level that the greatest disparities in participation occur. The *Investment in Education* report noted, for example, that 'the strong association between university entrance and social group is unmistakeable'.[46] It indicated that children of professional persons, managers, salaried employees (senior) and intermediate non-manual workers constituted 65 per cent of entrants to university in 1963. The report of the Commission on Higher Education (1967) also contained a report by Monica Nevin which showed that among full-time first year students attending UCD in 1964-65, children of semi-skilled and unskilled workers accounted for only 1 per cent of the total as compared with 21.6 per cent for children of employers and managers and 20.1 per cent for children of intermediate non-manual workers.[47] The introduction of higher education grants in 1968 was designed to increase participation at third level by the lower socio-economic groups. It would appear that this scheme has had only a marginal effect on participation by such groups.

Data on the socio-economic background of full-time students in UCD for the 1975-76 to 1978-79 period indicates that in 1975-76 the relative participation of students from a 'working-class' background had increased when compared with Nevin's survey in the mid 1960s (from 10.5 per cent to 16.2 per cent) but declined thereafter (to 10.5 per cent in 1978-79); the decline since 1975-76 was attributed to the decline in the real value of the higher education grants and their availability.[48]

In a survey of Dublin entrants to third-level education in 1978-79, Clancy and Benson have indicated that almost three-quarters (72 per cent) of these entrants come from the four higher socio-economic groups (higher professional, lower professional, employers and managers and salaried employees) although these groups constitute only one-fifth (20.7 per cent) of the population of Dublin.[49] They also established that, in general, the areas of Dublin which McGréil found to have the highest level of educational achievement are those which have the highest participation rates in higher education in 1978-79. Paradoxically, it is at third level that per-pupil public expenditure is highest (as will be indicated in the following pages) and yet it is at this level that participation of children from lower socio-economic groups is lowest.

It appears that one of the main reasons for the comparatively low participation in education of children from the lower socio-economic groups is the unfavourable environment of such children. The problem of compensating for deficiencies in the

environment of the disadvantaged child is the subject of
experiments in a number of countries. These experiments are
forms of positive discrimination. In Britain educational priority
areas have been established as a means of compensating for
disadvantages of the child's environment. In Ireland there is
only one such project, located at Rutland Street in the inner
city area of Dublin.[50]

Public Expenditure on education

Recent reports by Sheehan, McDonagh and Tussing[51] raise
important questions concerning expenditure on education in
general and relative expenditure between the various levels.[52]
Only some of the major findings and issues of these reports are
presented here.

In its comments on Sheehan's report NESC called for
increased relative spending on the compulsory school-going
age group (6-15 years) in the belief that this would lessen
inequalities of access to higher education, and therefore
improve job and earnings opportunities. It also makes the
observation that unless needy parents are enabled to keep their
children at school up to the age of 17, third level grants will
have little effect in achieving equality of opportunity. NESC
also stated that:

> ... the current system of financing the individual at third
> level may mean an over-production of some types of
> graduates (medicine being the most notable case) and a
> scarcity of others. Furthermore, because of the high earnings
> prospects of some graduates, the present method of
> university financing results in a very large discrepancy
> between the relatively low costs incurred by the individual
> (because of the very high subsidy from public funds) and the
> income he may subsequently earn.[53]

The report recommended that a mixed system of loans and
grants for students at senior second level and third level be
examined, as should the possibility of a graduated fee system
where the payment of fees is related to the ability of a student's
family to pay.

McDonagh's report deals, among other things with the

financing of education at first and second levels. He indicates that the financing of secondary education is cumbersome and too demanding from an administrative viewpoint. The report points out, for example, that the portion of secondary school teachers' salaries paid by school managers is really paid from supplemental grants to the school by the Department of Education. He recommends that the full salaries be paid directly by the Department. Other recommendations regarding financing of schools are that the Department of Education should pay 100 per cent of school building costs instead of the present 80 per cent, that existing capitation and supplemental grants be abolished and replaced by a 'capitation grant towards the operating costs of secondary schools' which would be pitched at a level to meet the essential unit costs computed in the report; secondary schools outside the free education system should be aided only by the payment of teachers' salaries. McDonagh indicates that the unit cost in vocational schools is higher than secondary schools. It has been pointed out that there are valid reasons for this difference.[54]

At primary level the administration is less complex but McDonagh indicates that, for historical reasons which are no longer tenable, primary-teacher training is heavily subsidised. He recommends that students attending training colleges should not only pay similar fees to those attending arts courses at universities but also an economic fee for their board and accommodation at training colleges.

In his report Tussing indicates that a number of trends are likely to increase substantially public expenditure on education in the near future. One of these is the decline in the proportion of teachers who are members of religious orders. These have traditionally ploughed money back into the educational system. Between 1974 and 1986 Tussing predicts that the proportion of religious will decline from 15 per cent to 9 per cent at first level and from 31 per cent to 20 per cent in secondary schools.[55] Tussing concludes that 'the era is virtually, if not completely, over in which the primary system could economise through use of large numbers of religious', and that the trend at second level will also increase school expenditures. A second factor is an increasing technical content in the curriculum mainly at second level which will inevitably raise the cost of instruction in the future. These trends will coincide with an 'explosive growth in school enrolments, partly as a result of a rapidly rising youth population and partly as a result of rising school participation rates'. Tussing estimates that by 1986 enrolment will rise at all levels, 14.3 per cent at first level, 27.1 per cent at second level and 21.9 per cent at third level. Increases in participation rates will inevitably mean that more teachers will have to be employed.

Because of the above trends Tussing estimates that real public expenditure on first and second level is likely to double over the period 1974-86 and more than double at third level. Consequently there will be great enrolment and budgetary pressures in the future. If this impending crisis is not planned for, it will be the poor and disadvantaged, according to Tussing, rather than the wealthy and the advantaged, whose opportunities will be reduced. Tussing's view is that 'scarce resources available for education should be reserved, in general for those aspects of schooling which benefit society as opposed to the individual, and in particular Irish society; and for the less advantaged'.[56]

To achieve these objectives Tussing recommends the abolition of free, post-primary education from Intermediate Certificate onwards with a system of grants to poorer children who cannot afford the fees. Tussing's argument is that the age span of compulsory schooling (6-15 years) is of public and general social value. Above that level, however, the potential earnings of the recipient are enhanced and the more so the higher he or she goes. Therefore, he argues, the individual should pay for this increased private benefit. Tussing also recommends that the fees in third level institutions be raised high enough to cover the current costs of such institutions. He advocates a system of loans to students at third level. His argument for such a recommendation is that only a small fraction of the population have the opportunity to attend third level institutions and those who do are subsequently rewarded handsomely in employment opportunities and higher earnings. Tussing agrees that the recommendations in his report may seem harsh but the alternatives may be even harsher.

In what was evidently a reply to Tussing's second level recommendations, the government's green paper, *Development for Full Employment* (1978), stated: 'The introduction of free second level education had socially progessive and far-reaching egalitarian consequences for the development of Irish society and the Government would be reluctant to seek economies in this area'.[57] The green paper, however, seemed to be broadly in agreement with Tussing's recommendation on third level education, namely that fees be increased and a loan scheme introduced. It also accorded with McDonagh's view that students in teacher training colleges enjoyed a level of support which far exceeded that of other third level students. It suggested that they be placed on the same basis as these students and that a charge might be levied for board and accommodation.

The subsequent white paper, *Programme for National Development 1978-81* (1979), stated:

> ... the Government feel that third level institutions should be moving towards a situation where they would collect a greater proportion of their incomes in fees and that this movement be accompanied by an appropriate improvement in the grants scheme for poorer students ... the subsidy for board and accommodation for student teachers should be reduced, with a view to placing these students more on a par with other third level students.[58]

If nothing else, the reports by Sheehan, McDonagh and Tussing have sparked off a much-needed debate on the future of the Irish education system.

Appendix: Circular on Community Schools from Department of Education, October 1970

1. The creation of community schools must be viewed against the background of government policy in relation to post-primary schools and in particular the following aspects of that policy:
   (a) the provision of free post-primary education for all

children irrespective of ability and without the use of selection procedures on transfer from primary to post-primary;

(b) the elimination of the barrier between secondary and vocational schools and the creation of a unified post-primary system of education;

(c) the provision of comprehensive facilities in each area of the country to cater for the varying aptitudes and abilities of pupils and to provide reasonable equality of educational opportunity for all our children irrespective of the area of the country in which they reside or the means of their parents;

(d) the elimination of overlapping and duplication in the provision of teachers, buildings and equipment so that the available resources in manpower and finance may be utilised to the best advantage and so make resources available to improve the level of services in our post-primary schools.

2. The optimum size for a post-primary school is a matter to which a lot of attention has been given both here and elsewhere. The Advisory Councils for Dublin and Cork have recommended the creation of school units of 400 to 800 pupils. OECD expressed the view a few years ago that the absolute minimum size was probably around the 450 mark. The Department's experience has been that in terms of the level of facilities which can be provided at a tolerable level, the optimum size is around 800 pupils. Generally the Department has accepted the views of the Dublin and Cork Advisory Councils, and aims at the creation of school units of 400 to 800 pupils. It is accepted that given the present distribution of post-primary schools in this country, it will not always be possible, at any rate in the forseeable future, to create school units of 400 to 800 pupils everywhere but there are a number of small towns throughout the country which at present have two or three post-primary schools with a total enrolment of something between 400 and 800 pupils. It is felt that in such areas a single post-primary school, if it could be achieved, would provide a better level of service to the area while at the same time removing the divisions that

at present exist in our post-primary sectors and the difficulties to which these give rise.

3. On another level there is growing acceptance throughout the world that education is a life-long process and that second chance education must be provided at all levels. It would seem clear, therefore, that there will be very substantial development of adult education facilities over the next decade. Allied with this, there is in all countries a growing community consciousness and an increasing demand for school facilities (halls, gymnasia, meeting rooms, playing fields, swimming pools etc.) to be made available out of school hours to voluntary organisations and the adult community generally.

4. Community schools are seen as resulting from the amalgamation of existing secondary and vocational schools or in city areas from the development of individual single schools instead of the traditional development of separate secondary and vocational schools. These schools would provide a reasonably full range of courses leading to Group Certificate, Intermediate Certificate and Leaving Certificate. The community school would provide adult education facilities in the area and, subject to reasonable safeguards against abuse or damage to buildings, equipment, etc, would make facilities available to voluntary organisations and to the adult community generally.

5. The community school would be governed by a board of management consisting of representatives of the secondary school managers and the local Vocational Education Committee with an independent chairman who might be the bishop of the diocese or other agreed chairman or with the chairmanship rotating amongst the representative members of the board. The representation of any particular interest would vary depending on the circumstances of each case and would be a matter for negotiation with the interests involved. It might prove possible to include representatives of parents or industrial/commercial interests but this would vary by way of nomination of the educational authorities involved or by some other way which was agreed by them in the course of negotiations. The site and buildings would be vested in trustees nominated by parties involved.

6. The board of management would be responsible for the administration of the school and its educational policy. The board would be solely responsible for the appointments of staff, including principals, vice-principals and other posts of responsibility, subject to the usual departmental regulations in regard to qualifications, overall quota of teachers, number, types and rates of pay to non-teaching staff. In the case of amalgamations existing permanent staff in the schools being amalgamated would be offered assimilation on to the staff of the community school if they applied for it. Rates of salary and allowances would be those applicable to secondary and vocational schools under the latest arrangements.

7. The capital costs involved (site, buildings, equipment, furniture, playing facilities, etc) would be met out of public funds subject to an agreed local contribution. This local contribution would be a matter for negotiation in each individual case.

8. The current costs of running the school would be met by the board of management which would be funded directly and in full by the Department. This Department favours an arrangement under which a budget would be agreed annually in advance with the board of management and within the limits of that budget the board would be free to decide how best to utilise the funds at its disposal. The board would be free, if it thought fit, to supplement its receipts by such local contributions as it might be possible for it to raise for general or specific purposes. The board's accounts would be subject to audit by the Comptroller and Auditor General in so far as expenditure of public funds was concerned.

Appendix: Schedule of annual benefits payable under the Higher Education Grants scheme, available only to students from lower income groups. See pages 143-144.

(1) Students whose normal family residence is not in or adjacent to a university town.

Income of Parent per annum	Rateable Valuation	Grant Category Number of dependent children in family				
		1 or 2	3	4	5	6 and over
Exceeding £5,885 and not exceeding £6,100	Exceeding £48.00 and not exceeding £50	—	—	—	—	F
Exceeding £5,675 and not exceeding £5,885	Exceeding £46.00 and not exceeding £48	—	—	—	F	D
Exceeding £5,460 and not exceeding £5,675	Exceeding £44.00 and not exceeding £46	—	—	F	D	C
Exceeding £5,250 and not exceeding £5,460	Exceeding £42.00 and not exceeding £44	—	F	D	C	B
Exceeding £5,035 and not exceeding £5,250	Exceeding £40.00 and not exceeding £42	F	D	C	B	A
Exceeding £4,825 and not exceeding £5,035	Exceeding £39.00 and not exceeding £40	D	C	B	A	A
Exceeding £4,610 and not exceeding £4,825	Exceeding £37.00 and not exceeding £39	C	B	A	A	A
Exceeding £4,400 and not exceeding £4,610	Exceeding £35.00 and not exceeding £37	B	A	A	A	A
Not exceeding £4,400	Not exceeding £35	A	A	A	A	A

ANNUAL VALUE OF GRANT CATEGORIES

Category A: Lecture fee (not exceeding £386*) plus £600 in respect of maintenance and other expenses.

Category B: Lecture fee (not exceeding £386*) plus £480 in respect of maintenance and other expenses.

Category C: Lecture fee (not exceeding £386*) plus £360 in respect of maintenance and other expenses.

Category D: Lecture fee (not exceeding £386*) plus £240 in respect of maintenance and other expenses.

Category F: Lecture fee only (not exceeding £386*).

(2) Students whose course is not provided in an educational institution adjacent to his normal family residence.

Income of Parent per annum	Rateable Valuation	Number of dependent children in family				
		1 or 2	3	4	5	6 and over
Exceeding £5,885 and not exceeding £6,100	Exceeding £48.00 and not exceeding £50	—	—	—	—	L
Exceeding £5,675 and not exceeding £5,885	Exceeding £46.00 and not exceeding £48	—	—	—	L	J
Exceeding £5,460 and not exceeding £5,675	Exceeding £44.00 and not exceeding £46	—	—	L	J	I
Exceeding £5,250 and not exceeding £5,460	Exceeding £42.00 and not exceeding £44	—	L	J	I	H
Exceeding £5,035 and not exceeding £5,250	Exceeding £40.00 and not exceeding £42	L	J	I	H	G
Exceeding £4,825 and not exceeding £5,035	Exceeding £39.00 and not exceeding £40	J	I	H	G	G
Exceeding £4,610 and not exceeding £4,825	Exceeding £37.00 and not exceeding £39	I	H	G	G	G
Exceeding £4,400 and not exceeding £4,610	Exceeding £35.00 and not exceeding £37	H	G	G	G	G
Not exceeding £4,400	Not exceeding £35	G	G	G	G	G

ANNUAL VALUE OF GRANT CATEGORIES

Category G: Lecture fee (not exceeding £386*) plus £240 in respect of maintenance and other expenses.
Category H: Lecture fee (not exceeding £386*) plus £192 in respect of maintenance and other expenses.
Category I: Lecture fee (not exceeding £386*) plus £144 in respect of maintenance and other expenses.
Category J: Lecture fee (not exceeding £386*) plus £ 96 in respect of maintenance and other expenses.
Category L: Lecture fee only (not exceeding £386*).

*This upper limit may be exceeded to the extent necessary to cover the total lecture fees (as defined in the Grants Scheme) payable in certain years of the degree courses in the medical, veterinary and dental faculties in the colleges of the National Universities of Ireland and in Trinity College, Dublin.

Chapter 5

Health Services

Introduction
As in housing and education, it is now widely accepted that at least a certain amount of state intervention in the provision of health services is necessary. It would be generally accepted, for example, that certain public and preventive health measures such as sanitation and immunisation against certain diseases should be provided by the state. Indeed the earliest intervention measures were of this nature. The degree to which the state should intervene beyond this level, however, has been a matter of debate, though less so in Ireland[1] than in Britain or the USA. On the one hand it may be argued that health care is essentially no different from other commodities and consequently its provision should be left to the play of market forces. On the other hand there would appear to be convincing arguments for treating health care as significantly different in many respects from other goods which are bought and sold on the market.[2]

In Ireland it has never been government policy to provide or endeavour to provide a fully free health service. The objective has been to ensure that economic circumstances will not prevent a person from seeking medical care. In the white paper of 1966 on *The Health Services and their Further Development* it is stated that in developing the health services to their existing level,

> ... the Government did not accept the proposition that the State had a duty to provide unconditionally all medical, dental and other health services free of cost for everyone, without regard to individual need or circumstances. On the other hand, no service is designed so that a person must show dire want before he can avail himself of it.[3]

The level of health in a community is not determined solely by the level or type of health service. These services constitute only one of the factors which contribute to the health of the community. In fact it appears that the major improvements in life expectancy during this century owe more to factors such as housing conditions, levels of nutrition and proper sanitation than to medical care.

Considerable advances have been made in the provision of health services in Ireland since the last century. On the administrative side the trend has been towards a rationalisation of the administrative structures. The bodies with responsibility for various aspects of the health services in the nineteenth century have been gradually reduced so that by the 1970s there were at local level only eight regional health boards dealing with the administration of health services.

Recent attempts to rationalise the hospital system, however, have been far less successful, and the existing pattern of hospital provision differs little from that in the late nineteenth century. Hospital facilities have improved considerably but the basic structure has remained virtually unaltered.

The present system of eligibility for health services represents a combination of a national health service, similar to that in Britain, and private practice. Approximately two-fifths of the population have free entitlement to all health services while the remainder have limited entitlement. An attempt to introduce a comprehensive hospital service for the entire community in 1974 failed but in 1979 the existing complex system of eligibility for hospital services was considerably simplified.

Of all the social services none has been subject to the same degree of examination and review as the health services. Many of the recent improvements in services have been preceded by a number of inquiries and reports on various aspects of the health services.

While the traditional pattern of health care in Ireland has centred on institutions such as hospitals, there has been a general shift in emphasis towards community care within the past two decades or so. This is reflected in the importance attached to health education and the improvements in community services such as the introduction of a choice-of-doctor scheme for eligible persons in 1972. The proportionate expenditure devoted to community services, however, is still considerably less than that devoted to institutional schemes.

Administration

Hensey[4] has already outlined in admirable detail the evolution of health care in Ireland and consequently, only the major developments are reviewed here. State health services were first provided in a rudimentary form under the Poor Law (Ireland) Act, 1838. The Poor Law administration provided infirmaries and other forms of medical care in association with the workhouses established in each poor law union. Unions were administrative units and the total number covering the present area of the Republic was 126. In 1851 the unions were further divided into dispensary districts, to each of which a physician was attached whose duty it was to attend without charge to the sick poor of the area. This dispensary system survived up to 1972.

In 1872 the Irish Poor Law Commissioners were abolished and replaced by the Irish Local Government Board which assumed control of both poor law and public health services. Central control became more pronounced following independence when in 1924 the Department of Local Government and Public Health was established. In 1947 this Department was divided into three, Local Government, Health and Social Welfare.

At local level the administrative structure for health services remained highly complex throughout the nineteenth century and well into the present century. There were a number of agencies with responsibility for various aspects of health care; boards of guardians, for example, which had been established in each poor law union continued in existence until 1923. By 1940 most health functions at local level had been transferred to county councils and the county manager became responsible for the formulation of local policy on health service. The transfer of responsibility for all health services to local authorities was completed in 1947 when they assumed responsibility in urban areas for preventive health services which up to then had been the domain of urban district councils. In 1947 there were thirty-one health authorities in the state corresponding to the same number of local authorities. In 1960, however, this number was reduced to twenty-seven when unified health authorities were established within the four counties containing the main cities of Dublin, Cork, Limerick and Waterford; the health functions of Dublin County Council and Dublin County Borough, for example, were amalgamated. The trend towards a reduction in the number of authorities with responsibility for health services was taken a stage further when the 1970 Health Act provided for the establishment of eight regional health boards.

The reasons for the regionalisation of health functions were outlined in a white paper in 1966.[5] They were based mainly on the following considerations:

1. The state had taken over the major share of the costs of running the services which were increasing substantially every year. It was therefore desirable to have a new administrative framework to combine national and local interests.

2. It was becoming more and more obvious that in order to develop the medical service itself especially in relation to acute hospital care it would be necessary to have the organisation on an inter-county basis. It was clear that the county as a unit was unsuitable; it was too small as an area for hospital services.

3. The removal of health affairs from the general local authority sphere had been foreshadowed as far back as 1947 when the Department of Health was separated from the Department of Local Government and set up as a separate ministry.

Under the provisions of the Health Act, 1970, the administrative structure of the health services was changed as from 1 April 1970. From that date the health services in the state were to be administered by eight health boards, each covering a number of counties (see Table 25, page 149).

In setting up the boards consideration was given to the area, size of population and the regions delimited for local government planning and development. As can be seen from Table 25, however, the regions vary not only in size but also in population with, for example, the Eastern Health Board area having a population more than five times that of the midland or north-western health board areas. Some of these differences, however, are explained by the location of existing facilities, especially hospitals.

The membership of each health board varies from twenty-seven to thirty-five and is a combination of three main interests:

Table 25: Counties comprising area (sq. miles) and population of health board areas in 1979

Health Board	Counties	Population	Total
Eastern	Dublin	982,586	
(1,800)	Kildare	97,063	
	Wicklow	83,793	1,163,442
North Eastern	Cavan	53,706	
(1,950)	Louth	86,180	
	Meath	90,589	
	Monaghan	50,358	280,833
South Eastern	Waterford	87,252	
(3,630)	Carlow	38,649	
	Kilkenny	69,115	
	Tipperary (S.R.)	72,215	
	Wexford	96,259	366,490
Midland	Laois	49,907	
(2,250)	Longford	30,777	
	Offaly	57,183	
	Westmeath	59,915	197,782
Southern	Cork	395,735	
(4,700)	Kerry	120,281	516,016
Mid-Western	Limerick	157,374	
(3,040)	Clare	84,823	
	Tipperary (N.R.)	58,448	300,645
Western	Galway	167,792	
(5,020)	Mayo	113,751	
	Roscommon	54,095	335,638
North Western	Donegal	121,599	
(2,600)	Leitrim	27,827	
	Sligo	54,609	204,035

1. Elected representatives drawn from county councils and borough councils; these account for more than half the membership.

2. Professional representatives of the medical, nursing, dental and pharmaceutical interests who are mostly officers of the board.

3. Nominees of the Minister for Health of which there are three on each board.

Each health board has a chief executive officer who is responsible for the day to day administration. The chief executive officer has, by statute, personal responsibility for the appointment, control and remuneration of staff and for deciding on the entitlement of individuals to health services. In addition, he may be delegated authority from the board to perform other functions. Policy decisions on services and expenditure, however, are the responsibility of the board.

Management

The blueprint for the development of the management of the health services after 1970 is contained in the report prepared by McKinsey and Co, management consultants, entitled *Towards Better Health Care — Management in the Health Board*. It proposed a management team headed by a chief executive officer with a team of six or four, depending on the size of the health board area, and including programme managers and functional officers. The basis of the approach, accepted by all the health boards, was (1) organisation to achieve objectives, (2) delegation to manage services, and (3) action to implement recommendations. The management team concept replaces the hierarchical system which was a feature of the county management system of administration. It provides for direct access to the chief executive officer by the team heads and is based on patient care needs rather than geographical areas. The team usually meets weekly under the leadership of the chief executive officer.

Other Bodies. As part of the administrative organisation of the health services under the Health Act, 1970, the following bodies were established in addition to the health boards —

Comhairle na nOspidéal, three regional hospital boards (based in Dublin, Cork and Galway) and advisory committees.[6]

The functions of Comhairle include the regulation of the number and type of consultant medical and certain other staff in the hospitals and advising the Minister for Health on matters relating to the organisation and operation of hospital services.

The regional hospital boards, whose establishment had been recommended in the *Report of the Consultative Council on the General Hospital Services* (1968), were charged with the general organisation and development of hospital services in an efficient manner by the health boards and voluntary organisations. They were not to be concerned with the day-to-day running of the hospitals. The areas covered by these boards were intended to be three regions, each comprised of a number of health board regions, for example, the Galway-based regional hospital board was to encompass the western and north-western health board areas. These boards were never fully activated, however, and in 1977 the National Health Council[7] called for their abolition.[8]

The 1970 Health Act also made provision for another body, the local advisory committee, which would function on a county basis and would have an advisory role together with any function delegated by the health board. Membership of this committee is made up of local councillors, the county manager, members of the medical profession and persons attached to voluntary organisations in the sphere of social services.

The question has sometimes been raised as to whether regionalisation of the health services has in fact led to greater efficiency in the provision of services. This concern arose in the context of rising expenditure on health services, including administration. The fact that health expenditure increased at an unprecedented rate shortly after the establishment of the health board structure is due principally to inflation rather than a consequence of a changeover from the county system. The National Health Council addressed itself to this topic during 1975 and from information supplied to the Council by the Department of Health concluded that the administrative cost was considered to be only marginally greater.[9]

One of the main reasons, given in the white paper of 1966, for the change to a regional structure was the inadequacy of the existing hospital services and the belief that they could only be properly developed on a regional basis. Since the establishment of health boards, however, little progress has been made in rationalising hospital services. During a debate in the Dáil in March 1976, Brendan Corish, Minister for Health and Social Welfare, discounted the notion of reverting to the county system stating that in his opinion, 'the most practical, sensible and logical thing is to improve the present system'.[10] He accepted the necessity for a review of the health board system. In June 1978 an all-party Dáil committee on health services was established and as part of its terms of reference it was to consider and advise on the effectiveness of the existing organisation structure for providing health care.

Finance
The major source of income for expenditure on health services at present is the exchequer; up to 1977, however, local taxation was an important and significant source of income.

During the nineteenth century local rates constituted the primary source of income for health services and only towards the end of the century was state aid provided. By 1947, state grants accounted for 16 per cent of the total cost of the services. Post-war developments in the health services necessitated increased state expenditure. Under the Health Services (Financial Provisions) Act, 1947, the state undertook to meet for each health authority the increase in the cost of its services over what that authority had spent in the base year (the financial year ended 31 March 1948) until the cost of the services provided by the authority was being shared equally between the exchequer and local authorities, on a fifty-fifty basis. The white paper of 1966 indicated that local rates were not a form of taxation suitable for collecting revenue on the scale required by proposed developments in the health services and proposed instead that the cost of further extensions of the services should not be met in any proportion by the local rates. By 1970 the exchequer's contribution amounted to 56 per cent of total costs. In 1973 the government decided to remove health charges from local rates over a four-year period and by 1977 the transfer had been completed.

An important source of revenue for hospitals — the Hospitals Trust Fund — dates from the 1930s. A small number of voluntary hospitals combined to run a sweepstake from horse racing in 1930 and this proved to be a financial success. More voluntary hospitals joined in the venture and the first three sweepstakes resulted in the distribution of £1.25 million among the participating voluntary hospitals. Under the Public Hospitals Act, 1933, available surpluses of ensuing sweepstakes were to be payable to the Hospitals Trust Fund, a statutory body appointed by the Minister for Health to administer the funds.

The Hospitals Commission was set up to report to the Minister on applications for grants from the fund. The income of the Hospitals Fund is used mainly for capital expenditure on all hospitals. The income from the sweepstake has, for some time, been insufficient to meet the capital requirements of the health services and exchequer capital grants are paid into the Hospitals Trust Fund to supplement the income from sweepstakes. At present about 90 per cent of income for capital expenditure is met by the exchequer. The total amount contributed to the Hospitals Trust Fund from sweepstakes up to the end of 1975 was approximately £81.5 million.[11] Up to 1974 voluntary hospitals were financed by capitation grants and grants from the Hospitals Trust Fund towards revenue deficits. This has now been replaced by a system of direct payments on behalf of health boards. These payments, related to budgets approved by the Minister for Health, are made on a monthly basis and are limited to 85 per cent of approved budgets in one year. The balance is paid the following year.

Another source of revenue for health services was introduced under the Health Contributions Act, 1971. This is a scheme whereby persons with limited eligibility for health services (see Section on Eligibility for health services, page 176) contribute towards the cost of the services available to them. In the case of insured workers the contribution is made as part of their weekly social insurance contribution while the self-employed, retired people and people with private means make an annual contribution (farmers' contributions are paid to health boards and others to the Revenue Commissioners). Where an insured worker has full eligibility the employer pays the contribution. Previously, people with limited eligibility (formerly the middle income group) made a nominal contribution towards the cost of hospitalisation when they actually availed of the service.

Another source of income since 1973 is receipts under EEC regulations. These receipts are mainly in respect of health services provided for people for whom Britain is liable under EEC regulations. They include recipients of British pensions, dependants of people employed in Britain and British holiday-makers.

Over 90 per cent of funds for health services are now derived from the exchequer (see Table 26, page 154) but following the introduction of pay-related health contributions in April 1979, the state's share should decline slightly.

Table 26: Sources of funds for non-capital expenditure on health services in 1978

	£ million	%
Exchequer	343.376	94.1
Health contributions	16.624	4.5
Receipts under EEC regulations	3.300	0.9
Hospitals sweepstake	1.700	0.5
Total	365.000	100.0

Source: *Statistical information relevant to the health services in 1978* Department of Health, Stationery Office, Dublin 1978, p. 64

Services

The work of health boards is divided into three broad programmes, each with a programme manager. The programmes are:

Community Care
General Hospital
Special Hospital
These provide a useful framework for an examination of health services.

Community Care Programme
The traditional pattern of health services in Ireland placed great emphasis on institutional care. The policy in recent years, however, has been to emphasise community rather than hospital services. The Community Care Programme stresses the need to provide and develop services in the community as opposed to within an institutional setting. The basic reasoning behind this is that it is justified on social as well as economic grounds and that an efficient community care health service will reduce the demand for hospital beds. There is now a widespread acceptance of the concept of delivering services, outside the hospital programmes, through community care teams which include representatives of the different disciplines involved in community care.

The emphasis on community care has been expressed by successive Ministers for Health and in government statements. In introducing the estimate for his Department in 1975, for example, Brendan Corish, Minister for Health, stated: 'My objective is to bring about a shift in resources in favour of community services, in the belief that this will lead to a better health service overall'.[12] The white paper, *Programme for National Development 1978-1981,* also stated:

> The Government's principal long-term aim in the health area is to bring about a shift in emphasis in the services from the curing of illness to its prevention by means of positive programmes designed to make people aware that their health is one of their principal assets .... It is intended that, where possible, illness will be treated in a community rather than institutional setting.[13]

The Community Care Programme includes all the health services in which care is provided outside hospitals and other institutions. As such it encompasses a wide range of health services. These may be broadly classified under two headings:

1. Primary medical and para-medical services, which include services provided by general practitioners, public health nurses, dentists, ophthalmologists, treatment of infectious diseases, vaccination, immunisation and other preventive services.

2. Personal social services and community welfare services, which include services provided by social workers, home helps, meals-on-wheels organisers and staff in day-care nurseries.

The McKinsey report recommended that community care be delivered by teams drawn from all those engaged in field services including doctors, nurses, dentists, social workers, health inspectors and assistance officers. They would bring to bear on the problems of the family or the individual the concerted efforts of a team rather than the fragmented work of individuals from different services. This system would lead to the devolution of services, the discontinuance of centralised specialist groupings and the formation of new multi-disciplinary teams, each to be headed by a Director of Community Care. In each health board area the region has been divided into a number of community care areas, each with a population of 100,000 to 120,000 with a community care team and a Director of Community Care. On the basis of population in the Eastern Health Board area, for example, the region is divided into ten community care areas — Kildare and Wicklow remaining as entities in themselves and Dublin being divided into eight areas.

It is not possible to deal at length with each of the services provided under the Community Care programme. Instead a few services are examined — the General Medical Service (which encompasses the choice-of-doctor scheme), dental services, child health services and the home help service.

General Medical Service. As already noted a free general practitioner service for poor persons was provided from 1851 in local dispensary districts. This system continued until the 1970 Health Act provided for its abolition. The white paper of 1966 had referred to the advantages of the dispensary system but indicated that the segregation of the population into fee-paying patients (who attended the doctor's surgery) and public patients (who attended the dispensary) outweighed any of its merits. Consequently the 1970 Health Act provided for the introducion of a choice-of-doctor scheme under which eligible persons would not be discriminated against in regard to place of treatment. The choice-of-doctor scheme comes under the General Medical Service which also subsumes the service provided by pharmacists to those eligible.

Following negotiations between the Minister for Health and the medical profession the choice-of-doctor scheme was introduced in 1972. It gave the eligible patient (people with full eligibility and their dependants) a choice of doctor to the greatest extent practicable and ended the discrimination and stigma attached to the dispensary system. The introduction of the choice-of-doctor scheme in 1972 has been described, with considerable justification, as 'a major landmark in the history of social development in Ireland'.[14] In 1978 a total of 1,313 doctors were participating in the scheme.[15] Most of these care for both private and eligible patients although the ratio between both categories of patients may vary considerably between different parts of the country. Participating doctors are paid a fee per consultation in accordance with a scale which varies depending on the time at which the service is given and, in the case of domiciliary consultation, on the distance travelled.

Under the dispensary system most of the doctors supplied drugs, medicines and appliances to eligible patients. Under the new scheme retail pharmaceutical chemists who have entered into agreement with health boards are the primary channel of supply of drugs prescribed for eligible persons. Prescriptions are dispensed without charge to the patient and the pharmacist recoups the cost of the drugs and in addition is paid a dispensing fee by the health board.

The number of pharmacies registered under the scheme in 1978 was 1,117. In rural areas where the doctor's practice is located three miles or more from the nearest retail pharmacist participating in the scheme, the doctor may dispense the medicines and is paid a dispensing fee (£1.63 in November 1977) for each patient. In 1978 there were 389 doctors dispensing.

Since its inception in 1972 expenditure on the General Medical Service has increased from £12.26 million in 1973 to £39.48 million in 1978, and the cost of providing drugs and medicine has accounted for about two-thirds of total expenditure in the General Medical Service each year. Between 1974 and 1978 the overall cost per eligible patient almost doubled (from £17.76 to £32.40) and the major part of this increase related to medicines. Detailed information on costs and other matters relevant to the General Medical Service is set out in Table 27, page 159. The overall increase in expenditure over the years is partly attributable to the increase in the number of those eligible and the increase in the price of drugs and medicines.

In 1975, however, the Minister for Health established a working party to examine prescribing patterns in the General Medical Service. The working party's brief was to consider the extent to which there might be over-prescribing or the prescribing of needlessly expensive medicines, to consider the question of prescribing with due regard to economy and to make recommendations in relation to these matters. The working party's report was published in July 1976. While acknowledging the practical difficulties involved in defining overprescribing the report concluded that within the General Medical Service there was:

... evidence that a number of doctors overprescribe to a significant extent. This overprescribing mainly consists in prescribing too many items, prescribing excessive quantities, constantly prescribing the more expensive drugs without regard to their cost and in the case of some patients prescribing more than one drug with the same action. While the majority of doctors prescribe in a reasonable manner they are under constant pressure from the public to prescribe drugs which are not really necessary. This manifests itself in the number and type of drugs and in the quantities which are ordered.[16]

The working party's recommendations to effect a reduction in the drug bill relate, on the one hand, to the possibility of

Table 27: Summary of statistical information on the General
Medical Services, 1974 and 1978

Year ended December	1974	1978
Number of persons covered by Medical cards at 31 December	1,083,136	1,219,178
Doctors		
Total number of visits	5,354,295	6,689,592
Surgery	4,125,245	5,310,768
Domicilary	1,299,050	1,378,824
Total Visiting Rate	5.51	5.64
Surgery	4.24	4.48
Domiciliary	1.27	1.16
Total cost	£6,822,817	£12,817,303
Cost per visit	£1.27	£1.92
Cost per patient	£7.02	£10.81
Pharmacists		
Number of forms	4,271,597	5,409,680
Number of items	8,752,966	11,100,484
Items per forms	2.05	2.05
Total cost of prescriptions	£9,908,798	£23,716,563
Ingredient cost	£6,694,929	£17,235,276
Dispensing fee	£3,127,893	£6,173,103
VAT	£85,976	£308,184
Cost per item	£1.13	£2.14
Cost per form	£2.32	£4.38
Ingredient cost per item	£0.76	£1.55
Total cost of stock orders (inc. needles & syringes)	£1,443,372	£2,945,709
Total cost of medicine	£11,352,170	£26,662,272
Overall cost of medicine per eligible patient	£10.74	£21.59
Overall payment per eligible patient	£17.76	£32.40

Source: *Report of the General Medical Services (Payments)
Board* 1978, p.50.

reducing the basic cost of the drugs available in the country and, on the other, to reducing the quantities of drugs consumed here.

Dental services[17]. The Community Care dental service provides for preventive (fluoridation of water supplies, education, screening) and treatment (extraction, filling, dentures) services. Persons eligible for dental treatment are:

1. Children under 6 years who attend health examination clinics, in respect of defects noticed at examination.
2. Pupils of national schools, in respect of defects noticed at a health examination at such schools.
3. People with full eligibility for health services (medical card holders and their dependants).
4. Insured people are entitled, under the Social Welfare Acts, to dental care from dentists on the Department of Social Welfare's dental panel. In the case of fillings, scalings and extractions there is no charge. For dentures the insured pay approximately two-thirds of the cost.

There are several unsatisfactory features about the dental services scheme at present. Eligibility for free dental services for children applies only to defects noticed at health examinations. Moreover, two groups of children at both ends of the school age range are missed out — children of parents without full eligibility who reside outside the towns where health examination clinics are held and also, children of parents without full eligibility no longer attending national school who are under 16 years of age (once over 16 they may be entitled to a medical card in their own right). In areas where there are no regular school health examinations the service does not, of course, apply. On the preventive side, the fluoridation of water supplies commenced in July 1964. By 1966, one-third of the population was served by a fluoridated water supply and by 1977, over half (56 per cent) of the population was served.

At present large sections of the population are not receiving the dental services to which they are entitled. In some areas there are long waiting lists;[18] in others, priority is given to the elderly and the most needy. A special sub-committee of the National Health Council, established to draft a report on the public dental service and to make recommendations for its improvement, indicated that:

> ... the existing service was most unsatisfactory and inadequate to deal with the demand from eligible persons. It was estimated that only one-third of the 600,000 eligible children estimated to need attention were examined each year under the scheme. Adults receiving treatment under the scheme number about 50,000 a year out of an estimated 570,000 eligible adults not catered for by other schemes.[19]

The Council made sixteen recommendations to the Minister for Health for improving the dental service. These included a free comprehensive service to be made available to all children up to the age of 16 years; a ratio of one dentist per 1,500 children under 16 years, as against the existing ratio of 1:6,300, to be aimed at immediately; a division of responsibility for dental services, for instance between public and private practitioners, to be carefully considered; where public dental facilities were not available, all priority groups to have the option, as an interim measure, of having routine treatment provided by a private practitioner in his own surgery subject to prearranged procedures; adequate dental anaesthetic facilities to be made available in each health board area as a matter of urgency since such facilities were non-existent in many areas. At present there are insufficient dentists at national level to cope with the workload and Ireland has the lowest ratio of dentists of all the EEC countries, 2.2 per 10,000 compared with 5.1 per 10,000 in Germany. It has been suggested that the use of hygienists and other auxiliaries in the dental service would help to improve the present unsatisfactory position.[20]

In 1979 a report prepared by a working party drawn from the Irish Dental Association, the Department of Health and health boards was published.[21] The report contained fifty-one recommendations dealing with manpower, career structures, treatment facilities, prevention, organisation and administration, auxiliary dental personnel and both professional and public education. The report was directed towards making constructive proposals to eradicate the serious deficiencies in dental care. The inability of the public dental service to fulfil its role is due, the report states, to the absence of a sustained preventive approach in the services provided and to a shortage of dentists. It points out that, in the absence of a preventive philosophy, an improved dental treatment service is unlikely to bring about an improvement in the dental health of the community. The only type of dental auxiliary immediately recommended in the report is the dental hygienist whose role is seen as being exclusively confined to health education and prevention under the prescription of a dentist.

In November 1979 a scheme was introduced for a trial period whereby adult medical card holders could attend private dentists for treatment. About 60 per cent of private dentists in the country agreed to participate in this choice-of-dentist scheme.

Child health services. No examination of child health services in Ireland would be complete without reference to the abortive attempt by Noel Browne, Minister for Health in the Inter-Party Government of 1948-51, to introduce a mother and child scheme. The subject and its considerable ramifications are dealt with at length elsewhere[22] and only a brief summary of the main events is offered here.

The 1947 Health Act provided for a free mother and child scheme and it fell to Dr Browne as Minister for Health to implement such a scheme. At that stage the maternity and child care services consisted of attendance by dispensary doctors and midwives on poor patients (with hospital care if necessary) and clinics and nursing services provided by health authorities or voluntary agencies. The legislative base for the latter services dated from 1915 when local authorities were permitted, but not obliged, to make suitable arrangements for looking after the health of expectant mothers, nursing mothers and children under 5 years of age. Subsequent regulations envisaged the formulation by local authorities and voluntary agencies of maternity and child welfare schemes incorporating a range of facilities such as the establishment of health centres and employment of nurses and health visitors. By 1939, a total of 148 approved schemes were in operation, thirty administered by local authorities and the remainder by voluntary agencies.[23]

The 1947 white paper on the health services noted that the child welfare service 'had developed unevenly over the country as a whole and has not grown beyond the health visitor stage, save in the cities and a few urban centres. In the cities the service is for all practical purposes confined to the poorer classes'.[24] The details of the new scheme were based on recommendations submitted by a consultative Child Health Council, representative of the various interests concerned, and established by Dr Browne in 1948. The draft proposals were completed in 1950. The scheme provided for free health services for all mothers before, during and after childbirth and for all children up to 16 years of age. It was to be based on dispensary doctors although, as an interim measure, private practitioners were to be allowed to participate in the scheme. There was to be no compulsion on the public to avail of the scheme, no means test and no contributions.

Such a scheme was necessary, in Dr Browne's view, because at the time Ireland had the highest overall infant and maternal mortality rates in Europe. The Irish Medical Association, however, opposed the scheme on the grounds that it represented a dangerous advance towards complete state control of medicine and a referendum among its members indicated that a clear majority of those who replied were also opposed to working such a scheme. The Catholic hierarchy also opposed the scheme and in a letter to the Taoiseach, John A. Costello, in October 1950 outlined their objections. The hierarchy's opposition was based on the principle of subsidiarity, that is, that the state should not undertake functions which could be adequately fulfilled by individuals on their own or by the local community. The letter stated that: 'The right to provide for the health of children belongs to parents, not to the state. The state has the right to intervene only in a subsidiary capacity to supplement not to supplant.'[25] These objections were reiterated in a further letter of April 1951 in which the hierarchy stated that the scheme was 'contrary to Catholic social teaching'.

The cabinet which initially supported the scheme now decided that it should be abandoned and informed the hierarchy of this decision, 'expressing the complete willingness of the Government to defer to the judgement as given by the hierarchy that the particular scheme in question is opposed to Catholic social thinking.'[26] Dr Browne's resignation from the cabinet in April 1951 was followed shortly afterwards by a general election. Fianna Fáil assumed office in 1951 and Dr James Ryan as Minister for Health now became responsible for implementing the mother and child sections of the 1947 Health Act.

The 1953 Health Act provided for a considerably modified version of the original mother and child scheme. Under the Act, eligibility for hospital services was extended to the middle income group so that women in the lower and middle income groups which accounted for approximately 85 per cent of the population became entitled to a full maternity service with choice of doctor and midwife and, subject to a financial contribution, choice of hospital or maternity home. Comprehensive medical care and nursing care for expectant mothers in the lower and middle income groups and for their infants up to six weeks were also provided. Health authorities became obliged to establish clinics in towns of 3,000 or more population and the age limit for children covered by the child welfare service was raised by one year to include children up to 6 years of age. Another important difference was that women in the higher income group (approximately 15 per cent of the population) were to be entitled to use the service for expectant mothers and their infants but only if they paid a small insurance contribution. This part of the Act was never implemented, however, and was formally repealed by the Health Act, 1970.

The remainder of this section is devoted to two aspects of child health services, developmental services and school health examination services.

The study group which reported to the Minister for Health on the child health services in 1968 recommended the medical screening of all children at specified ages so as to monitor the extent to which they were developing within the normal range, to detect and keep under review any children who were showing deviation from normal development and to refer for appropriate care any suspected or identified cases of disease or defect. It was envisaged that initially the service would be provided in the cities and towns with populations of 5,000 and over. It was hoped that at a later stage, similar services would be provided in the remainder of the country and that consideration would be given to the extent to which general medical practitioners could be involved in that service. Routine child welfare clinics, which had been in operation in most towns with populations of 3,000 and over, were to be reduced substantially or completely phased out and reliance was to be placed on scheduled examinations which were to take place at six months, twelve months and twenty-four months. The children were to be examined in developmental paediatric clinics. It is estimated that in 1971 two-thirds (66 per cent) of eligible children were examined at the first stage, i.e. six months (or 6 to 10 months in practice). By 1976, 85 per cent of eligible children were examined at the first stage[27] and approximately one in five children examined at each of the three stages required further attention. Under section 66 of the 1970 Health Act each health board is required to provide these examinations free of charge to all children under 6 years. Yet, as the figures indicate, all children are not receiving the examinations, particularly at the first stage. This is largely explained by the fact that developmental clinics are confined in the main to towns of 5,000 population and over. While in some areas the service is well developed, in others it is totally lacking; for instance, there is not one developmental paediatric clinic in counties Roscommon or Leitrim.

Each health board is also obliged under the 1970 Health Act to make available an examination service, free of charge, for pupils in national schools. This service originated in 1919 when local authorities were required to provide for the medical inspection and treatment of children attending national schools. The purpose of the service is to ensure that children who have defects will receive treatment as quickly as possible and will then be able to develop and derive the maximum educational benefit while at school. The service provides for free out-patient specialist treatment for all such children in respect of defects discovered at examination together with dental, ophthalmic and aural treatment (including hearing aids) and spectacles. Where in-patient hospital treatment is necessary the service is only free of charge for children of parents who have full or limited eligibility. The aim was that the school doctor should visit all schools with fifty or more pupils each year (and smaller schools once every two years) and give all school entrants a comprehensive medical examination when they were approximately one year at school. A further examination would be made of a limited number of children between the ages of 9 and 10 years, selected on the basis of information obtained from parents, teachers, nurses or other interested parties. Other children on observation by the school doctor would also be medically examined. It was also intended that nurses would carry out annual testing of vision, posture and cleanliness amongst all national school children and new entrants would receive a special audiometric test by a nurse trained in that technique. Routine medical examinations were to be phased out. In 1976 almost all new entrants to national schools were examined and over one-third required further attention.[28]

The generally unsatisfactory nature of child health services was referred to at the Waterford Seminar[29] on Irish health services. The seminar recommended that:

> Because of its preventative nature and the long-term financial saving that would result, a critical study should be made of the child health services. Such a study should consider: what are we doing? What gaps are there in the service? What needs are we not meeting? And, on the basis of the answers to these questions, what new services do we need to develop?[30]

Home help service. Section 61 of the 1970 Health Act empowers but does not require health boards to make arrangements to assist in the maintenance at home of the following categories of persons:

1. A sick or infirm person or dependant of such a person;

2. A woman availing herself of medical surgical and mid-wifery services, or receiving similar care, or a dependant of such a woman;

3. A person who but for the provision of a home help service would require to be maintained otherwise than at home.

The Act does not preclude any income group from availing of the service but, because of funding limitations, the great majority of beneficiaries are likely to be people with full eligibility for health services. Each health board has statutory authority to provide a home help service and may employ its own personnel or may involve appropriate voluntary agencies. The home help may be either full-time or part-time. Between 1974 and 1977 the number of beneficiaries under the home help service has fluctuated (see Table 28, page 167). In 1976, when health services in general came under budgetary pressure, the number of beneficiaries declined from 5,810 at the end of 1975 to 5,097 at the end of 1976; in the same year there was a slight fall in expenditure on the service. These changes during 1976, however, are largely attributable to the situation in the Western Health Board where the expenditure was almost halved (from £271,705 to £140,516) and where the number of beneficiaries fell by two-thirds (from 1,541 to 563).[31] These cutbacks in the Western Health Board area were largely due to the fact that the practice of employing relatives as home helps was terminated in 1976.

Table 28: Number of home helps, beneficiaries and expenditure on home help service 1974-1977

	1974	1975	1976	1977
Number of home helps	4,734	4,840	3,980	4,664
Number of beneficiaries	5,563	5,810	5,097	6,021
Expenditure (£000s)	627.6	1,132.3	1,114.5	1,565.0

Source: *Report on Home Help Service* National Social Service Council, Dublin 1978, pp.16-17

In 1977, almost all (97.6 per cent) home helps were part-time and in 1976 the largest category of beneficiaries was the elderly who accounted for 83.2 per cent of all beneficiaries in that year. The National Social Service Council, in their report on home help services, made twenty-five recommendations among which were that the paid home-help service should be seen as supplementary to a good neighbour response; that rates of payment be at least on a par with comparable types of employment in order to attract suitable candidates and that a greater investment was urgently required to improve the provision of home helps to families in stress situations and eligible groups other than the elderly.[32]

Comment. The necessity of providing adequate community care services is widely acknowledged. Yet the cost of providing these services fully is an obstacle to the development of efficient services. Some of the existing services, for instance, child health services and dental services, are far from adequate; in order to provide these services fully and even to provide services for those entitled to them free of charge the cost would be substantial. Furthermore, achieving the 'shift in resources in favour of community services' is hindered by the fact that hospital services account for a high proportion of health costs (see Table 29 page 169). Hospital services must be maintained and improved and this postpones the possibility of diverting resources to community services. The demands to improve hospital care are still, and are likely to continue for a considerable time, at a high level. The almost infinite possibilities for raising the level of technology and care in the hospital service, however, should not be used as a justification for continually postponing development in community care.

General Hospital Programme
This programme covers the treatment of patients in medical, surgical and maternity hospitals including treatment in outpatient consultant clinics associated with these hospitals. These services are provided either directly by health boards in hospitals under their control or by contract with voluntary and private hospitals.

Table 29: Allocation of non-capital expenditure by health programme in 1978

	£ million	%
Community Care	88.217	24.2
General Hospital	176.588	48.4
Special Hospital	77.545	21.2
General Support Services (i.e. central and local administration)	22.650	6.2
Total	365,000	100.0

Source: *Statistics Relevant to the Health Services 1978* Department of Health, Stationery Office, Dublin 1978, pp. 64-66

There are three categories of hospital ownership in Ireland.[33] Firstly, there are 97 hospitals which were formerly operated by local authorities and are now administered by health boards. These hospitals originated mainly in the nineteenth century[34] and in 1976 accounted for just under half (47 per cent) of hospital beds. Secondly, there are 47 voluntary public hospitals, some of which date from the early eighteenth century and they account for over two-fifths (44.9 per cent) of hospital beds. Thirdly, there are 16 private hospitals and these account for 8.1 per cent of hospital beds. The present distribution of general hospitals in Ireland is due largely to historical circumstances. As might be expected, the voluntary public hospitals tend to be concentrated in the larger urban areas, principally Dublin, where the greatest demand for services existed and where financial support was also likely to be forthcoming. At present, these hospitals are funded from the Department of Health. The public hospital system evolved from the workhouses of the nineteenth century Poor Law and, following the foundation of the state, a county system of hospitals was established.

In the period 1973 to 1976 the total number of patients treated in health board and voluntary public hospitals increased by 13 per cent (from 418,279 to 472,731); over the same period the average duration of stay by patients was reduced from 12.5 days to 10.9 days in health board hospitals and from 12.4 days to 10.7 days in voluntary public hospitals.

In 1967, the then Minister for Health, Sean Flanagan, appointed a consultative council with the following terms of reference:

> To examine the position in regard to general hospital in-patient and out-patient services in the State and to report in outline on the future organisation, extent and location of these services ... so as to secure ... that the public is provided in the most effective way with the best possible services.

The chairman of the council was Professor Patrick Fitzgerald and the report, published in 1968, is usually referred to as the *Fitzgerald Report*.[35] In general, the report indicated that the existing hospital system was defective in staffing, equipment, quality of service and teaching standards. It suggested that the system could only be improved by a radical re-organisation involving, among other things, a considerable reduction in the number of centres providing acute treatment and a planned and co-ordinated hospital organisation embracing both the public and voluntary hospitals. It recommended that the hospital system be re-organised into three regions based on the medical teaching centres at Dublin, Cork and Galway. Each region would have a regional hospital of 600-1,000 beds offering a full range of services supported by a number of general hospitals of about 300 beds throughout the region. The existing district hospitals would be staffed by general practitioners catering for non-acute cases needing care. The existing county hospitals were to be community health centres providing in-patient services as suggested for district hospitals but backed by increased diagnostic facilities and a more comprehensive consultant out-patient organisation. The report also recommended increasing emphasis on out-patient care and referred, though rather vaguely, to a need to explore the relationship between the hospital service and the general practitioner. The report indicated that the number of beds in use in the 169 acute care hospitals was 21,000, representing 7.2 beds per 1,000 population, a figure which was high by comparison with other countries. The report recommended that 4.15 acute beds per 1,000 population be adopted as the standard for future planning.

The General Hospital Development Plan (GHDP) issued by Brendan Corish, Minister for Health, in October 1975 differed substantially from the Fitzgerald Report. The major difference between the plans was the number of acute care hospitals to be established. In reference to the Fitzgerald Report the Minister stated:

> While the general concept of this report was accepted in principle by the then Government and while, from the medical point of view, the recommendations were logical, it became clear in subsequent years that the detailed concept as set out did not have sufficient regard to the practical needs and wishes of the people.[36]

In 1973 the Minister initiated a process of widespread consultation, involving the profession, local bodies and Comhairle na nOspidéal. Guidelines drawn up by Comhairle modified the earlier recommendations of the Fitzgerald Report and proposed that:
1. The general aim should be to organise acute hospital services so that the population served would be within a radius of 30 miles of the hospital centre.
2. The minimum staff of such an acute hospital should consist of two consultant surgeons and two consultant physicians with other consultant medical personnel and other staff as required by the case-load.
3. A minimum scale consultant-staffed hospital conforming to the guidelines should usually serve a population of about 100,000 but where there were special considerations such as low population density, a lower figure would be appropriate, ranging down to 75,000 in exceptional circumstances.

The Minister accepted the Comhairle guidelines as a

reasonable basis for improving the hospital service and for decisions on the future system. For each health board area, a working group drawn from the health board, the Comhairle and the
regional hospital board surveyed the available facilities and
considered, in the context of the guidelines, what realistic options existed for future policy. Each county health advisory
committee within the health board area had an opportunity to
express its opinion. The GHDP envisaged the development of
general hospitals in twenty-three locations (about twice as
many as envisaged in the Fitzgerald Report) and speculated on
the further development of community hospitals in formats and
locations to be decided on. The plan contained no detail of the
future development of hospital services in either Cork or
Limerick cities beyond tentative mention of the possibility of a
major hospital in the north east area of Cork city. In addition,
the siting of a general hospital in south Tipperary was left for a
later decision, pending further consultation between the
Minister and the South Eastern Health Board. The major differences between the GHDP and the Fitzgerald Report were
distance of population from a general hospital (30 miles versus
60 miles) and the number of general hospitals (23 versus 12).

The plan could be viewed as a balance between professional
medical opinion and broader political considerations. The
editorial of *The Irish Times* commented at the time: 'Indeed, it is
not so much a national plan of any substance as an interim
political statement on the state of play at local level.'[37]

In its pre-election manifesto of 1977, the Fianna Fáil party
included an undertaking 'to preserve the role of the County
Hospital in providing the necessary level of services for the
local community.'[38]

Since the GHDP was not comprehensive and in the absence
of a detailed policy statement from the new government, Comhairle na nOspidéal was obliged to approve consultant posts in
several hospitals whose future status was unclear.[39] From the
sequence of decisions, or lack of them, Comhairle na
nOspidéal concluded that the country would in the future be
served by a limited number of large specialised hospitals in
Dublin, Cork and Galway (at least 7 and possibly 9) and by a
large number of smaller general hospitals (about 24 or 26).

Comhairle indicated that: 'Inherent in such a situation of many small hospitals is the danger that medical deficiencies spelled out in the Fitzgerald Report and for which that body proposed medical solutions, will continue to exist.'[40]

The Comhairle is of the belief that in order to overcome the limitations of small hospitals, the concept of joint departments involving the staffs in particular specialities in two or more separate hospitals is worthy of examination and experimentation.

Special Hospital Programme

This programme covers the services for the mentally ill and the mentally handicapped. The services for the mentally ill are provided primarily by consultant psychiatrists on the health board's staff to patients either in hospitals, at outpatient clinics, or by giving advice to other professionals attached to voluntary organisations concerned with the prevention and treatment of mental illness. Institutions for the care of mentally handicapped persons are mainly provided by voluntary and religious organisations and patients are maintained there by health boards on a contract basis. In 1977 there were 41 psychiatric hospitals, 29 of which were run by health boards.

In 1961 a commission of inquiry on mental illness was appointed to examine and report on the health services available for the mentally ill and to make recommendations on the measures required to improve these services. The commission's report, published in 1966, indicated that in 1961 there were 7.3 psychiatric beds per 1,000 of the population which appeared to be the highest in the world.[41] No clear explanation emerged for the exceptional rates of residence in psychiatric hospitals here but the commission suggested a possible combination of reasons — high rate of emigration, low marriage rates, unemployment, social and geographic isolation in rural areas, unhelpful public attitudes towards mental illness which does not help discharge.

It is accepted that large and overcrowded institutions are a hindrance to progress in this field of health, particularly in regard to the developments in the effectiveness of psychiatry in modern times. The Commission stated:

... a successful programme for mental health requires in-culcation throughout the community of the basic principles of mental hygiene and an appreciation of, and sympathy with, mental illness and its problems. Many patients can now be successfully treated while living at home or conti-nuing with their work. The Commission's recommendations, therefore, envisage a positive programme of public educa-tion, especially for those most likely to come into contact with the mentally ill; services for certain classes, such as children, adolescents and others, who may be in need of special care; the development of community services such as out-patient clinics, day hospitals, hostels, family care, domiciliary consultations; the use in the community, not on-ly of psychiatrists, but also of general practitioners, psychologists, nurses, psychiatric and other social workers, voluntary organisations and public health personnel; the development of preventive services and facilities for research and the co-ordination of all these services with the general programme of preventive and curative medicine.[42]

The commission emphasised the need for active and early treatment of mental illness and for the integration of psychiatry and general medicine, and thus favoured a concept of psychiatric units in or associated with general hospitals.

For long-stay patients the Commission recommended that mental hospitals should be regarded not merely as centres for custodial care, but that planned and purposeful activity for the patients should be featured, with a view to their rehabilitation and restoration to the community as far as possible. The Com-mission felt that the aim should be to reduce the 10,000 long-stay places to 5,000 over fifteen years. The Commission also stressed the need to give priority to the development of out-patient services.

According to the Psychiatric Hospital Census of 1971, undertaken by the Medico-Social Research Board, there were 16,661 patients in Irish psychiatric hospitals on 31 March 1971.[43] One of the more striking features of the psychiatric population was the high proportion (82.2 per cent) who were unmarried. Almost one-third (30.4 per cent) were aged 65 and over. Schizophrenia accounted for half (50.1 per cent) of all occupied beds with mental handicap the next highest contributor (16 per cent) to the 1971 resident hospital population. The highest rate per 100,000 people by social group was among other agricultural occupations and fishermen[44] where the rate was 1,771.7 and the lowest rate (183.1) was among employers, managers and salaried employees. The hospitalised rate of psychiatric illness was highest in the western counties, the rate in the Western Health Board area being more than twice that in the Eastern Health Board area (see Table 30, page 175).

Table 30: Number of psychiatric patients and rates per 100,000 persons by health board area, 1971

Health board	Number	Rate per 100,000 persons
Eastern	3,916	424.7
Midland	1,165	653.7
Mid Western	1,815	685.4
North Eastern	1,445	610.7
North Western	1,305	685.4
South Eastern	1,969	616.1
Southern	2,001	442.2
Western	2,922	912.7

Source: O'Hare, A. and Walsh, D. *The Irish Psychiatric Hospital Census 1971* Medico-Social Research Board, Dublin 1974

In 1961 a commission of inquiry on mental handicap was appointed to examine and report on the arrangements for the care of the mentally handicapped. The Commission's report, published in 1965,[45] stated that, as in many other countries, the development of most of the special services for the mentally handicapped in Ireland had been of comparatively recent origin. The report defined mental handicap as 'arrested or incomplete development of mind' and made a distinction between three categories, mild, moderate and severe, related to intelligence quotients. It estimated the total number of mentally handicapped persons to be 17,000, considered the social, economic and organisational features that their existence presented and made detailed recommendations how the various needs of different age groups and categories of mentally handicapped persons should be met. These included the setting up by each health authority for its area of a diagnostic, assessment and advisory service related in the first instance to the school medical service and backed by a general service. Continued extensive reliance on the work of voluntary organisations, religious and lay is recommended in providing pre-school and school care, adult care including training and employment, sheltered employment, short-term admissions and training of personnel and research. As in the case of mental illness, emphasis is laid on the need for community care as far as possible. The Commission's recommendations, particularly those relating to the provision of additional places, have largely formed the basis of policy in this field since the report was published. No special legislation exists in regard to services for the mentally handicapped, who are covered by the provisions of the Health Acts.

Between 1964 and 1976 the number of mentally handicapped persons catered for in residential centres increased by three-fifths (60.8 per cent) but there was a dramatic increase in the numbers catered for at day centres where the increase was practically ten-fold (see Table 31, page 177).

Eligibility for health services
The 1970 Health Act codified earlier legislation regarding entitlement to health services. It defined two groups, those with full eligibility (replacing the lower income group whose eligibility originated under the dispensary system in 1851), and those with limited eligibility (the middle income group of the 1953 Health Act). In April 1979 the limited eligibility group was redefined and, at present, the population may be divided into three categories for purposes of health service eligibility as follows:
Category 1: the full eligibility group which accounts for approximately 40 per cent of the population. Subject to a means test people in this group are entitled to all health services free.

Table 31: Number of mentally-handicapped children and adults catered for in residential and day centres on 31 December 1964 and 1976

	Residential Centres		Day Centres	
	1964	1976	1964	1976
Children[a]	1,784	2,531	594	4,713
Adults	1,317	2,454	38	1,205
Total	3,101	4,985	632	5,918

[a]Children up to 16 years of age.

Source: *Statistical Information relevant to the Health Services, 1978* Department of Health

Category 2: the former limited eligibility group which accounts for approximately 45 per cent of the population. This group includes people (other than those with full eligibility) whose income in the year ended 5 April 1979 was less than £5,500 or farmers whose rateable valuation was less than £60. They pay a 1 per cent contribution based on income and they are entitled to 'free' services in public hospitals.

Category 3: the higher income group which accounts for about 15 per cent of the population and includes people with incomes in excess of £5,500 in the year ended 5 April 1979 or farmers with rateable valuations exceeding £60. People in this group also pay a 1 per cent contribution related to income up to a ceiling of £5,500, and are entitled to maintenance in public hospitals.

The above is necessarily a simplification of what in practice is a highly complex system although, following changes in April 1979, the present system is much less complex than it used to be.Before examining each of the categories in more detail it is well to note here that some services are available to all members of the community. These include treatment for infectious diseases; hospital in-patient and out-patient services for children under 16 years suffering from certain prescribed illnesses such as mental handicap, cystic fibrosis, spina bifida, and cerebral palsy; free drugs, medicines and appliances for children suffering from mental handicap or mental illness and other persons suffering from prescribed illnesses such as cystic fibrosis, spina bifida, epilepsy, parkinsonism and multiple sclerosis.[46]

Category 1
Those with full eligibility are defined in the 1970 Health Act as 'adult persons unable without undue hardship to arrange general practitioner, medical and surgical services for themselves and their dependants' and dependants of such people. People with full eligibility receive a General Medical Service card (medical card) which entitles them to free health services. Each health board keeps a register of people with full eligibility which is updated regularly. The Minister for Health may make regulations specifying a class or classes of people within the category having full eligibility but in practice this has not happened.

The decision who is entitled to medical cards rests with the chief executive officer of each health board. Formerly, different criteria were used in assessing means in each area. Since 1974, however, the chief executive officers of health boards have jointly agreed on general guidelines which have been used in determining those categories which have full eligibility. These criteria which are issued as guidelines have no statutory effect and are issued primarily to inform each health board and the public in general of the broad categories of persons who normally qualify for full eligibility. In assessing means, regard is had to the means of the spouse (if any) of the head of the household who is assessed in his/her own right. The means test is based on the gross income of the applicant. The annual income limits have risen considerably since they were first introduced in January 1974 (see Table 32 page 179) and in July 1975 a second revision was made in order to offset the effects of inflation. Expenses necessarily incurred in travelling to and from work may be allowed in some circumstances especially where they create hardship.

People with no income other than the following pensions and allowances under the Social Welfare and Health Acts are generally entitled to medical cards:

Old age (care) allowance
Old age (non-contributory) pension (maximum rate)
Widows' (non-contributory) pension
Orphans' (non-contributory) pension
Deserted wife's allowance
Blind pension
Infectious diseases (maintenance) allowance
Disabled person's (maintenance) allowance.
Persons with full eligibility are entitled to a range of free services including:
1. a general medical practitioner service with choice of doctor;
2. drugs, medicines and appliances (supplied through retail pharmacies or, in some cases, doctors);
3. maternity care service and infant welfare service (for infants up to six weeks old);
4. hospital and specialist services;

Table 32: Income guidelines for medical cards in January 1974-1979 (£ per week)

Category	1974	1976	1978	1979
Single person (living alone)	14.00	19.50	26.00	28.00
Single person (living with family)	12.00	17.00	22.50	24.00
Married couple	20.00	28.25	37.50	40.50
Allowances Dependent children under 16	1.75	2.60	3.50	4.00
Other dependants	2.75	3.75	5.00	5.50
Outgoings on rent and house mortgage in excess of:	2.00	2.60	3.50	4.00

5. a supply of milk for expectant and nursing mothers and for children under five years of age;

6. a maternity cash grant (£8 for each child born in a confinement);

7. dental, ophthalmic and aural services;

8. limited travelling facilities for parents of children who are long-stay patients in hospital.

Since the improvements in the General Medical Service with the introduction of the choice of doctor scheme in 1972, the number of people with medical cards and the total number covered by medical cards, that is, holders of cards and their dependants, has increased steadily up to 1977 as Table 33 on page 181 indicates. The percentage of the 1979 population covered by medical cards varies considerably between health board areas. In 1978, the percentage in the North Western Health Board was 57.1 per cent (the highest) as compared with 22.4 per cent (the lowest) in the Eastern Health Board area. Even within a health board area there is likely to be variation between counties, for example in the North Eastern Health Board where Cavan had 50.7 per cent while Meath had 35.3 per cent. As might be expected the counties with the highest proportion of their populations covered by medical cards are those in the west and north west where there is a high dependence on agriculture but where farm incomes and incomes in general are low[47] and which also contain relatively high proportions of elderly people.[48] In 1978, Mayo with 63 per cent had the highest percentage while Dublin with 21.3 per cent had the lowest (see Table 34 page 182). It has been pointed out, however, that these factors do not fully explain the variation between areas and that the individual health board area is a significant determinant of the population covered.[49] This is partly attributable to the variation which occurs in assessing farmers' income.[50]

A survey of medical card holders, carried out by the Department of Health in 1977, indicated that welfare recipients (excluding those on unemployment benefit and unemployment assistance) accounted for about one-third of the medical card population. Over one-fifth were wage-earners (excluding farm labourers), a similar proportion were unemployed and one-

Table 33:   Number of persons and percentage of population
covered by medical cards on 31 December 1972-
1978

Year	Number of persons	Percentage of total population
1972	864,106	29.0[a]
1973	1,010,090	32.9[b]
1974	1,083,136	34.1[b]
1974	1,162,386	36.6[b]
1976	1,193,909	37.0[b]
1977	1,233,150	37.7[b]
1978	1,219,178	36.2[c]

[a] Based on 1971 Census of Population
[b] Based on Central Statistics Office estimates
[c] Based on 1979 Census of Population

Sources: *Reports of the General Medical Services (Payments)
Board; Census of Population 1971 and 1979; CSO
estimates*

tenth were farmers. These proportions varied between health
board areas (see Table 35, page 184).

Category II
This category is one which has given rise to a certain amount of
controversy in recent years not only because of anomalies
which arose between this category and that of full eligibility but
also because of anomalies within it, for instance insured
manual workers had eligibility irrespective of income whereas
insured non-manual workers were subject to an income limit,
and the complex criteria involved.[51] Under a revised scheme
announced in July 1978 by the then Minister for Health,
Charles Haughey, many of these anomalies have been removed. The revised scheme came into operation in April 1979 and
under its provisions the previous distinction between manual
and non-manual workers was abolished.

All persons whose gross income was less than £5,500 per

Table 34:   Number of persons covered by medical cards on 31 December 1972-79, percentage change 1972, 1978, and percentage of 1979 population covered in December 1978.

	1972	1978	% Change	% 1979 population covered December 1978
Eastern	162,187	260,851	60.8	22.4
Dublin	124,261	209,215	68.4	21.3
Wicklow	18,063	23,166	28.3	27.6
Kildare	19,863	28,470	43.3	29.3
Midland	65,060	92,881	42.8	47.0
Longford	11,392	15,840	39.0	51.5
Westmeath	17,505	25,749	47.1	43.0
Offaly	21,620	29,029	34.3	50.8
Laois	14,543	22,263	53.1	44.6
Mid Western	77,516	116,628	50.5	38.8
Clare	23,070 [a]	31,240	35.4	36.8
Limerick	41,099	63,408	54.3	40.3
Tipperary (NR)	13,347	21,980	64.7	37.6
North Eastern	77,629	117,294	51.1	41.8
Cavan	18,489	27,214	47.2	50.7
Louth	17,485	33,712	92.8	39.1
Meath	25,960	31,965	23.1	35.3
Monaghan	15,695 [a]	24,403	55.5	48.5
North Western	73,733	116,511	58.0	57.1
Donegal	46,274	74,090	60.1	60.9
Leitrim	11,731	16,368	39.5	58.8
Sligo	15,728	26,053	58.2	47.7

Table 34 (Continued)

	1972	1978	% Change	% 1979 population covered December 1978
South Eastern	122,512	156,078	27.4	42.6
Carlow	14,904	16,608	11.4	43.0
Kilkenny	24,348	29,724	22.1	43.0
Tipperary (SR)	28,784	33,831	17.5	45.0
Waterford	24,979	34,666	38.7	39.7
Wexford	29,497	41,249	39.8	42.9
Southern	153,471	168,033	9.5	32.6
Cork	96,146	115,043	19.7	29.1
Kerry	57,325	52,990	-7.6	44.1
Western	131,998	190,902	44.6	56.9
Galway	55,284	87,177	57.7	52.0
Mayo	56,501	71,650	26.8	63.0
Roscommon	20,213	32,075	58.7	59.3
Total	864,106	1,219,178	41.1	36.2

[a] Estimated

Sources: *The General Practitioner in Ireland*, Stationery Office, Dublin 1974, pp 85-6; *Reports of the General Medical Services (Payments) Board* 1973-1978.

annum in the year ended 5 April 1979 or farmers whose rateable valuation is £60 or under are in Category II, unless of course they have full eligibility. Persons under the income or valuation limits pay 1 per cent of income up to a maximum of £55 per annum and in return are entitled to a number of 'free' health services including:
1. hospital services as in-patients
2. out-patient specialist services (including X-ray examination)
3. a maternity care service and infant welfare service (for infants up to six weeks old)

Table 35: Percentage distribution of the medical card population by income source of medical card holder 1977/8

| | Health Board | | | | | | | | |
	Eastern	Midland	Mid Western	North Eastern	North Western	South Eastern	Southern	Western	Total
Total Persons (000s) = 100 per cent	259	92	114	122	121	157	175	191	1,234
Farmers	1.3	10.8	8.7	12.7	18.3	4.7	4.3	26.2	9.6
Farm Labourers	2.2	4.9	3.2	4.5	3.4	5.2	1.0	1.8	2.9
Other Wage Earners	18.9	37.9	22.4	26.4	16.0	26.4	19.7	17.5	21.9
Self-Employed persons	1.0	1.1	2.4	1.9	1.7	1.9	1.8	1.2	1.6
Students	10.4	5.1	6.7	5.9	4.0	6.5	10.7	8.5	7.94
Unemployed	31.5	12.1	23.9	20.7	24.0	17.7	19.2	13.9	21.4
Welfare Recipients	30.4	20.7	30.3	25.3	31.3	35.8	41.3	29.6	31.6
Other	3.9	7.1	2.1	2.4	0.9	1.4	1.7	1.0	2.4

Source: *Medical Card Survey*, Planning Unit, Department of Health, 1979.

4. assistance towards the cost of prescribed medical requisites in excess of £5 per month (£8 a month from 1 March 1980).

The income limit for Category II is similar to that for pay-related social insurance (see Chapter 2) and is to be reviewed periodically.[52]

Category III

This category is frequently referred to as the higher income group. Up to April 1979 this group, which accounts for approximately 15 per cent of the population, did not have entitlement to any health service with the exception of services available to all people, already referred to, and some other minor exceptions.[53] For people in this group, protection against the high cost of hospital services was afforded by taking out insurance with the Voluntary Health Insurance Board (VHI). From April 1979, however, persons in this group are also liable for a 1 per cent contribution up to an income ceiling of £5,500 or £60 rateable valuation in the case of farmers. All persons in this group are liable for the maximum contribution. In return for this contribution, such persons have 'free' entitlement to the maintenance element of hospital services but are liable for hospital consultants' fees. They may take out insurance with the VHI to cover such fees and/or cover themselves against charges for private or semi-private hospital accommodation and treatment in voluntary or private hospitals. Persons in this group are also eligible for assistance towards the cost of prescribed medical requisites.

The VHI was established under the Voluntary Health Insurance Act of 1957 and is charged with providing health insurance schemes. The Act made it illegal for any other body to offer health insurance without a licence from the Minister for Health. The VHI is a non-profit-making body and any surplus on its income is devoted to the reduction of insurance premiums or increases in benefits. The policy-holder chooses the cover which he/she wishes to take out for hospital maintenance and treatment and following increases in hospital charges the VHI normally advises its members of the corresponding increase in premiums required. A major exception to hospital cover under VHI up to April 1979 was normal maternity treatment, which was excluded initially because it was felt that its inclusion would mean raising premiums to unacceptable levels.[54] From April 1979, the VHI introduced considerable changes in its insurance schemes[55] and now has three basic plans, as follows: *Plan A* covers the full charge for semi-private and private accommodation in public hospitals; *Plan B* covers the full charge in public hospitals and also up to semi-private level in private hospitals and nursing homes; *Plan C* covers the full charge in all hospitals and nursing homes including all private rooms.

Insurance premiums are related not only to the type of plan chosen but also to marital status and the number of children in the family, no additional premiums being paid where the number of children exceeds three. The full amount of insurance premiums may be offset against income tax.

By 1958, one year after its establishment, a total of 57,000 persons were covered by the VHI schemes. The numbers have increased steadily since then so that by February 1978 there was a total membership of 645,165 persons, consisting of 232,329 registered members and 412,836 spouses, children and other dependants.[56] Since the total membership of VHI (approximately one-fifth of the population) is in excess of the estimated number in Category III it is clear that some people in Category II have also invested in supplementary cover to enable them to have private or semi-private accommodation and treatment in hospitals. An estimated 25 per cent to 28 per cent of persons covered by VHI are in Category II and are therefore entitled to 'free' hospitalisation in public wards of hospitals only and, more surprisingly, it has been estimated that one-third of patients not in Categories I or II have no health insurance cover of any kind.[57] In 1977-78 the annual subscription income of VHI was £15,671,337 of which 80.9 per cent was distributed on claims.

Comment on eligibility for health services

In August 1973, Brendan Corish, Minister for Health, announced that from April 1974, every member of the community without limit of income would be entitled to free hospital in-patient and out-patient services, free maternity and infant welfare services and assistance towards the cost of drugs and medicines. The effect of this would have been to extend to the higher income group the same eligibility for services as that being enjoyed by those in the limited eligibility category. Persons to whom eligibility was being extended would also have been liable for a health contribution.

This proposed extension of services did not occur, because discussions between the Department of Health and hospital consultants were not successful regarding the latters' conditions of employment, and remuneration in particular, under the new scheme. It was also considered that under the proposed scheme, demand for hospital service in public wards would rise, thus placing a heavy burden on hospitals and their staffs and necessitating an improvement in facilities and an adequate remuneration for consultants who might be expected to lose their private practice and experience a consequent decline in income.[58] The argument that there would be increased demand was highly questionable.[59] Furthermore, as already noted, a considerable proportion of people in Category II also opt for insurance cover with the VHI to enable them to have semi-private or private accommodation in hospitals and it is unlikely that consultants' private practice would have been seriously affected. In a discussion document on the feasibility of a compulsory specialist and hospital insurance scheme, published in 1976, the Irish Medical Association stated:

> We are strongly opposed to a comprehensive 'free' health service because of the inevitable weakening in the doctor-patient relationship which occurs, the loss of incentive and independence of the doctor, and the loss of the patient's sense of personal responsibility towards the service.[60]

Shortly before 1 April 1974 the Minister for Health announced that the proposed scheme had been deferred indefinitely. In an effort to introduce the scheme as quickly as possible and reach some compromise with the hospital consultants, the Minister established an independent review body with the following terms of reference:

> To examine and report on the systems and rates of payment and conditions of employment of consultants in hospitals engaged in the provision of services under the Health Act, 1970, which would be appropriate in the context of the abolition of income and valuation limits for limited eligibility.

The review group produced an interim report in February 1978 which favoured private practice. The report stressed that:

> The community's inherited beliefs in matters concerning sickness and death are of profound importance to all members of the community. In this country they tend to require a strongly personalised relationship between doctor and patient generally, and to seek it also in the case of hospital consultants. This inheritance is naturally different from those of communities elsewhere in the world. Its distinctiveness means that conditions currently existing in the health systems of other countries might not be at all appropriate here.[61]

A few months after the publication of the review body's report, the Minister for Health, Charles Haughey, announced that the existing system of eligibility for hospital services would be improved considerably from April 1979. As already indicated, the revised scheme has eliminated many of the anomalies in the former 'limited eligibility' category although an estimated 25,000 manual workers lost eligibility as a result of the change. One of the major anomalies which still remains is that no allowance is made for dependants in determining income as is the case in Category I, for instance a single person with an income of £5,490 is in Category II whereas a married person with a large family and an income of £5,510 is not. Despite the fact that people in the higher income group are still liable for consultants' fees the revised scheme has gone some way towards the introduction of a comprehensive hospital service for the entire community.

Chapter 6

Welfare Services

Introduction
The basic social services, housing, education, health and income maintenance, cater for needs which are common to all members of society. However, certain groups have special needs, and services over and above the basic services have evolved to cater for these needs. Such groups include the elderly, deprived children and the handicapped (both mental and physical). While these groups are catered for to some extent by the basic services, special provision is also required. Hence services such as residential care for deprived children or sheltered employment for the handicapped have been developed.

It is in the field of welfare services that voluntary effort plays its greatest role. This is mainly because of the state's traditional preoccupation with providing satisfactory basic services for all members of society. In more recent years, however, state involvement in providing special provision for certain groups has improved and for this, voluntary organisations which frequently paved the way must take some credit.

This chapter examines the services for three groups, the elderly, the handicapped and deprived children. It also examines the role of voluntary organisations and contains a brief review of social work services in Ireland.

The Elderly
The age at which a person may be said to be elderly or aged is an arbitrary one. However, it is usual to classify those aged 65 or over as elderly since this is the generally accepted age of retirement from employment.

A demographic feature common to most developed nations is the relatively high proportion of people aged 65 and over. This is mainly due to the reduction of mortality rates in infancy and childhood which has led to a considerable increase in life expectancy. The average life expectancy at birth in Ireland during the period 1925-27 was 57.4 for males and 57.9 for females. By 1970-72 these had increased to 68.8 and 73.5 respectively.[1] In some European countries the proportionate increase in elderly persons is associated with a declining birth rate and a consequent proportionate decline in the younger age groups. In Ireland, similarly, the elderly have formed an increasing proportion of the total population up to the 1960s. In 1841, the proportion was approximately 3 per cent and by 1961 this had increased to 11.2 per cent. While the absolute numbers of elderly persons increased between 1961 and 1971 the proportion of such persons remained stable (see Table 36, page 190) This is largely explained by the general population increase in the same period.

Table 36: Number of persons aged 65 and over, 1926-71

Year	Number	Percentage of total population
1926	271,700	9.1
1936	286,684	9.6
1946	314,322	10.6
1961	315,063	11.2
1966	323,007	11.2
1971	329,819	11.1

Source: *Census of Population 1971*

The percentage of elderly persons varies considerably between urban (defined as towns containing populations of 1,500 or over) and rural areas of the state. In 1971 the figures were 9.1 per cent and 13.2 per cent respectively. Considerable differences also exist between counties, ranging from 8.2 per cent in Kildare to 17.3 per cent in Leitrim. In general, western counties have relatively high proportions of elderly people compared with other counties. One of the principal reasons for the relatively high proportion of elderly persons in rural areas has been persistent migration. This migration has been selective in that members of the young adult age group have tended to migrate, leaving behind an imbalanced population structure with disproportionate numbers of elderly people.

A feature of the elderly population is the increasing proportion living alone. In 1966 there were 35,024 such persons, representing 10.8 per cent of all elderly people. By 1971 these figures had increased to 43,109 and 13.1 per cent respectively. Those elderly persons living alone are acknowledged to constitute a vulnerable group, a group with high demands on health and welfare services.

Growing concern over the increasing numbers of elderly persons and the inadequacy of existing services was recognised in 1965 when the Minister for Health, in consultation with the Minister for Local Government and Social Welfare, appointed an inter-departmental committee whose function was 'to examine and to report on the general problem of the care of the aged and to make recommendations regarding the improvement and extension of services.' The report, entitled *The Care of the Aged,* was published in 1968 and contained ninety-four recommendations. The recommendations on improved services were, in the committee's view, 'based on the belief that it is better, and probably much cheaper, to help the aged to live in the community than to provide for them in hospitals or other institutions'.[2] This emphasis on community as opposed to institutional care had at this time gained acceptance in Britain. It was to influence subsequent policy in Ireland not only in relation to the elderly but also to services for other groups such as the mentally ill, and health services in general.

The development in services for the elderly may be examined under the two main headings, community and institutional.

Community services

Reeves has indicated that:

> ... many of the factors complicating old age are non-medical. Old people, like the young, have basic human needs — for understanding and sympathy, security and shelter, relatives and friends, money and adequate food supply, activity and facilities to maintain good health. These basic needs must be provided adequately long before they have a social breakdown and enter hospital disguised as medical casualties.[3]

A variety of services therefore must be provided in order to enable the elderly to live in the community. These range from income maintenance services to the activities of voluntary bodies.

Income maintenance. The main state income maintenance schemes are the contributory and non-contributory old age pensions. The former are paid to persons who have been in insurable employment and have made a sufficient number of contributions while the latter are paid subject to a means test. In recent years there has been a considerable increase in the number of recipients of these two pensions (see Table 37, page 192). Over two-thirds of pensioners are in receipt of the means-tested non-contributory pension.

The increase in the number of pensioners is mainly due to changes in the pension schemes. The major innovations were the lowering of the qualifying age and the easing of the means

Table 37: Number of recipients of old-age contributory and non-contributory pensions 1966, 1971 and 1978[a]

	31/12/66	31/3/71	31/12/78	% increase 1966-1978
Contributory	40,556	46,549	61,838	52.5
Non-contributory	112,621	113,570	133,669	18.7
Total	153,177	160,119	195,507	27.6

[a] It should be noted that a retirement pension at age 65 for insured persons was introduced in 1970. By 31/12/78 there were 29,585 persons in receipt of this pension.

Source: *Reports of the Department of Social Welfare*

test. Between 1973 and 1977 the qualifying age was reduced from 70 to 66 years. This was the first time that the qualifying age had been lowered since the introduction of the old age pension in 1908. Since 1973 the means test has been eased considerably so that by 1976 the first £6 of weekly income was disregarded for the full rate of the non-contributory pension. Prior to 1973 only persons with no means qualified for the maximum rate of pension and these accounted for 20 per cent of the total number of non-contributory pensioners. By 1976 approximately 90 per cent were in receipt of the full pension. In 1977 pensioners living alone became entitled to an additional £1 weekly (£1.10 in 1978) and approximately 30,000 pensioners benefit from this. In recent years also the rates of payment have been increased considerably, in the main to keep pace with inflation. There still remains the need, however, to relate these welfare payments to some established index.[4]

A number of other innovations have been made which, while not directly income maintenance in nature are linked with the Department of Social Welfare's pension schemes and indeed are operated under the general control of that Department. These include the introduction in 1967 of free travel for all persons aged 70 and over (now 66 years), the electricity allowance scheme for certain categories of old age pensioners (mainly those living alone) and the introduction in 1968 of free television licences for pensioners entitled to the electricity allowance. Furthermore, with the introduction by health boards of uniform income guidelines for determining entitlement to medical cards, those in receipt of the non-contributory pension at the maximum rate have become automatically entitled to medical cards.

Housing. Over the past two decades various provisions have been made by the state for housing the elderly. The 1957 Housing Act, for example, made provision to cover out of public funds the entire cost of essential repairs to dwellings occupied by elderly people living in unfit conditions in remote areas. The 1962 Housing Act provided for state and local authority grants for dwellings provided by an approved body on a philanthropic basis for the accommodation of elderly persons. These grants may be given for the construction, purchase, reconstruction or conversion of dwellings. Local authorities also provide mobile or demountable dwellings mainly for elderly persons living in deteriorating dwellings or for those living in remote areas. In local authority housing estates a certain number of dwellings may be reserved for elderly persons.

Domiciliary services. Perhaps the most socially significant domiciliary service to be introduced in recent years has been the home help service which enables health boards, either on their own or in conjunction with voluntary agencies, to provide services for families in stress situations and for the elderly, especially those living alone. One of the primary objectives of this scheme is to encourage persons who can remain in their own home to do so rather than seek institutional care. From modest beginnings in 1971 this service has grown and by December 1976 there were 5,097 beneficiaries (83 per cent of whom were elderly persons) but this figure represented a decrease over the previous year (see the section 'Home Help Services' in Chapter 5, pages 166-8).[5] While the scheme has much potential it would appear as if it is vulnerable in a period of economic restraint.

In some urban areas, voluntary organisations, with financial assistance from health boards, provide a meals-on-wheels service. Approximately three out of every five elderly persons live in rural areas where it is difficult to supply such a service. In the context of domiciliary services it is also worth noting that many voluntary organisations provide a variety of services such as visiting, laundry service, supply of fuel, holidays and outings.

Institutional services

In the *Care of the Aged* report it was estimated that in 1968 approximately 20,000 elderly persons were receiving institutional care. Of this number, 8,057 were in county homes and the remainder in hospitals (psychiatric and general) or private nursing homes.[6] The categories of elderly persons in county homes were: chronic sick (4,574), aged other than chronic sick (2,721), mentally handicapped (642) and casuals (120). The last group referred to is mainly homeless persons who remain for a few nights only. Some of the county homes originated as Poor Law workhouses. The avowed purpose of the Poor Law was to discourage applications for relief so thoroughly that only those who were destitute would apply. There has therefore been a stigma attached to the workhouses and to their successors, the county homes.

The *Care of the Aged* report pointed out that the county homes catered for a variety of patients and that persons were frequently admitted without any medical or social assessment and without any effort to determine whether some form of help in the community would obviate the need for admission. Similarly, a report by the Medico-Social Research Board in 1975 on admission to county homes indicated that such homes were catch-all institutions — the major change over the past century being that whereas the nineteenth-century institution (the workhouse) catered for all age groups, the twentieth century county home caters for all groups of the aged, including the ill, the incapacitated, the isolated and the homeless.[7] The report stated that while all these groups are characterised by their inability to live in the community, both the extent and the causes of this inability vary from group to group. The lack of community services and 'half-way houses', the report stated, means that all have recourse to the county home. This results in numbers of relatively healthy and capable old people entering these homes because 'they have no other choice'. A report on psychiatric and geriatric services published by the Western Health Board in 1974 also referred to the admission of persons to county homes and stated:

All the demands for in-patient care for the elderly do not arise from purely medical reasons. Pressure for admission may come from relatives, friends or neighbours who have become over anxious, sometimes as a result of guilt feelings. Occasionally motivation is more questionable. The house or property is wanted by a relative or neighbour and the old person is standing in the way. Community care if adequate and well organised can provide an answer to some of these dangers. Support may relieve pressure and anxiety and sometimes community workers are able to prevent the unscrupulous from getting their way.[8]

The *Care of the Aged* report recommended that four main types of accommodation should be provided for the elderly:

General hospitals. To provide specialised general medical and surgical care. They should continue to admit the elderly who are acutely ill or in need of urgent treatment or in any other emergency.

Geriatric assessment units. Specially equipped and staffed units for the full investigation and assessment of elderly people who are clearly not in need of the acute treatment which the general hospitals can provide, for their short term treatment and rehabilitation, where this is possible, and for the assignment to the most appropriate accommodation of those in need of long-term care.

Long-stay hospital units. To provide, for example, for patients who are so mentally ill or confused or disturbed that they require long-stay hospital care, patients who need continuous nursing care, patients who are bedfast and need nursing care.

Welfare homes. To provide institutional care for people who have no relations or other people to provide them with the help they need in their own homes.

A number of welfare homes have been established since the publication of the *Care of the Aged* report and many of the county homes have been rebuilt or reconstructed; in fact the term 'county home' is no longer in official use and 'geriatric hospital' is now the appropriate term. By 1975 there were 177 institutions for the elderly containing almost 13,000 patients. The categories and number of patients are set out in Table 38 on page 197. Almost two-thirds of the patients were aged 75 or over and one-quarter had been institutionalised for five years or more.[9]

The Handicapped
A handicap has been defined as:

Any limitations, congenital or acquired, of a person's physical or mental ability which affects his daily activity and work by reducing his social contribution, his vocational employment prospects or his ability to use public services.[10]

This definition covers people with a wide range of disabilities, the blind, the mentally or physically handicapped and the mentally ill. While the nature and severity of the handicap will differ from one individual to another all handicapped persons have one need in common, the need to be aided to overcome their handicaps and to become as integrated as much as possible into society.[11]

Table 38: Types of institutions for the elderly and number of patients in each, 1975

	Number	Number of patients
Geriatric hospitals	46	8,411
Welfare homes	23	896
Voluntary and private institutions	108	3,681
Total	177	12,988

Extent of the problem

In 1974 the Medico-Social Research Board carried out a census of mentally handicapped persons in *residential care* in Ireland.[12] The census was conducted in all known residential centres. It indicated that there were 8,138 mentally handicapped people in these centres. More than half (52.3 per cent) were in mental handicap centres and one third (33.7 per cent) in psychiatric hospitals. Almost one quarter (22.6 per cent) were diagnosed as mildly mentally handicapped and the remainder as more severely handicapped. Of all the health board areas, the Midland Health Board area had the highest number per

100,000 population in residential care (386.2), followed by the Western (323.1) and North Western (323) areas.

The census indicated that both the scattered nature of the population within these health board areas and the relative lack of day facilities contributed to the high rate of residential provision. Half of the residents were aged between 5 and 25 years, 30 per cent were aged 25 to 50 and 18 per cent were aged over 50.

The Medico-Social Research Board also carried out a census of mentally handicapped in *non-residential care* in 1974.[13] The census forms were completed by public health nurses and medical officers of health. The census was confined to the moderate, severe and profound categories of handicap, of persons aged 4 and over. Forms for 4,863 people were returned. Of these two-thirds were diagnosed as having moderate mental handicap, 26.3 per cent severe handicap and 6.8 per cent profound mental handicap. There was a wide disparity between the rates for different health board areas. The highest rate at 236 per 100,000 population occurred in the Western area, while the lowest was 130 per 100,000 in the Eastern area. The disparity between the areas is even greater among persons aged 20 and over, 223.6 and 53.2 respectively. The census suggests that the effect of migration has to be considered as a significant factor as well as the presence or otherwise of adequate day facilities.

The censuses, therefore, indicated that, in all, there were 13,000 mentally handicapped persons in the community.

It is much more difficult, however, to estimate with any degree of accuracy, the total number of persons suffering from all kinds of handicap in the community. The report on *Training and Employing the Handicapped* estimated that there were approximately 100,000 handicapped adults.[14] The estimate included people receiving disabled person's maintenance allowance from health boards and people receiving invalidity and long term sickness benefits under the social insurance scheme. The breakdown is set out in Table 39 on page 199.

In addition to the above, the report states that there are probably thousands of unidentified persons living in the community who are not in receipt of public allowances either because they are ineligible because of means or because they have not sought them.

Table 39: Distribution of handicapped adults in institutions and in the community.

	Number of handicapped
In Institutions	
Mental hospitals (excluding short-term patients)	12,000
Mental handicap institutions (residential and day)	3,000
County homes and other institutions for infirm and handicapped	10,000
In the Community	
On disabled persons maintenance allowances	26,000
On Department of Social Welfare benefits	
— long-term disability benefits	20,000
— invalidity pensions	8,000
— occupational injuries benefits	5,000
Blind persons	6,000
Other handicapped persons (estimate)	10,000
Total	100,000

Services

With the exception of the Mental Treatment Acts (for the mentally ill) there is no special legislation dealing with handicapped persons. Health boards operate some special institutions for the care, treatment or training of the handicapped and contribute towards the cost of maintaining such persons in centres conducted by voluntary bodies, mainly religious orders. In recent years the emphasis has been on increasing the number of places in day centres as opposed to residential centres. In the case of mental handicap, for example, the numbers catered for in 1964 in day centres was

632 and in residential centres 3,101. By 1976 these numbers had increased to 4,985 and 5,918 respectively.[15] This trend is also evident in the provision of special national schools for handicapped children all of which are aided by the Department of Education. The numbers of such schools, of pupils attending and of teachers have increased substantially between 1967-68 and 1977-78, especially in relation to the mentally handicapped (see Table 40, page 201).

The object in increasing the number of places in schools and other centres has been to integrate the handicapped into ordinary community life. The report on *Training and Employing the Handicapped,* points out that:

A great many handicapped persons are willing and able to work. Some require special training; others need special conditions of employment. The important thing is that no one should be denied the opportunity to work, even if it requires a special effort by society to enable him to do so. The alternative of providing financial assistance, no matter how generous, to compensate the disabled person for his impairment is not a sufficient answer. It may be the only one in some instances, but for many it ignores the deeper psychological needs of the individual, the satisfaction derived from being a useful member of the community, the enhanced dignity of the worker.

The report also estimates that of the 100,000 handicapped persons, some 15,000 might benefit from preparation and training for work. By comparison, the total number of places in one form or another available for the preparation of handicapped persons for work is, according to the report, about 3,000.[16]

Rehabilitation in Ireland is carried out at two levels: open employment and sheltered employment.

Open employment. The main work in this field is carried out by the Rehabilitation Institute, a voluntary organisation which runs centres in Dublin, Cork, Limerick and in other large urban centres. Work in this area is also carried out at the

Table 40: Number of special national schools by category, together with numbers of pupils and teachers 1967-68 and 1977-78.

Special School	Schools	Pupils	Teachers
		1967-68	
Mentally handicapped	35	2,846	169
Children with impaired hearing	3	615	75
Blind and partially sighted	2	157	16
Physically handicapped	21	827	60
Emotionally disturbed	4	158	16
Other special schools	—	—	—
Total	65	4,603	336

Special School	Schools	Pupils	Teachers
		1977-78	
Mentally handicapped	58	5,673	426
Children with impaired hearing	4	831	142
Blind and partially sighted	2	142	22
Physically handicapped	17	684	58
Emotionally disturbed	12	424	53
Other special schools	11	394	50
Total	104	8,148	751

Source: Department of Education, *Statistical Reports.*

Toghermore centre in Tuam (an independent centre) and at the RETOS centre at Shannon, a centre under the aegis of the National Rehabilitation Board. The RETOS centre is specially orientated to deal with psychiatric cases. Its purpose is to train persons suffering from psychiatric illness for re-entry to open employment and trainees are selected from psychiatric hospitals within a 50-mile radius of Shannon. The other centres were established with a view to handling the physically handicapped but lately have begun to absorb some psychiatric and mildly mentally handicapped cases. In all, these centres provide approximately 500 approved training places. The regional health boards pay the various bodies involved a capitation fee per month.

Sheltered employment. There are many handicapped persons who even with training will never be able to compete with other workers. For these persons some form of sheltered employment is required. In Ireland, training for sheltered employment and sheltered employment itself is provided by a number of institutions and agencies. The Central Remedial Clinic (CRC), for example, is a voluntary organisation established in 1951 whose aim was to provide an after-care service for victims of polio. Since its foundation both the establishment itself and the range of services it provides have expanded considerably. The clinic's range of operations now includes occupational therapy, physiotherapy, a primary school for the physically handicapped, a sheltered workshop, and research into the causes of handicap. The ultimate aim of the sheltered employment provided by the CRC is to equip handicapped workers for open employment. The CRC draws the bulk of its finance from private fund-raising activities. In addition it receives a capitation payment yearly for each person employed in its sheltered workshop.

Co-ordination
The National Rehabilitation Board (NRB) established in 1967 under the Health (Corporate Bodies) Act, 1961, has as one of its main functions the co-ordination of the work of voluntary organisations engaged in rehabilitation. In addition, the NRB

has several other functions including advising the Minister for Health on all aspects of rehabilitation and arranging for the provision of services for the treatment, assessment, vocational guidance, training and placement of disabled persons. Its activities include: medical/vocational assessment, including psychological testing; placement services for the adult disabled; an advisory employment service for handicapped children of school leaving age; a national hearing aid and educational advisory service; an industrial therapy service; colleges for the training of occupational and speech therapists.

The NRB provides a wide range of services for the handicapped either on its own or in conjunction with other agencies. In 1977, 883 adults and 289 youths were placed in employment by the NRB.[17]

The report on *Training and Employing the Handicapped* set down general principles and guidelines for the future development of facilities for training and employing the handicapped. Recommendations, under 109 headings, dealt with aspects as diffuse as the overall state co-ordination of services and as particular as the staff qualifications required in sheltered workshops or the curriculum content of training programmes. One of the main recommendations was that the NRB be charged with responsibility for implementing the report's recommendations.

Since Ireland's entry into the EEC in 1973 an important source of finance for agencies involved in providing services for the handicapped has been the European Social Fund (ESF). In 1973 a total of £184,448 was received in grants from the ESF. By 1977 the grants approved amounted to £3,076,892.[18]

Deprived children

Deprived children have been broadly defined as 'those who because of family circumstances, or the environment in which they live, are deprived of the care, the opportunities and the facilities which they need and to which they are entitled'.[19] Not all children fall within this broad definition. Indeed the majority who live in stable families where material and emotional support is available do not. The importance of the family unit where children are socialised is stressed in the Irish

Constitution which also, however, pledges that the state will safeguard the weaker sections of society. More particularly, the state reserves the right to intervene in certain circumstances.

> In exceptional cases, where the parents for physical or moral reasons, fail in their duty towards children, the State shall endeavour to supply the place of parents, but always with due regard for the natural and imprescriptable rights of the child.[20]

In recent years considerable attention has been focused on the plight of deprived children and especially on those in residential care. In 1966 a Tuairim report highlighted the inadequacies of residential care for deprived children in Ireland.[21] In the following year the government established a committee under the chairmanship of District Justice Eileen Kennedy, 'to survey the Reformatory and Industrial Schools systems and to make a report and recommendations to the Minister for Education'. The Committee's report (usually referred to as the Kennedy Report) was published in 1970.[22] At the end of the same year and shortly after the publication of the report, an organisation called CARE — Campaign for the Care of Deprived Children — was established. Comprised of persons involved with or interested in the care of deprived children, its main objectives were to publicise the problems of deprived children, to highlight the inadequacies in existing services and to campaign for improved services. In 1972 CARE published a memorandum analysing the problems of deprived children.[23]

Extent of the problem
It is virtually impossible to estimate with any degree of accuracy the number of deprived children. Indications of the extent of the problem, however, are available from a variety of sources. In this context it is useful to use the classification of deprived children adopted in the CARE memorandum: children in families under stress, children with no family, children of broken homes and children in trouble with the law.

Children in families under stress. The type of families in this situation would include those living in overcrowded conditions; where the father is continuously unemployed and there is not an adequate income; where there is a problem of alcoholism or chronic illness.

Children with no family. This refers mainly to illegitimate children whose numbers have been increasing in the past few decades. In 1961 for example there were 975 illegitimate births as compared with 2,514 in 1975.[24] Such children may be either cared for by their natural parent(s), adopted, fostered or committed to residential care. Between 1952 when adoption was legalised in Ireland and the end of 1977 a total of 24,848 adoption orders was made.[25]

Children of broken families. The type of situation here would be where one or both parents die; where a parent deserts or where a parent is committed to hospital on a long-term basis. Children from such families may be fostered or committed to residential care.

Children in trouble with the law. Ironically, those children who break the law are more likely to be noticed and dealt with than their deprived counterparts who are non-offenders. In 1976 the number of juveniles (persons under 17 years) convicted for indictable offences was 2,622 as compared with 3,168 in 1966.[26]

Obviously there will be some overlap between the children in the above categories. Research has indicated, for example, that delinquency is associated with obvious forms of deprivation such as poor housing conditions, poverty and broken families. A range of services is available to deal with deprived children in the community. These services may be of a statutory (e.g. social work service) or voluntary (e.g. the work of the Irish Society for the Prevention of Cruelty to Children) nature. Children and youths committed to residential care or prison represent those who for one reason or another cannot be catered for in the community. Statistics are available on such children and over the period 1967-77 the number of children in care in residential homes and special schools and the number of admissions declined sharply (see Table 41 page 207). Over the same period, however, the number of persons aged under 21 years who were committed to prisons increased up to 1972 and declined subsequently.

The number of admissions to residential homes because of lack of guardianship or because children did not have any home amounted to 156 or 41.2 per cent of the total in 1967. By 1977 these figures had declined to 31 and 22 per cent respectively. Over the same period the numbers committed to residential homes or special schools as a result of being charged with indictable offences declined from 182 (48 per cent of total) to 77 (54.6 per cent of total).[27]

The services for deprived children may be broadly categorised as community or institutional. It is not the intention to describe and comment on all of these services. Instead a few key services are selected for particular attention.

Community services
The School Attendance Act, 1926, provides for the issue of a warning notice to parents who fail to send a child to school and the fining of parents who fail to comply with such a warning. The Act also provides that 'the Court, if it thinks fit, may order the child to be sent to a certified industrial school'. In county boroughs school attendance committees, composed of members of the local authority and educational interests, employ a staff of school attendance officers. In other areas members of the Garda Síochána are appointed as school attendance officers. The report of the Dublin School Attendance Department for the year ended June 1977 indicates that 933 statutory notices were served, £320.11 imposed in fines, 59 children were sent for assessment and 37 were committed to special schools. The work of school attendance officers brings them in contact with a wide range of social problems. The 1973 report of the Dublin School Attendance Department points out that:

Non-attendance at school (in 95 per cent of the cases that come to the notice of the School Attendance Department) can be cured by persuasion, advice and the intelligent use by the School Attendance officer of the provisions of the School

Attendance Act. Irregular school attendance in itself is not a tremendous social problem but, unfortunately for a number of Dublin children, non-attendance at school is a mere symptom of a greater malaise. Investigation by School Attendance officers uncovers problems of such magnitude that the mild misdemeanour of irregular attendance pales into insignificance.[28]

Table 41: Number of admissions and number of children in care in residential homes and special schools and number of persons under 21 years committed to prisons 1967, 1972 and 1977

	1967	1972	1977
Residential homes and special schools[a]			
Number of admissions	379	219	141
Number in care	2,252	1,113	584
Prisons			
Number committed	252	782	487

[a] Up to 1970-71 residential homes and special schools were referred to as industrial and reformatory schools respectively.

Source: *Statistical Reports, Department of Education, Annual Report on Prisons*

Of late, the role of school attendance officers as defined in the 1926 Act and the archaism of the Act itself have been questioned, particularly by the officers themselves. A report of the National Association of School Attendance Officers published in 1975 recommended that school attendance officers be replaced by education welfare officers 'with the emphasis on child welfare rather than law enforcement'. The report also recommended the reorganisation of the system of school attendance committees and that the new committees, to be called education welfare committees, be given quasi-judicial powers to protect children's interest in all matters relating to their welfare during the periods of compulsory schooling. No child should be taken into care merely for not attending school, it stated.[29]

In 1889 a branch of the National Society for the Prevention of Cruelty to Children (founded by Benjamin Waugh in Britain) was established in Dublin. In 1956 the Irish branch became autonomous and has since been referred to as the Irish Society for the Prevention of Cruelty to Children (ISPCC). Since its foundation the Society has promoted and pioneered the care and protection of children at risk from injury, neglect, emotional deprivation and unhappiness. At one time the usual course of action in cases of child neglect was to remove the children from their unsatisfactory home environment and place them in institutions.

The Society has had to re-assess its role in recent years and it now endeavours to project an image of a helpful rather than punitive agency.[30] It established a family casework service for the protection of the child with the express purpose of keeping families together, but its functions have been undermined by the provision of new statutory services, especially the social work services of health boards. In 1977 the Society established a working party to examine and appraise the structure and function of the Society. The most important recommendation made by the working party was that the ISPCC which had pioneered the way for statutory family casework services for children and their families should now create a new role for itself that would supplement the work carried out by health boards. By 1978 the Society had established a number of family centres and therapeutic pre-schools and was gradually phasing out its family casework service.[31]

In Ireland legal adoption is governed by the Adoption Acts of 1952 to 1976 which are administered by the Adoption Board (An Bord Uchtála). The Adoption Board does not arrange adoptions or nominate or recommend a child for adoption. Adoptions are mainly arranged by voluntary adoption societies which are registered with the Adoption Board. There are twenty adoption societies and they are denominational in character. Of the 1,127 adoption orders made in 1977 the breakdown by type of placement was as follows:[32] by registered adoption societies, 938; by health boards, 79; by natural mother with relatives, 104; by natural mother with persons other than relatives, 3; by third parties, 3.

Owing mainly to geographic location there is considerable variation in the level of activity of adoption societies. Four societies were responsible for half the 938 placements in 1977.[33] Since the first Adoption Act was passed in 1952 a number of changes have been made in the law. Up to 1974, for example, adopters were required to be of the same religion as the child and its parents, or if the child was illegitimate, its mother. This section of the 1952 Act was found to be unconstitutional in 1974 and the present position is that an adoption order shall not be made unless the consenting parties know the religion of the applicant or applicants and give consent.[34] In 1977, out of 1,127 adoption orders made, 1,082 were made in favour of Catholic adopters, twenty-three in favour of adopters of mixed religion (one of the parties a Catholic) and twenty-two in favour of adopters of a religion other than Catholic. An adoption order can only be made in respect of a child who is an orphan, illegitimate or who has been legitimated by nature of the Legitimacy Act, 1931, but whose birth has not been re-registered under the Act. The child must be resident in the state, not less than six weeks old and not more than 21 years of age. The Adoption Board is bound to give consideration to the wishes of the child if he or she is over 7 years old. The child may be adopted by the mother, natural father, a relative of the child, a widow, a married couple living together and, since the 1974 Act, a widower under certain circumstances. Despite some recent changes, Shatter[35] makes a number of criticisms of the present law governing adoption, for instance a legitimate child (other than an orphan) cannot be adopted despite the fact that in some circumstances it would be beneficial for the welfare of the child; the time between the placement of the child and the adoption order being made is too long (usually six months), thus adding 'unnecessary uncertainty to the adoption process and... considerable anxiety to the applicants'; the natural father cannot directly intervene in the adoption process. Further criticisms of the adoption process have been made by Darling[36] who indicated disparities in the modus operandi of adoption societies.

Health boards take three categories of children into care, orphans, deserted or abandoned children and children of parents who are unable to provide for their children. While it is health board policy to avoid, except as a last resort, the removal of children from the home, they can arrange to have a child cared for in a number of ways, for example by adoption in the case of orphans, by fostering the child, by placing the child in a residential home or by placing him or her in employment if he or she is over 15 years old. In addition, child care staff of health boards supervise children placed by others in foster care. Under the provisions of Section 61 of the Health Act, 1970, health boards may also contribute towards the running costs of day nurseries operated by voluntary agencies. Such nurseries are primarily day care centres and their main purpose is to provide an alternative to residential care for children whose parents cannot care for them during the day. The *Report of the Commission on the Status of Women* (1972) had recommended that:

> Where new housing schemes are being erected provisions should be made for the building of creches or day-nurseries and the provision of facilities of this nature should be a condition for the grant of planning permission for such schemes where many women may have an economic necessity to take up part-time work.[37]

Three years after the publication of the report it was noted that:

> There has been little development in the provision of day-care facilities. Approximately thirty day nurseries operate in the country. The Health Boards in the areas in which they are situated meet between 50 per cent and 100 per cent of the running costs. No action has been taken to make the provision of creches or day nurseries a condition for the granting of planning permission for new housing schemes.[38]

The Juvenile Liaison Officer Scheme was introduced in Dublin in 1963 and subsequently extended to other large urban areas. The underlying principle of this scheme is that juvenile liaison officers (members of the Garda Síochána specially chosen for the work) are empowered to deal with children and young persons who commit certain offences such as burglary or larceny without resorting to court proceedings. Normally the offender must be under 17 years of age, must have committed a minor offence and must admit to the offence. He or she must not have previously come under the notice of the Gardaí. The parents or guardian must agree to co-operate with the Gardaí by accepting help and advice concerning the child's future and the injured party must agree to the child being cautioned rather than prosecuted. In general, it is the policy to caution rather than prosecute a juvenile who is known to be a first offender and who satisfies the above conditions. Juveniles dealt with under the scheme are either those who have broken the law or potential delinquents, i.e. those not known to have committed any offence but whose known behaviour could lead them into crime.

By 1978 there were 4 sergeants, 35 Gardaí and 2 Ban Ghardaí employed in the operation of the scheme.[39] Outside the urban areas where juvenile liaison officers have been appointed there is also provision for the cautioning of juveniles under the age of 17 years for minor offences and they are subject to an informal type of surveillance. Between 1963 when the scheme was introduced and 1978 a total of 12,374 offenders had been cautioned and supervised. Of these, 1,480 (12 per cent of the total) are known to have committed further offences and received Court convictions. This figure suggests that the scheme helps to prevent recidivism. However, it should be noted that the figure relates only to the period for which juveniles are supervised and that convictions of persons over 17 years are not included even though they may have been in the scheme up to the age of 17. This is not to deny the undoubted merits of the scheme, particularly the advantage that one-time offenders do not have the stigma of a criminal record and this in itself may lessen the incidence of crime.

Children may be brought before the courts if they have committed an offence or if they are in need of care and protection as laid down in the Children Act of 1908.[40] When dealing with children under 17 years of age a court is required to sit in a different place or at a different time from the ordinary sittings of the court and such courts are referred to as Juvenile Courts. In Dublin there is a special full-time Children's Court. Considerable criticism of the court system and its application to children has been made in the Kennedy Report[41] and the CARE Memorandum.[42] The age of criminal responsibility in Ireland, for example, is seven years, the lowest in Europe. The Kennedy Report recommended that this be raised to twelve years initially.[43] While supporting this proposal CARE rightly pointed out that the main concern should be the provision of effective means of dealing with children on either side of the limit. The type of 'court' system favoured by CARE is one in which the District Justice is accompanied by experienced lay people in making decisions on the best course of treatment for children, whether they be offenders or otherwise.[45]

Institutional services
Young convicted offenders or children in need of care are catered for in either residential homes, special schools or prisons.

The reformatory schools (now special schools) date from the Reformatory Schools Act, 1858, when it was recognised that the criminal offences of children were different in kind and degree from those of adults and therefore required different treatment. Such schools were run by religious orders. In order to meet the need for neglected, orphaned and abandoned children industrial schools were subsequently established and these were also operated by religious orders. The maximum number of such schools was ten (reformatory) and seventy-one (industrial).[46] By the time the Kennedy Report was published in 1972 there were three reformatory and twenty-nine industrial schools. The Report indicated that the closure of reformatories was due to the decrease in the number of committals while the reduction in the number of children committed to industrial schools was due to various factors such as 'the decline in population, improvements in living standards, improved social services, adoption and boarding-out (fosterage)'.

The report recommended that the system of residential care for children should be abolished and be replaced by group homes which would approximate as closely as possible to the normal family. It found the reformatory system completely inadequate and recommended the closure of the boys' reformatory at Daingean, County Offaly, and its replacement by modern special schools conducted by trained staff. The report was also critical of the regime in St Patrick's Institution (a prison for offenders between the ages of 16 and 21) and of the lack of educational facilities in particular.

Since the publication of the Kennedy Report a number of developments have occurred. The boys' reformatory at Daingean has been closed and two modern special schools at Finglas and Lusk in Dublin have been opened. Many of the former large industrial schools have been replaced by family type units; training courses are now available for staff engaged in residential care of children; educational facilities have been provided in St Patrick's Institution.[47] Other recent developments in institutional care have been the establishment of 'open' prisons at Shanganagh Castle, County Dublin, and Shelton Abbey, County Wicklow, for offenders under 21 years.

In what many regarded as a retrograde step a new detention centre for young offenders aged 12 to 16 years was opened at Loughan House, County Cavan, in October 1978. Loughan House was formerly an open prison for offenders aged 16 to 21 years and was specially refurbished for its new role. The proposal to establish the centre led to considerable controversy and several organisations such as CARE, the Irish Association of Social Workers, the Prisoners' Rights Organisation, the ISPCC, the Fine Gael and Labour parties as well as individuals opposed its establishment. Even prison officers, whose members were to staff the centre following a concentrated training course in child care, expressed reservations about the proposal initially. Among the reasons for opposition to the proposal were the location of the centre which would make visiting by relatives difficult, the employment of prison officers rather than qualified child care workers to man the centre and the prison-like atmosphere of the centre which would not be conducive to the rehabilitation of the inmates.[48]

Some support for the proposal, however, was also forth-coming, mainly from individuals. An editorial in the *Garda Review* supported the establishment of the centre and suggested that the lack of a proper custodial facility for young offenders had played a major role in the rise of crime. The Minister for Justice, Gerard Collins, repeatedly justified his plan on the grounds that it was a necessary interim measure 'to accommodate boys between the ages of 12 and 16 years, who because of their behavioural problems or their tendency to abscond are not currently acceptable in the existing special schools'.[49] In June 1978 it was announced that a purpose-built special school for young offenders which would eventually replace the controversial Loughan House would be completed by 1980.

One of the major criticisms of the child care services in general made by the Kennedy Report was that no one govern-ment department had overall responsibility for such services. It recommended that administrative responsibility for all aspects of child care should be transferred to the Department of Health.[50] In 1974 the government allocated main responsibility, in relation to child care including that of co-ordination, to the Minister for Health, Brendan Corish. He in turn established a task force to report on the necessary updating and reform of child care legislation and of the child care services. In November 1975 the task force issued an interim report.[51] This report dealt mainly with residential services and recommended the establishment of thirteen new residential centres, the modification of another and the establishment of neighbour-hood youth projects. The proposed residential centres were for disturbed, homeless and itinerant children mainly in the Dublin area.

Voluntary Organisations[52]
Voluntary organisations may be classified in a number of ways. The term voluntary is used in two quite distinct contexts. Firstly, it may refer to the activity of volunteers, people who give of their own time and energy, generally without payment, in the service of others. Secondly, it may refer to independent organisations as distinct from statutory agencies.

Some voluntary bodies are completely financed and administered by voluntary funds and voluntary workers and employ no paid professional staff. There are also voluntary bodies largely financed by voluntary funds and which also receive state grants and employ paid professional staff.

During the Victorian era a large number of charitable organisations grew up in Britain to help such categories as prisoners, prostitutes, orphans, widows, unwanted children and the poor in general. Parallel to the voluntary efforts, the state began to become more and more involved in the provision of services, the predominant body in this sphere being the local authority. At the beginning of the century several important state measures were taken to protect the individual against the contingencies of life, for example old age pensions introduced in 1908, sickness and unemployment benefit in 1911. Since then the state income maintenance services have expanded greatly. The state has also become increasingly involved in the provision of housing, education and health services.

With the increase in state activity in the social field a corresponding decline in voluntary effort might be expected. If anything the opposite would appear to be the case. Irrespective of the number of services provided by the state there will always be cases which defy help channelled through official agencies. Voluntary bodies can provide the flexibility to pick up such cases. Examples might be the organisations which attempt to help chronic alcoholics and travelling people. It is difficult to imagine a bureaucracy providing a service such as that provided by the Samaritans whose volunteers provide only a personal relationship when the stress of modern living becomes too much and the client contemplates ending his or her life. Voluntary organisations may also play an important role as pressure groups which focus attention on existing needs or gaps in existing services. Examples of such organisations are CARE and Free Legal Advice Centres (FLAC). It is important that groups exist to speak on behalf of the underprivileged. Some are recognised by the government as having such a role; the Society of St Vincent de Paul, for instance, makes an annual submission to the government prior to the introduction of a Budget. This important aspect of the work of voluntary agencies was recognised in the Seebohm Report in Britain which stated:

> Voluntary organisations pioneered social reform in the past and we see them playing a major role in developing citizen participation, in revealing new needs and in exposing shortcomings in services.[53]

While voluntary organisations play an important part in the social services there is a danger that if they provide adequate services the state might relinquish responsibility for such services or refuse to give them the support which they deserve. For over a century the state allowed voluntary bodies to bear the brunt of child care services and in the provision of services for the handicapped it still does to a large extent. If there had not been religious orders willing to provide residential child care services the state would have had to face up to its responsibility much earlier. A further example is the work of FLAC, an organisation which has repeatedly stated that it is the state's duty to provide a comprehensive system of free legal aid as is the case in other European countries. FLAC sees its role as a temporary one until a state scheme is introduced.[54]

Changing role of voluntary organisations

It does at first seem paradoxical that despite the increased involvement of the state in the provision of social services not only are voluntary organisations still flourishing but that new organisations are in fact being established. A number of such organisations have been established in Ireland in the last few years. Some have been established owing to a change in the climate of opinion and changed attitudes — ALLY and CHERISH for unmarried mothers. Others have been founded in order to meet new needs which have become more acute in recent years — ADAPT for deserted and alone parents, or Irish Women's Aid Society for battered wives. There are basic differences between the new voluntary organisations of today and their predecessors in the nineteenth century. As the Aves report points out:

The new and heartening characteristic of today's pioneers is that, unlike most of their predecessors, they start as a rule without social or financial privilege or an assumption that they are entitled to make moral judgements about their neighbours. The pioneering drive tends to come from the young, from egalitarians, from those who resent social dysfunctioning and individual misery and have sufficiently passionate convictions to try to do something about it. There is evidence that such movements are able to draw upon a considerable supply of volunteers.[55]

Others have been obliged to change their structure or philosophy in order to remain relevant to present-day problems. The Society of St Vincent de Paul, for example, underwent a soul-searching period recently and has adapted to changing circumstances. It is no longer totally male-dominated, it is now more ecumenical in its membership and has branched out into various new activities. The ISPCC has also undergone change recently and is now no longer solely concerned with physical cruelty to children and the prosecution of guilty parents or removing children from their homes but has become involved in other activities such as the establishment of family centres.

Other voluntary organisations still continue to function long after their raison d'être has disappeared. In some cases the very titles of these societies are archaic or reflect a climate of opinion which is scarcely tenable in modern society — Catholic Protection and Rescue Society (Adoption Society) or the Sick and Indigent Roomkeepers' Society. For whatever reasons, many organisations still linger on despite the fact that other statutory or voluntary agencies may perform their original functions far more effectively. As Leaper stated:

It becomes very difficult for those so totally absorbed with a special interest to see it in its context or to adapt themselves to other social or civic demands. This becomes all the more difficult if one has to renounce the cherished chairmanship, secretaryship, executive committee membership, in which the individual takes pride and satisfaction. Yet at a given moment in history the best possible course for certain independent bodies may well be to go out of existence and let voluntary activity take a new form in a new organisation.[56]

Co-ordination

Commenting on the need for co-ordination among organisations the *Care of the Aged* report pointed out that a host of public and voluntary organisations were involved in the provision of social services. Annex 1 of the report listed a total of 156 voluntary bodies at national and local level which were providing community care services for the elderly. The large number of organisations dealing not only with the elderly but other groups as well suggests certain problems. In general, voluntary bodies operate as free agents without any central direction. This situation may lead to the futile expenditure of energy, funds or skills which are in short supply. Duplication can easily arise where there are a large number of bodies working in isolation from each other, the possible result being fragmented and inadequate services.

The *Care of the Aged* report recommended that social service councils be established whose main function would be the co-ordination of services provided at local level. The report also envisaged them as serving other useful purposes such as creating an understanding between health authorities and voluntary bodies; acting as a mouthpiece for local bodies, thus avoiding unnecessary individual effort by these bodies and employing skilled staff which many voluntary bodies could not afford to do.[57]

The Directory of Social Service Organisations (1978) published by the National Social Service Council lists 229 social service councils and care of the aged committees. While the majority of councils were established since the publication of the *Care of the Aged* report, a few of the more notable councils were established in the early 1960s, for instance in Kilkenny and Limerick. Social service councils are usually representative of the voluntary organisations in an area. Their aim is to work together in the provision of social services; to co-ordinate existing activities; to identify needs and to try to ensure that they are met. Through discussion, the existing activities of the voluntary organisations can be co-ordinated. Frequently, they can employ a social worker to undertake activities on behalf of all the voluntary agencies concerned. There is a great variation in the range of services provided by social service councils. Some concentrate almost exclusively on services for the elderly while others provide comprehensive services embracing the needs of various groups in the community and may be providing as many as fifty different types of services.

National Social Service Council

The NSSC was established in 1971 by the then Minister for Health, Erskine Childers. At the inaugural meeting of the Council the Minister referred to the fact that there was no one focal point of voluntary social work activity in this country; no specific agency to which someone, conscious of the need for a new service or sensitive to the deficiencies in an existing one, could come with proposals of change or offers of help. Nor, he said was there then any place in which a person might obtain comprehensive and up-to-date information about the range of voluntary work in the social field in Ireland. The establishment of the Council would, he said, lead to the creation of such a focal point and would also be a source of encouragement, assistance and advice to existing agencies. He said that the NSSC was being established at a time when it was more generally accepted than ever before that there was an obligation on all of us to ensure that in a society which, overall, was becoming more affluent, the weak, the needy, the old were not neglected.

The aims of the NCCS are:

1. to promote co-operation between voluntary social service organisations at local and regional level by encouraging the formation and development of social service councils or similar bodies or by other means

2. to promote co-operation between statutory and voluntary social services

3. to provide information and advice on the social services and related fields

4. to offer advice on policy and services to government and to statutory and voluntary bodies engaged in the provision of social services

5. to encourage the development of social services as an integral part of community development.

The NSSC publishes a monthly information bulletin, *Relate,* which contains up-to-date information on changes in social services and is a most useful source.

Social work

The Charity Organisation Society (COS) was established in London in 1869 to co-ordinate the activities of the city's charitable bodies. It also introduced family casework, that is counselling of individuals and families with a view to reforming the clients so that they might become independent, self-respecting individuals.[58] This method of personal inquiry and follow-up was not original but it was the COS which developed casework fully as a professional activity by its insistence on rigorous inquiry into the nature of the problems facing applicants and their families.

The fact that casework required special qualities and qualifications was early recognised. As a result, the COS in 1896 instituted for its social workers a scheme of training through lectures and practical work. In due course the COS promoted the establishment of a school of sociology from which grew the Department of Social Science and Administration of the London School of Economics in 1912. Thereafter similar departments were established in nearly all universities in Britain. By the turn of the century, therefore, states Woodroofe, social casework 'had evolved from a set of rules to guide volunteers in their work as friendly visitors of the poor into a philosophy which embodied many of the principles of modern casework and a technique which could be transmitted by education and training from one generation of social workers to another.'[59]

With the expansion of the statutory social and medical services, social workers had a very practical job to do, learning exactly what help was available to their clients and enabling them to get it. A trend towards specialisation also emerged and social workers began to specialise in such areas as psychiatric problems, child-care, geriatric problems and medical problems.

In 1965 a committee was established in Britain 'to review the organisation and responsibilities of local authority personal social services in England and Wales and to consider what changes are desirable to secure an effective family service'. The committee published its report in 1968 and it is popularly known as the Seebohm report after the chairman of the committee, Frederic Seebohm. Its central recommendation, which was adopted, was that all welfare services be brought together in a single unified social service department. Social service departments were established with the passing of the Social Services Act of 1970. Prior to the Seebohm reorganisation there was little contact or co-ordination between the various local authority departments concerned with the provision of services to, for example, the elderly or children in need. Attention was focused on the individual rather than the family. As a result the situation sometimes arose where two or three social workers from different departments became involved with different members of the same family (either the children, parents or grandparents) without ever coming in contact with each other.

The Seebohm report accepted the widely held view that specialisation, both in work and in training, had gone too far, causing a fragmentation of the service and encouraging what is called a 'symptom centred approach' to cases. A family with several problems might be visited by several workers independently, not one of whom was concerned to assess the situation as a whole.

Only recently have social workers been employed on any extensive scale in Ireland. The main impetus to the development of social work has been the establishment of the Community Care Programme by health boards. Prior to this, the majority of people trained in social work in Ireland emigrated. In 1963 Binchy could write that, 'we must be one of the few countries in the world exporting the bulk of our newly qualified social workers each year.'[60] In 1971 there were 235 social workers in Ireland of whom 145 were employed by statutory bodies and 90 by voluntary agencies. By 1977 the total number had increased to 370.[61]

A study of social work services in Tallaght, County Dublin,

indicated that these services needed to be co-ordinated.[62] The study showed that the present fragmented services do not reach all those in need of them, only about 2 per cent of the estimated 28,000 population being clients of sixty-one social workers employed by a variety of agencies. Of the fifty-eight social workers who completed a questionnaire, all but one came from outside Tallaght and they represented forty agencies. The extent of overlapping of clients was not measured, as names and addresses were not used in the survey for reasons of confidentiality. But the fragmentation of services is obvious. The study details the types of agencies with which clients in Tallaght deal — 40 per cent were seen by social workers in voluntary agencies including the Tallaght Welfare Society; over 18 per cent were seen by social workers in general hospitals and 15 per cent by statutory social workers. Other clients were seen in children's hospitals and child guidance clinics, by social workers with agencies for the handicapped or social workers in specialist hospitals and 3 per cent in psychiatric hospitals and out-patients clinics.

Basically there are three main types of social work, casework, groupwork and community work. Casework is the oldest and most traditional type of social work. It has as its focus the social and emotional problems of individuals. Groupwork is an extension of casework in that instead of dealing with one individual a social worker may at one time deal with a number of individuals who share a common problem. Community work has a very different set of assumptions, theories and practice from those of casework. The aim of community work is to bring people together so that they can participate in changing their society. The major focus in both Britain and Ireland at present is on casework although an increasing number of social workers engage in groupwork as a logical extension of work with individuals and families. Most social workers also are generic though there is some specialisation in Ireland and a tendency to return to specialisation in Britain.[63] Social workers are also involved in supplying information about various social services and in helping clients obtain their entitlements.

At the Social Service Councils Conference held in Limerick

in 1976, Sister Stanislaus, from the Kilkenny Social Service Centre (also chairman of the National Committee on Pilot Schemes to Combat Poverty), expressed some reservations about the increasing reliance on casework:

> It's interesting, though often overlooked, that over the past twenty years whenever the British people identified or investigated a social problem there was a national call for more social workers. No matter how intense the criticism of the services the need for more trained social workers was never challenged. We are doing precisely the same thing without ever asking what we want them to do. My fear is that as Health Boards employ more and more social workers operating as caseworkers, we will find sooner or later the community beginning to evade its responsibility, forcing social workers to become the modern workhouse or institution on whom we dump our social problems, who will carry our ills and become our scapegoats. Health Boards are paying a lot of attention to the qualifications which they require of social workers but scarcely any attention has been given to how they will use them. While I am not denying for a minute the need for casework, I think that much more thought needs to be given to the use of community and group workers — community workers who will represent the interests of the local community, who will provide a vehicle for the community to assess its local needs and enable it to participate in the planning, provision and delivery of services to meet these needs; community workers who will act as sources of information, stimulators and catalysts and encouragers and who will help local communities to think and work through the potential of a real local response to need.[64]

Since 1978 some health boards have employed community workers whose functions include liaising between voluntary groups engaged in the provision of social services and the relevant statutory agencies.

Chapter 7

Some EEC Comparisons

Introduction
A referendum held in Ireland in May 1972 indicated an over-whelming majority in favour of Ireland's entry into the EEC. Accompanied by the United Kingdom and Denmark, Ireland's formal membership began on 1 January 1973. The three new states joined the existing six — France, Germany, Holland, Luxembourg, Belgium and Italy — which in 1957 had signed the Treaty of Rome establishing the EEC.

Within the EEC are a number of institutions, the main ones being the Commission, the Council of Ministers, the European Parliament, the Economic and Social Committee and the European Court of Justice. The Commission is the executive body headed by thirteen commissioners. Ireland's first Commissioner, from 1973 to 1976, was Dr Patrick Hillery who had responsibility for Social Affairs, and the current Irish representative is Richard Burke, Commissioner for Consumer Affairs, Transport, Taxation and relations with the European Parliament. The Council of Ministers representing the nine member states has the responsibility of deciding on proposals from the Commission. The European Parliament and the Economic and Social Committee are consultative bodies which advise the Council of Ministers on actions it should take with regard to Commission proposals. Commission proposals may take one of three forms — regulations which are automatically enforced in member states, directives which member states are obliged to adopt in principle but which allow for some flexibility to suit national circumstances, and finally, recommendations which have no legal force.

In this chapter it is proposed to examine the meaning of social policy in an EEC context, and to examine the broad similarities and dissimilarities between member states in regard to the provision of social services. It is not intended to examine the social services in any EEC country in depth but merely to place Irish services in an EEC context, to indicate what features are held in common with other member states or what major differences exist.

Social Policy

The term European Economic Community, or the more popular 'Common Market' suggests that the EEC is almost exclusively concerned with economic problems. Indeed it is true to say that its main preoccupation has been with economic affairs. The Treaty of Rome, however, also contained social provisions with two basic aims which are closely related, the promotion of employment and the raising of living and working conditions. During the 1960s, however, the main emphasis was on the promotion of high living standards through steady economic expansion. But as Shanks[1] indicates, this economic growth had been bought at a price and certain regions (mainly peripheral) and certain groups in society (the young, the old, women, the handicapped, migrant workers) were losing ground.

At the Paris summit meeting in October 1972 the heads of government of the nine member states requested the Community institutions to draw up a programme of action providing for concrete measures in the area of social policy. A statement issued at the meeting stated that: 'The Heads of State or Government emphasise that they attach as much importance to vigorous action in the social field as to the achievement of economic and monetary union'. The Commission subsequently drew up a Social Action Programme (SAP), a draft of which was submitted to the Council at the end of 1973 and finally incorporated in a resolution of the Council in January 1974. In adópting the SAP which was to run from 1974 to 1976 the Community expressed its intention to take the various measures necessary to achieve three broad aims, (1) the attainment of full and better employment; (2) the improvement of living and working conditions; (3) the increased involvement of management and labour in the economic and social decisions of the Community and of workers in the life of under-takings (e.g. firms, companies, factories). The full implementation of the SAP, however, was quickly hindered by the economic recession which followed the oil crisis of 1973. Another factor was that since the SAP had no sanction in the Treaty of Rome its implementation depended entirely on the political will of the nine member states which, during the recession, became preoccupied with their own affairs.

In particular, the objective of full employment became increasingly difficult to achieve. Simply put, the objective was 'to create enough jobs for the present and future working population of the Community so that no worker is forced to migrate in search of work'.[2] Between 1973 and 1977 the annual average number unemployed in the EEC more than doubled, from 2.6 million to 5.7 million.[3] Of particular concern was the fact that over the same period the number of young people (under 25 years) unemployed had trebled and accounted for 40 per cent of the total unemployed.[4]

Some progress was made, however, in implementing aspects of the SAP. These included the issuing of directives on equal pay and mass dismissals; a directive on equality of opportunity for women in the labour market; the initiation of pilot schemes to combat poverty; the extension of the Social Fund to cater for migrant and handicapped workers and workers aged under 25 and the establishment of the Foundation for Improved Living Conditions.

Since 1977 the question of unemployment has continued to be a priority in member states. The only notable official statement in 1977 of Community intentions in the social field was an address by the Commissioner of Social Affairs, Hank Vredeling, to the Council of Ministers in which he outlined five main objectives for the next few years: (1) the return to full employment; (2) 'humanisation' of work; (3) the reduction of inequalities; (4) progress in social security and public health; and (5) strengthening participation and co-determination at all levels.[5]

In a submission to the President of the Commission and the Commissioner for Social Affairs, the International Committee of the United Kingdom National Council of Social Service (NCSS) stated:

In practice and in spite of the statement by the Heads of

Government in 1972, community social policy had tended merely to play a remedial rather than a preventive role, being used as a means of mopping up the undesirable consequences of economic growth (unemployment in declining industries, for example).[6]

The NCSS recommended that the Commission should promote a close relationship between economic and social policy, strengthen the sense of Community identity, redistribute wealth between regions, recognise Europe's responsibilities to the poorer nations and introduce greater democracy in the Community institutions.

In his critique of social policy in the EEC Shanks[7] suggests that in the future a fourth key objective, social justice, should be added to the original three aims of the SAP. This, in his view, is essential if the Community is to help overcome the social friction which has been one of the major effects of the inflationary spiral seen in Europe in recent years. He also maintains that the Community's effectiveness in the social field is not confined to passing legislation and distributing Community funds but that it can be equally, if not more, effective as catalyst, educator, co-ordinator, data-bank and standard setter.

Income maintenance
There are considerable differences between countries in the evolution of their income maintenance systems. Thus, Germany and Denmark played pioneering roles in introducing schemes such as pensions (both old age and survivors) yet were the last to introduce family (child) benefits (see Table 42, page 228).

Administration
One of the major differences between Ireland, the UK and the rest of the EEC is in the administration of income maintenance payments. In Ireland and the UK income maintenance services are centrally administered whereas in other EEC countries administration is in the hands of a multitude of autonomous funds. This situation is very similar to that which

Table 42: Year in which various income maintenance schemes
were first introduced in EEC countries

Country	Old age pensions	Survivors pensions	Unemployment
Belgium	1900	1900	1944
Germany	1889	1889	1927
France	1910	1910	1940
Italy	1919	1919	1919
Luxembourg	1911	1911	1921
Netherlands	1913	–	1949
UK	1908	1925	1911
Ireland	1908	1935	1911
Denmark	1891	1891	1907

Country	Invalidity	Industrial injuries	Families (child) benefits
Belgium	1944	1903	1930
Germany	1889	1884	1954
France	1910	1898	1932
Italy	1919	1898	1937
Luxembourg	1911	1902	1947
Netherlands	1913	–	1939
UK	1911	1897	1945
Ireland	1911	1897	1944
Denmark	1921	1898	1950

Source: *Comparative Tables on the Social Security systems
in the Member States of the European Communities*
(9th Edition) 1976

existed in Ireland and the UK up to approximately forty years
ago. Many of the funds in other EEC countries operate on a
vocational basis with special funds for groups of workers such
as civil servants, miners, railwaymen and farmers. This

structure embodies what James and Laurent[8] have referred to as 'the concept of group solidarity, whereas the British, Irish, Danish and to some extent the Dutch systems emphasise the fact of common citizenship'. The group solidarity on the continent is due in large part to the important role played by trade unions and employers in developing and administering social insurance schemes originally. Lawson and Reed state that:

> In most continental EEC countries, social insurance was originally conceived as a partnership between the state, employers and unions, concerned as much with regulating and containing industrial conflict as with the problem of poverty. As a result the unions, and indeed both sides of industry, played an important role in the administration of many of the early schemes and in policy making at different levels.[9]

Finance

The emphasis on the occupational group rather than common citizenship is manifest in a further respect in that most social security benefits in Europe are earnings-related with the exception of family allowances. By contrast, Ireland, the UK, Denmark and the Netherlands still rely to some extent on flat-rate benefits though the recent emphasis has been on a shift towards pay-related contributions and benefits.

Countries with well developed earnings-related systems naturally depend more on contributions from employers and employees than on general taxation. The flat-rate countries on the other hand rely more on general taxation as a means of financing benefits. In this respect Denmark depends less on employer/employee contributions than any other country and it is followed closely by Ireland (see Table 43, page 230). It should be noted that the figures in Table 43 include expenditure on health and certain other services and therefore are not strictly comparable. Nevertheless they are indicative of the overall trend in relation to expenditure. With a further shift towards pay-related contributions in 1979, Ireland should move closer to other EEC countries. One of the major reasons

Table 43: Source of finance as percentage of total finance for
social security benefits in EEC countries, 1970 and
1975

Country	Employers		Insured persons	
	1970	1975	1970	1975
Germany	47.1	44.1	24.2	24.1
France	59.8	59.0	19.2	19.8
Italy	55.0	58.2	15.4	14.2
Netherlands	43.3	40.4	36.0	33.8
Belgium	46.8	43.3	21.1	19.9
Luxembourg	36.0	38.2	24.8	24.1
UK	33.6	37.3	18.7	16.6
Ireland	19.3	22.9	12.4	13.3
Denmark	10.1	9.9	6.5	2.7

Country	Public Funds		Other sources[a]	
	1970	1975	1970	1975
Germany	23.7	27.4	5.0	4.4
France	18.6	18.8	2.4	2.4
Italy	23.3	19.8	6.3	7.8
Netherlands	12.4	16.4	8.3	9.4
Belgium	25.5	31.2	6.6	5.6
Luxembourg	30.1	30.3	9.1	7.4
UK	38.3	39.3	9.4	6.8
Ireland	67.6	61.8	0.7	2.0
Denmark	80.2	84.3	3.2	3.1

[a] Includes income from investments and other receipts

Source: *Social indicators for the European Community
1960-1975*, Brussels 1977, pp 188-9.

for the dependence on public funds in Ireland, however, is the
absence of an insurance scheme to cover self-employed persons

and the consequent reliance on assistance schemes, which are financed entirely from the exchequer, to cater for this group.

Benefits provided

All EEC countries provide benefits to cover the main contingencies of life such as old age, unemployment and invalidism but the level of benefits and the qualifying conditions vary considerably. An examination of each of the schemes in detail is neither practicable nor appropriate in this chapter. Instead some indication of the variety which exists may be gleaned from a brief examination of family or child benefits, an area to which most EEC countries attach importance.

The degree of commitment to this particular form of income maintenance, however, varies considerably between countries as do the motives which inspired the introduction of such schemes in the first place. France introduced the family allowance shortly before the outbreak of World War II for demographic reasons, to encourage an increase in the birth rate. At that time the number of deaths exceeded births and large families were becoming very rare.[10] Associated with child benefits in France are a number of other ancillary benefits, for example those relating to childbirth and housing allowances. At one stage expenditure on family allowances in France exceeded that of any other form of income maintenance. More recently, however, there has been less importance attached to family allowances, though the proportion of social security expenditure devoted to them is still higher than in any other EEC country. The demographic factor appears to have been of little importance in other countries in introducing family allowances. Germany, for example, placed little emphasis on such benefits until very recently. Similarly, in the UK only the 'rediscovery' of poverty in the 1960s heightened the importance of child benefits as a means of alleviating hardship among low-income families. A major reform of the UK scheme of child benefits was completed in 1979 and is very similar to that introduced in Germany in 1975, that is the abolition of tax concessions for children, increased benefits and their extension to the first child in families.

A common feature is that family allowances in all EEC countries are flat-rate although the rates may be scaled according to the order of birth and sometimes the age of the child. Furthermore they now embrace all categories of the population with the exception of self-employed non-agricultural workers in Italy.[11] The upper age limit for receipt of allowances is normally 16 to 18 years but in some countries there is considerable extension beyond this period to cover those engaged in higher education (27 years in the Netherlands, 26 years in Italy, 25 years in Germany, Belgium and Luxembourg), girls remaining at home (27 years in the Netherlands, 25 years in Germany and Belgium) or the handicapped (no limit in the case of Germany, Belgium, Italy and Luxembourg)[12]

Apart from the actual allowances for children some countries have ancillary family benefits. Supplements which vary with the age of children exist in Denmark, Belgium, France and Luxembourg. In Belgium a family holiday allowance equal to the family allowances granted for April is paid the following month.[13]

Dynamisation
One of the standard differences between member states is the mechanism for adjusting social security payments. The term 'dynamisation' is used to describe a system whereby payments are automatically adjusted with increases in standards or costs of living. Germany pioneered this with pensions which are also governed by a formula which takes account of the retired person's previous income and duration of employment.[14] In the Benelux countries a system of index-linked automatic read-justments of pensions occurs. In Ireland and the UK increases in payments depend on legislative intervention. In 1975 both governments made an exceptional commitment to increase all social security payments twice in the one year to take account of inflation. This was repeated in Ireland in 1976, 1977 and 1979, the second increase in 1976 (for long-term recipients only) being given only after a period of campaigning by some organisations, principally the Irish Congress of Trade Unions.

Most EEC countries have some form of index-linking, though different methods are used and a distinction is often made between long-term and short-term benefits. The position is summarised in Table 44.

Table 44: Methods of adjustment of social security benefits in EEC countries

Country	Long-term benefits[a]	Short-term benefits[b]
Belgium	Periodically by monthly price index and annually by the general standard of living	Periodically by monthly price index
Denmark	By prices every six months and by the general economic situation every two years	Annually by wages
France	By wages every six months	Annually by wages or prices
Italy	Annually by wages and prices	
Luxembourg	By wages and monthly price index	Annually by wages
Netherlands	By wages every six months	By wages every six months
UK	Annually by prices or earnings	Annually by prices at least
Germany	Annually by wages and overall economic situation	
Ireland	Annually, in line with prices at least	

[a] e.g. old age, invalidity and survivor's pensions
[b] e.g. sickness, maternity and unemployment

Source: *Look Europe,* National Council of Social Service, May 1977, pp 3-4

The importance which the EEC Commission attaches to 'dynamisation' of income maintenance benefits was recognised in the Social Action Programme which summed up the existing situation as follows:

Mechanisms for maintaining the purchasing value of social security benefits exist in varying forms throughout the Community. The real income of pensioners, widows, the permanently disabled, etc may thus remain constant, but their relative income, as compared with the average earnings of the working population, declines. The existence of systems of linking the real value of social security benefits to the rise in real incomes is still fairly exceptional.[15]

The SAP objective was to bring about a situation in which all recipients of social benefits could share in rising prosperity 'by linking the real value of social benefits to the increases in incomes enjoyed by the productive sector of the population.'[16] The Commission subsequently admitted, however, that 'in view of the present troubled economic climate it is difficult to see the Member States taking a rapid decision in this field'.[17]

Health Services

Coverage
Over the past decade or so there has been a general trend throughout the EEC towards universal coverage for medical care (see Table 45, page 235).

Ireland, with approximately 40 per cent of the population covered for all health services and another 45 per cent for free hospital services, is the major exception in the EEC, although an attempt was made to move towards universal coverage for hospitalisation in 1974.

The Netherlands is another country somewhat out of step with developments within the EEC, with three-quarters of the population (composed of compulsorily insured wage and salary earners) entitled to free medical care. The remaining quarter of the population is usually insured with private insurers or the public funds but in the case of serious illness coverage extends to the entire population. Preparations began in 1975 for the establishment of a general health insurance scheme which will cover the entire population of the Netherlands.

In Belgium, compulsory insurance for health care was introduced in 1945 for certain sections of the population. In 1964 the self-employed were included and finally in 1969, all other groups previously without compulsory insurance.

Table 45: Percentage of population entitled to medical care in EEC countries 1960 and 1975

Country	1960	1975
Belgium	73	100
Germany	85	92
France	66	99
Italy	78	93/100[a]
Luxembourg	83	100
Netherlands	76[b]	76[b]
United Kingdom	100	100
Ireland	30/90[c]	30/90[c]
Denmark	90	100
EEC Total	87	95

[a] Only hospital care
[b] 100 per cent in the case of serious illness
[c] 30 per cent (full eligibility) and 90 per cent (limited eligibility). These figures should now read 40/85.

Source: *Report on the Development of the Social Situation in the Community, 1976* Brussels 1977, pp 220-221

In Germany, compulsory health insurance was introduced for certain sections of the population over a century ago and in time the scope of insurance was extended. By 1975, 92 per cent of the population was covered, the remaining 8 per cent relying on private insurance. As in Ireland those compulsorily insured may supplement their cover by purchasing private insurance.

In France, coverage is almost universal with 99 per cent of the population being covered by one form of compulsory insurance or another. The main reason for the increase in coverage during the 1960s was the inclusion of the self-employed.

In Italy, the number of persons insured, as a percentage of the population, has increased steadily since 1960. By 1975, 93 per cent of the population was compulsorily insured and 100 per cent covered for hospital care.

In Luxembourg, coverage was extended to all wage earners in two stages in 1925 and 1954. Salaried employees were brought within the system of compulsory coverage in 1951 and,finally, farmers in 1962.

Since 1948 coverage for health services has embraced the entire population of the United Kingdom.

In Denmark the entire population has been entitled to health services since 1972.

Finance and Organisation
James and Laurent,[18] in analysing the medical care systems in EEC countries, have ranked them according to the degree of 'integration' achieved in the relationship between doctor (or other agent of care), patient and financing organisation. The starting point on the scale would be a situation where doctors and patients freely contract with each other for items of care and any insurance is voluntary on the part of the patient and confined to the recovery of fees fixed by the contracting parties.

The first stage away from this is the institution of compulsory insurance so that it becomes universal for three parties to be involved. Every nation in the EEC has gone further than this at least to the extent of bringing the insurance fund into direct contact with the doctors and other medical agencies to establish an agreed scale of fees. This is the usual situation in France, Belgium, Luxembourg and (for non-specialist care) Italy. In these countries the patient pays his doctor according to the scale and is reimbursed by his social security fund. The reimbursement is usually only partial, 75 per cent or 80 per cent, leaving the patient to carry some direct charge. Lawson and Reed[19] suggest that the reimbursement principle in France and Belgium can be traced back to voluntary societies (out of which compulsory schemes later developed) which made cash payments to the insured when they incurred medical expenses rather than contracts with the providers of the services. They also suggest as another reason for the retention of this principle, the strength of the medical profession in these two countries when the state moved into health insurance, at a later stage than in Germany or Britain for instance, and conclude that any attempt to change the reimbursement principle would be resisted by doctors in France and Belgium.

The second stage is for the fund to pay the doctors directly, dispensing with any immediate financial participation by the patient. Such is the situation in the Netherlands although examples of this can be found in France, Belgium and Luxembourg.

In the third stage we reach the German situation where the triangular relationship becomes quadrangular, the fourth element being the doctors' associations. Neither the fund nor the patient now pays the doctor directly, but the fund remits an agreed global sum to the doctor's association, leaving it to the association to share it among its members on a complex formula involving both items of service and capitation payments.

The British National Health Service (NHS) represents the highest degree of integration achieved in the EEC. In Britain over 85 per cent of the NHS is financed out of general taxation. The purpose of the NHS when introduced was that a comprehensive service should be available to everyone regardless of 'financial means, age, sex, employment or vocation, area of residence or insurance qualification'. The whole system is largely financed and therefore regulated by the state. Everyone is entitled to go on the list of a NHS family doctor and through him has access to treatment in a nationally-financed network of hospitals. Until recently the British NHS was unique among the medical care systems of Western Europe but variants have now begun to appear elsewhere. In Italy, legislation passed in 1974 and 1977 provided for the abolition of sickness funds and their replacement by a national health service. The new service was introduced gradually and became fully operational in 1979. The Italian NHS is financed by earmarked taxation and administered by the area health authorities and the professions.

Denmark has launched a variation of the NHS. For the majority of the population there is a free service operated by the local and regional authorities out of regional and central taxation. The top 20 per cent of the income range must pay for their own care (apart from hospitalisation) and may then call on a system of partial reimbursement. Since 1 April 1976 all Danish citizens have been able to choose between a free health system (conditional upon choosing a doctor for a specified period) and a system of partial reimbursement of medical expenses (in this case with complete freedom of choice of doctor). The two possibilities existed previously but the divison was necessarily made on the basis of the level of income of those concerned.

The different stages outlined above apply (in most cases) to hospital as well as doctors' services. The majority of doctors working in hospitals in Europe also work in the outside community and are not salaried by the hospitals. The usual situation is that the hospital is free to enter into an agreement with the insurance fund governing the scale of charges and related matters and the fund either pays for its members' care or reimburses their expenses as the case may be. A large number of the hospitals in Europe are owned by private non-profit agencies such as church organisations or the Red Cross.

One of the basic differences between the original six and the three new entrants to the EEC (Britain, Denmark and Ireland) is in the organisation of health services. The continental health insurance schemes are highly decentralised and fragmented.[20]

In Germany there are approximately 2,000 sickness funds. These funds set the contribution rates within limits determined by the central government which is frequently obliged to make good the deficits which arise. As in Germany the Dutch central government is not directly involved in the provision of medical care. The ninety-one Dutch sickness funds receive their income from a general fund administered by the national Sickness Funds Council and provide insurance cover for those compelled to be members of the system and those who opt in.

Cover is provided by private insurers for those persons who are not members of the sickness funds. In Belgium all contributions are paid to an independent organisation (the National Social Security Organisation) of the Ministry of Social Affairs which redistributes part of the funds to another autonomous institution — the National Sickness and Invalidity Insurance Institution. This latter distributes the funds to six health care organisations, five groups of sickness funds and an auxiliary fund set up by the government. The funds negotiate fees with doctors and hospitals. The pattern is somewhat similar in France. The general scheme which covers 70 per cent of the population is financed by contributions paid to a central fund (the National Sickness Insurance Fund). The sickness funds (regional and local) receive their finance from the central fund and provide cash refunds (partial) to individual health care customers. There are special funds for civil servants, miners and railwaymen. In Luxembourg, the eleven sickness funds are responsible for organising the provision and meeting the cost of some medical care. The government provides hospitals and is responsible for the general supervision of the system. In Italy up to 1979, there were six large and 200 small funds providing insurance coverage which varied from fund to fund. The largest of the funds covered over half of the Italian population and like other funds agreed fees with the providers of medical care. As already mentioned a national health service has been introduced in Italy.

In Denmark the sickness funds which operated prior to 1973 have been abolished and finance is largely met from local taxation and central government subsidies. In the UK, medical care is largely financed out of general taxation and is provided by a structure which is directly controlled by the Department of Health and Social Security. The area health authority is responsible to the regional health authority which in turn is directly responsible to the Secretary of State for Health and Social Security. In Ireland the organisation is somewhat similar to the UK with the health boards being responsible for providing medical care subject to the overall control of the Department of Health.

In general, the health care systems in the EEC are complex

with tremendous variation between countries. The most noticeable common feature, however, is the trend towards universal coverage. The administration and organisation vary considerably, the multiplicity of sickness funds on the continent being in marked contrast with the position in Britain, Ireland and Denmark. The method of financing the providers of medical care, doctors and hospitals, also varies considerably between countries. Nevertheless throughout the EEC a pattern emerges of increasing state control to impose a fairer distribution of services, to restrain escalating costs and to act as arbiter in the negotiations between doctors and sickness funds. This does not necessarily mean that all the original members of the EEC are inclined to embrace the political ideology of the state system but rather that efficiency is the main appeal of the state system. Apart from ensuring more even distribution of services and saving on the separate administration of hundreds of sickness funds, the state is seen as the only institution which can counteract the monopolistic stranglehold of the medical profession. If the state is the sole buyer of services it has much greater bargaining power with the sole sellers (doctors) than individual insurance funds could ever have. Maynard[21] presents this argument convincingly and suggests that this is one reason why British expenditure on health care may appear relatively low compared with other European countries. However, he also points out that state control may create its own stranglehold, resulting in a brain drain and, by its hold over the pharmaceutical industry, a reduction in profits thereby restricting research.

Housing

Housing quantity

The massive postwar housing shortage which characterised many EEC countries has been eliminated. By about 1970 when the last national censuses were taken, the nine member states of the EEC averaged 341 dwellings per 1,000 inhabitants and estimates for 1975 indicate the dwellings/population ratio to be 365. In 1960 by comparison, there were only 304 dwellings per 1,000 inhabitants in the present member states (see Table 46, page 242). Housing balances have in general improved, partly as a result of falling rates of population increase and also because of expanded housing programmes. By 1975, therefore, there were between 32 and 40 dwellings available for each 100 inhabitants. Only Ireland with 26 was appreciably below this figure. This is largely due to the fact that despite substantial increases in housing output in Ireland the average family is larger than in other countries and in recent years the rate of population increase has been greater than in other member states.

While too much emphasis should not be assigned to quantity of dwellings it is nevertheless true that numbers of dwellings are basic to improvements of all kinds. At the very least they mean less overcrowding and are instrumental in the removal or improvement of the worst housing.

With the exception of Ireland, house building appears to be slowing down in the EEC countries. In 1975, 6.8 dwellings per 1,000 inhabitants were completed in the EEC as a whole. This represented a lower figure than for 1960 and was considerably less than the high figure of 8 in 1965. This overall trend, however, tends to conceal important differences between countries. While housing output in some countries has declined it has increased in others, notably Ireland, France and Belgium (see Table 47, p 243). In 1960, Ireland ranked ninth in regard to completed dwellings per 1,000 inhabitants but by 1975 it ranked fourth.

Housing Quality
As already noted in Chapter 3, a measure of the general quality of housing is its age. Statistics indicate that approximately two-fifths of the dwellings stock in the EEC is postwar and ought therefore to be of a relatively high standard. Given the extensive damage to dwellings in Germany during the war it is hardly surprising that the postwar proportion is high (see Table 47 page 243). The proportion of dwellings with bathrooms is another indicator of housing quality. In this context, considerable progress has been made in virtually all EEC countries during the 1960s, notably in Italy and the Netherlands where the proportion of dwellings having a bathroom increased

dramatically during the decade. The large discrepancy between countries may be partly explained by rural/urban differences and countries with substantial rural populations might be expected to come out worst in any comparison. Thus France (41 per cent) and Belgium (49 per cent) rank ninth and eighth respectively with Ireland (56 per cent) in seventh place. By contrast the proportions for highly urbanised societies like Britain and the Netherlands were 87 per cent and 81 per cent respectively (see Table 48, page 244).

Table 46: Number of dwellings per 1,000 inhabitants in EEC countries 1960-1975

Country	1960	1970	1975
Belgium	351	372	389[a]
Germany	289	341	383
France	349	375	399
Italy	275	320	327[a]
Luxembourg	300	319	n.a.
UK	315	345	363
Ireland	241	244	256
Denmark	320	370	398
EEC	304	341	365

[a]   1974

Source: *Report on the Development of the Social Situation in the Communities in 1976*

Owner Occupation
Owner occupation in EEC countries is, with some exceptions, rising (see Table 49 page 245). Ireland ranks first in this regard, for reasons more fully outlined in Chapter 3. By contrast, Germany is propping up the table, only one-third of its dwellings being owner occupied.

Subsidisation
In all EEC countries governments intervene in the housing

market by providing subsidies particularly to those whose needs can be regarded as priorities. The extent to which governments intervene, however, varies considerably (see Table 50 page 246). According to the EEC definition a subsidised dwelling is one, 'whose cost of construction, purchase or rental is kept at such a level that it can be rented or purchased by financially less-favoured population groups through financial means made available by public authorities (loans, bonuses, subsidies, low-interest rates'[22] It is important to note that this definition does not give any indication of the level of subsidisation. Table 50 therefore merely indicates broad differences in emphasis between countries. Bearing this in mind it would appear that Ireland is considerably ahead of other EEC countries in terms of subsidised dwellings. This is largely due to state grants for private dwellings which were cut back, however, in 1976, a fact which is reflected in the provisional figure of 87.7 per cent for 1976.

Table 47: Dwellings completed per 1,000 inhabitants in EEC countries 1960-1975

Country	1960	1965	1970	1975
Belgium	5.1	6.9	4.8[a]	7.9[a]
Germany	9.4	9.2	7.9	7.1
France	6.9	8.4	9.0	9.8
Italy	5.8	7.2	7.0	3.9
Luxembourg	4.2	7.2	5.1	9.2
Netherlands	7.3	9.4	9.0	8.9
U.K.	5.8	7.2	6.6	5.6
Ireland	2.1	4.1	4.6	8.6
Denmark	5.9	8.5	10.3	7.0
EEC Total	6.9	8.0	7.6	6.8

[a] Refers to dwellings already started

Source: *Report on the Development of the Social Situation in the Communities in 1976*

Table 48: Proportion of dwellings built prior to 1945 and proportion of dwellings with a bathroom in EEC countries

Country	% built before 1945	% with a bathroom	
	circa 1970	circa 1960	circa 1970
Belgium	62	24	49
Germany	49	49	68
France	71	25	41
Italy	n.a.	29	65
Luxembourg	62[a]	46	69
Netherlands	45	27	81
U.K.	61	77	87
Ireland	65[a]	33	56
Denmark	63	48	63
EEC Total	59[b]	45	65

[a] Before 1949
[b] Excluding Italy

Source: *Report on the Development of the Social Situation in the Communities in 1976*

Education
It is not the intention in this section to deal with educational policies in member states of the EEC. Instead the emphasis will be mainly on some comparative statistics regarding participation and expenditure.

Compulsory schooling in the EEC countries is in the range 5-7 years to 14-16 years. No change occurred in minimum age in any member states between 1960 and 1975 but some countries (Denmark, Ireland, the Netherlands and the UK) increased the maximum school leaving age during that period. By 1975 school attendance in most countries was compulsory from the age of six, the exceptions being Denmark (7 years) and the United Kingdom (5 years); in the same year the maximum compulsory age varied from 14 (Belgium and Italy) to 16 (Denmark, France and the UK).[23]

In all EEC countries the school-going population (excluding pre-primary and university) expressed as a percentage either of the total population or the population aged 5-24 years has increased over the decade 1965-75 (see table 51 page 247). By

Table 49: Proportion of dwellings which are owner occupied in EEC countries circa 1960 and 1970

Country	Circa 1960	Circa 1970
Belgium	50	55
Germany	35	34
France	42	45
Italy	46	53
Luxembourg	55	57
Netherlands	29	36
UK	43	51
Ireland	64	69
Denmark	47	47
EEC Total	42	46

Source: *Report on the Development of the Social Situation in the Communities in 1976*

1975-76 the school-going population in Ireland represented almost a quarter (23 per cent) of the total population, the highest in the EEC, although the Netherlands and the United Kingdom had proportions near this level. Over two-thirds (67.6 per cent) of the population aged 5-24 years in the UK were attending school in 1975-76 and in all other EEC countries, with the exception of Luxembourg, the figure was over 60 per cent.

The proportionate distribution of the school-going population by level (first, second, third) has changed considerably in the decade 1965-75. In general the proportions in first level declined in all countries and the major shift was to second level with smaller proportionate increases in third level (see Table 52, page 248). In 1965-66, for instance, almost three-quarters (72.6 per cent) of the school going population in Ireland was engaged in first level education but by 1975-76 the proportion had fallen to less than three-fifths (57.7 per cent). Over the same period the proportion engaged in second level education increased from 24.1 per cent to 37.8 per cent and at third level the increase was from 3.2 per cent to 4.6 per cent. By 1975, Ireland had the lowest proportion in second level and yet over the decade it recorded the highest percentage point increse of all countries at this level. At third level, Ireland, Luxembourg and the UK had considerably lower proportions than other countries and in this context Denmark ranked first with slightly more than one in ten of the school-going population engaged in third level education.

Table 50: Subsidised dwellings as a percentage of total dwell-ings built each year in EEC countries 1971-1975

Country	1971	1972	1973	1974	1975
Belgium	61.0	65.0	66.7	45.1	39.6
Germany	21.0	18.3	16.7	24.5	29.1
France	78.1	75.1	70.0	71.0	69.1
Italy	6.2	7.7	7.1	10.5	10.9
Luxembourg	28.0	31.2	39.0	39.0	35.6
Netherlands	83.7	82.6	80.1	75.5	81.5
UK	54.8	87.6	37.5	48.2	51.8
Ireland	96.8	97.5	96.9	97.3	96.1
Denmark	27.1	24.1	22.8	23.1	24.0
EEC Total	43.9	49.8	42.1	45.0	47.7

Source: *Report on the Development of the Social Situation in the Communities in 1976, 1977*

Table 51: School population[a] as percentage of total population and population aged 5-24 years in EEC countries 1965-66 and 1975-76

Country	% of population		% of population aged 5-24 years	
	1965-66	1975-76	1965-66	1975-76
Belgium	18.0	19.7	61.4	63.6
Germany	13.5	18.5	49.3	61.2
France	19.1	20.4	60.2	63.4
Italy	15.2	19.1	50.1	62.6
Luxembourg	14.6	16.4	51.9	55.5
Netherlands	19.8	22.4	55.9	64.9
U.K.	17.0	20.6	58.5	67.6
Ireland	20.4	23.0	56.9	62.1
Denmark	15.9	19.0	n.a.	62.5

[a] Excluding pre-primary and university

Source: *Social Indicators for the European Community 1960-1975*

It is in regard to educational expenditure per inhabitant and per person aged 5-24 years that wide disparities exist between member states (Table 53, page 248). Ireland comes out poorly by comparison with other countries. In 1973, educational expenditure per inhabitant in Ireland was half the average for the EEC as a whole and represented only one-third of expenditure per person in the Netherlands. Similarly, expenditure per person aged 5-24 years in Ireland was less than half the average for the EEC and less than a quarter of expenditure in Denmark.

Some of the reasons for the low level of expenditure on education, especially primary education, have been outlined by Tussing.[24] These include the contribution of the Catholic Church to the financing of the system and the traditional emphasis on academic as opposed to technical subjects in the curriculum.

Table 52: Percentage distribution of school population by level in EEC
countries, 1965-66 and 1975-76

Country	First level		Second level		Third level	
	1965/66	1975/76	1965/66	1975/76	1965/66	1975/76
Belgium	57.5	49.6	36.2	42.3	6.3	8.2
Germany	45.6	38.5	47.9	52.6	6.5	8.9
France	60.3	45.0	35.2	46.3	4.5	8.8
Italy	56.9	45.7	38.0	45.4	5.1	8.9
Luxembourg	65.5	54.9	31.4	40.5	3.0	4.6
Netherlands	60.1	49.8	35.0	42.3	4.9	7.9
UK	56.9	50.7	39.7	44.8	3.3	4.5
Ireland	72.6	57.7	24.1	37.8	3.2	4.6
Denmark	49.3	43.9	44.1	45.4	6.7	10.7

Source: *Social Indicators for the European Community 1960-1975.*

Table 53: Educational expenditure (European units of account) per
inhabitant and per person aged 5-24 years in EEC countires,
1973

Country	Per inhabitant	per person aged 5-24 years
Belgium	204.9	657.9
Germany	187.0	631.8
France	173.6	531.7
Italy	98.5	320.7
Luxembourg	171.1	585.3
Netherlands	238.8	686.7
UK	125.5	412.7
Ireland	79.2	214.8
Denmark	285.6	930.0
EEC Total	156.0	501.9

Source: *Social indicators for the European Community, 1960-1975*

The Treaty of Rome made no direct reference to education policy. In 1976, however, an action programme was agreed between member states. One of the major areas of concern was the children of migrant workers; in 1975 there were 2 million such children in the EEC and they pose a special educational problem. Policies have therefore been introduced to ensure that they are helped to adapt to their new school surroundings. Other areas of concern include mobility of students, teachers and research workers; the teaching of foreign languages and adult education.[25] The precise type of action to be adopted in these areas, however, is left to each member state.

Notes

Chapter One: Introduction

1. *National Income and Expenditure 1976* (Dublin: Stationery Office, 1978)
2. NESC Report No 25 *Towards a Social Report* (Dublin: Stationery Office, 1976) p. 139
3. Department of Education *Statistical Report 1976-77* (Dublin: Stationery Office, 1978) p. 2
4. *Household Budget Survey 1973* (Dublin: Stationery Office, 1976); *Quarterly Bulletin of Housing Statistics* (Dublin: Stationery Office)
5. Department of Health *Statistical Information relevant to the Health Services 1978* (Dublin: Stationery Office, 1978) p.40
6. *Trade Union Information* Irish Congress of Trade Unions (Summer 1978) p. 9
7. P. Kaim-Caudle *Comparative Social Policy and Social Security: A Ten Country Study* (London: Martin Robertson, 1973) p. 18
8. See NESC Report No 19 *Rural Areas: Social Planning Problems* (Dublin: Stationery Office, 1976)
9. *Development for Full Employment* (Dublin: Stationery Office, 1978)
10. Irish Bishops' Pastoral *The Work of Justice* (Dublin: Veritas Publications, 1977)
11. A. Coughlan 'Public affairs, the social scene' *Administration* 14,3 (1966) 205
12. R.A.B. Leaper 'Subsidiarity and the welfare state' *Administration* 23,4 (1975) 448
13. A. Coughlan *Aims of Social Policy* Tuairim pamphlet No 14 (Dublin, 1966) p. 4
14. F. Kennedy *Public Social Expenditure in Ireland* (Dublin: Economic and Social Research Institute, 1975)
15. NESC Report No 8 *An Approach to Social Policy* (Dublin: Stationery Office, 1975) p. 30
16. NESC *An Approach to Social Policy* pp 33-45
17. NESC *An Approach to Social Policy* p. 32
18. Kennedy *Public Social Expenditure* pp 11-20
19. For further details regarding Dr Dignan's paper which is now out of print see P. Kaim-Caudle *Social Policy in the Irish Republic* (London: Routledge & Kegan Paul, 1967) pp 40-44
20. Other works by the same author and published by the Economic and Social Research Institute, Dublin, include *Social Security in Ireland and Western Europe* (1964), *Housing in Ireland: Some Economic Aspects (1965), Dental Services in Ireland* (1969), *Ophthalmic Services in Ireland* (1970), *Pharmaceutical Services in Ireland* (1970) and *Irish Pensions Schemes 1969* (1971)
21. S. Ó Cinnéide *A Law for the Poor* (Dublin: Institute of Public Administration, 1970)

22. S. Ó Cinnéide 'The extent of poverty in Ireland' *Social Studies* 1,4 (1972)
23. M. Sheehan *The Meaning of Poverty* (Dublin: Council for Social Welfare, 1974)
24. For further information on voluntary organisations see *Directory of Social Services Organisations* 3rd edition, (Dublin: National Social Service Council, 1978)

Chapter Two: Income Maintenance

1. P. Kaim-Caudle *Comparative Social Policy and Social Security: A Ten Country Study* (London: Martin Robertson, 1973) p. 6
2. *First Report of the Department of Social Welfare 1947-1949* (Dublin: Stationery Office, 1950) p. 2
3. NESC Report No 26 *Towards a Social Report* (Dublin: Stationery Office, 1976) p. 139
4. P. Townsend 'Poverty as relative deprivation: resources and style of living' in D. Wedderburn (ed) *Poverty, Inequality and Class Structure* (Cambridge University Press, 1974) p. 15
5. A. Sinfield 'We the people and they the poor: a comparative view of poverty research' *Social Studies* 4,1 (1975) 3-9
6. J. Kavanagh 'The concept of poverty' *Social Studies* 1,4 (1972) 374
7. S. Ó Cinnéide 'The extent of poverty in Ireland' *Social Studies* 1,4 (1972) 381-400
8. All the conference papers were published in *Social Studies* 1,4 (1972). A second conference on poverty was held in Kilkenny in 1974 and the papers of the conference are published in *Social Studies* 4,1 (1975)
9. M. Sheehan *The Meaning of Poverty* (Dublin: The Council for Social Welfare, 1974)
10. Commission of the European Communities *Social Action Programme* (Bulletin of the European Communities, Supplement 2/74) pp 17-18
11. For further details see *Pilot Schemes '78, Interim Report* (National Committee on Pilot Schemes to Combat Poverty, Dublin 1978)
12. *Pilot Schemes '78* p. 2
13. See for example, P. Townsend *Poverty in the United Kingdom A Survey of Household Resources and Standards of Living* (Harmonds-worth: Penguin Books, 1979) Chapter 27
14. See NESC Report No 37 *Integrated Approaches to Personal Income Taxes and Transfers* (Dublin: Stationery Office, 1978)
15. *Combat Poverty: An introduction to the working of the National Committee on Pilot Schemes to Combat Poverty* (Dublin, 1975) p. 2
16. Details concerning all insurance and assistance schemes are contained in *Summary of Social Insurance and Social Assistance Services* issued annually by the Department of Social Welfare; for analysis and comment on individual schemes see NESC Report No 38 *Universality and Selectivity: Social Services in Ireland* (Dublin: Stationery Office, 1978)

17. Statistics used throughout this chapter are, unless otherwise stated, derived from the reports of the Department of Social Welfare, the most recent being that covering the period 1976-78.

18. For details concerning the various categories of contributors and rates of contribution see *Summary of Social Insurance and Social Assistance Services.*

19. Persons who cease to be covered by compulsory social insurance by becoming self-employed may opt to continue insurance on a voluntary basis for limited benefits (see *Summary of Social Insurance and Social Assistance Services*). In 1978, voluntary contributors accounted for 0.1% of all insured persons, *(Dáil Debates* Vol. 308 (1978) cols. 629-30)

20. Department of Social Welfare *Social Insurance for the Self-employed — A Discussion Paper* (Dublin: Stationery Office, 1978)

21. Department of Social Welfare *A National Income-Related Pension Scheme — A Discussion Paper* (Dublin: Stationery Office, 1976)

22. Quoted in Kaim-Caudle *Comparative Social Policy and Social Security: A Ten Country Study* p. 167

23. People who, for example, were in receipt of indoor or outdoor relief under the Poor Law, people who before becoming entitled to a pension had habitually failed to work according to their ability, opportunity and need for their maintenance and the maintenance of their dependants. See D. Farley *Social Insurance and Social Assistance in Ireland* (Dublin: Institute of Public Administration, 1964) pp 18-19

24. *Report of the Commission on the Status of Women* (Dublin: Stationery Office, 1972) Chapter 5

25. For a review of progress made in this and other areas covered by the *Report of the Commission on the Status of Women* see *Second Progress Report on the implementation of the recommendations in the Report of the Commission on the Status of Women* Final Report of the Women's Representative Committee (Dublin: Stationery Office, 1979)

26. For an excellent critique of means-testing in social services in general see NESC Report No 38 *Universality and Selectivity: Social Services in Ireland* (Dublin: Stationery Office, 1978) Chapter 3

27. Several anomalies were removed in 1979, see *Budget 1979* (Dublin: Stationery Office, 1979) pp 55-58

28. *Budget 1979* p. 25

29. See S. Ó Cinnéide 'The development of the home assistance service' *Administration* 17,3 (1969) 284-308

30. S. Ó Cinnéide *A Law for the Poor* (Dublin: Institute of Public Administration, 1970)

31. *Dáil Debates* Vol. 282 (1975) col. 1335

32. Farley *Social Insurance and Social Assistance in Ireland* p. 71

33. F. Kennedy *Public Social Expenditure in Ireland* Broadsheet No. 11 (Dublin: Economic and Social Research Institute, 1975) p. 85

34. *Development for Full Employment* (Dublin: Stationery Office, 1978) p. 76

35. *Programme for National Development 1978-1981* (Dublin: Stationery Office, 1979) p. 88. The issues related to family income support including

Alternative Strategies for Family Income Support (Dublin: Stationery Office, 1980)

36. For further details see *Guide to the Redundancy Payments Scheme* Department of Labour (1979); see also B.J. Whelan and B.M. Walsh *Redundancy and Re-employment in Ireland* (Dublin: Economic and Social Research Institute, 1977)

37. Farley *Social Insurance and Social Assistance in Ireland* p. 37

38. *A Statement on Social Policy* (Dublin: The Council for Social Welfare, 1972) pp 15-16

39. National Social Service Council *Relate* 6,1 (1978) 8

40. NESC *Universality and Selectivity: Social Services in Ireland* p. 89

41. Kennedy *Public Social Expenditure in Ireland* p. 63

42. In a submission on social welfare services to the Minister for Social Welfare in October 1978, the National Social Service Council stated: 'Local pensions' committees should be abolished, in the opinion of the Council. They are anachronistic, objectionable and tend to cause delay.' *Recommendations for Improvements in the Social Welfare Services* (Dublin: National Social Service Council, 1978) p. 7

43. *Budget 1975* (Dublin: Stationery Office, 1975) p. 23

44. *A National Partnership* (Dublin: Stationery Office, 1974) p. 40

45. *Action Plan for National Reconstruction* Fianna Fáil Manifesto, General Election (1977) p. 22

46. *Budget 1978* (Dublin: Stationery Office, 1978) p. 21

47. NESC Report No 17 *Statistics for Social Policy* (Dublin: Stationery Office, 1976) p. 48

48. *A Statement on Social Policy* p. 12

49. Examples of newspaper headlines during this period were: 'The social spongers' (*Irish Independent* 21/3/75); 'Dole money goes into the pubs' (*Irish Independent* 3/12/75); 'Abusing Social Welfare' (*Irish Independent* 19/3/76); 'Farmers should not get £3m. handouts — Councillor hits at dole system abuse' (*Irish Press* 19/11/76). For references to similar popular criticism of social security abuses in Britain during 1976 see P. Golding and S. Middleton 'Why is the press so obsessed with welfare scroungers?' (*New Society* 26/10/78).

50. A document entitled 'Work-Rewards-Recovery' (1977) issued by the Irish Farmers' Association, the Construction Industry Federation and the Chambers of Commerce, stated (p. 15) that 'unemployment benefit levels in Ireland are among the highest in Europe both in amount and length of time, resulting in a strong disincentive to work. This situation encourages abuses by a significant minority.'

51. See J. Murray 'Unemployment payments' (Dublin: National Social Service Council, 1977 and 1978). In these 2 papers Murray analyses the live register of unemployment for one week in October 1976 and in October 1977.

52. For a discussion of the issues relating to the smallholders' assistance scheme see NESC Report No 19 *Rural Areas: Social Planning Problems* (Dublin: Stationery Office, 1976) pp 57-62

53. For references to research carried out elsewhere see M. Jahoda 'The psychological meanings of unemployment' *New Society* 6 September 1979.

54. This particular form of fraud was singled out as a cause of concern in *Development for Full Employment* pp 77-78

Chapter Three: Housing

1. *Housing in the Seventies* (Dublin: Stationery Office, 1969) p. 3

2. There are two county councils in Tipperary, North Riding and South Riding.

3. This section contains a summary of developments up to the mid 1960s as outlined by P.J. Meghen *Housing in Ireland* (Dublin: Institute of Public Administration, 1966)

4. *Economic Development* (Dublin: Stationery Office, 1959) p. 46

5. F. Kennedy *Public Social Expenditure in Ireland* (Dublin: Economic and Social Research Institute, 1975) p. 15

6. NESC Report No 14 *Population Projections 1971-86: The Implications for Social Planning — Dwelling Needs* (Dublin: Stationery Office, 1976)

7. *Report of the Committee on the Price of Building Land* (Dublin: Stationery Office, 1974)

8. NESC Report No 23 *Report on Housing Subsidies* (Dublin: Stationery Office, 1977) pp 21-22

9. See *A Home of Your Own* 2nd edition (Dublin: Department of the Environment, 1978) p. 21

10. For details of the points system operated by county borough councils see NESC Report No 38 *Universality and Selectivity: Social Services in Ireland* (Dublin: Stationery Office, 1978) pp 218-22; see also National Social Service Council *Relate* 7 (1979) pp 2-7

11. *Dáil Debates* Vol 308 (1978) cols. 293-7

12. *Report on the Development of the Social Situation in the Community 1976* (Brussels, 1977) pp 214-5

13. P. Pfretzschner *The Dynamics of Irish Housing* (Dublin: Institute of Public Administration, 1965) p. 112

14. See *A Home of Your Own* pp 36-38

15. J. McKeon and R. Jennings *Public Subventions to Housing in Ireland* (Dublin: An Foras Forbartha, 1978) p. 11

16. See *A Home of Your Own* pp 39-43

17. NESC Report No 19 *Rural Areas: Social Planning Problems* (Dublin: Stationery Office, 1976) p. 39

18. See *A Home of Your Own* p. 25

19. For further details see T.J. Baker and L.M. O'Brien *The Irish Housing System: A Critical Overview* (Dublin: Economic and Social Research Institute, 1979) pp 99-100

20. P. Kaim-Caudle 'The economic and social cost of housing' *Administration* 22,3 (1974) 279

21. NESC *Report on Housing Subsidies* pp 8-12
22. Baker and O'Brien *The Irish Housing System*
23. Baker and O'Brien *The Irish Housing System* pp 223-4
24. Address by John O'Leary, Minister of State at the Department of the Environment, at the opening of the Bunnscourt/Ballyporeen Group Water Scheme, Cahir, County Tipperary, 23 August 1979.
25. *Irish Times* 15 November 1974
26. Pfretzschner *The Dynamics of Irish Housing* p. 115

Chapter Four: Education

1. There are many excellent works dealing with the development of first-level education and the education system in general. They include D.H. Akenson *The Irish Education Experiment* (London: Routledge & Kegan Paul, 1970) which deals with the national system of education in the 19th century; N. Atkinson *Irish Education, A History of Education Institutions* (Dublin: Allen Figgis, 1969); P.J. Dowling *A History of Irish Education* (Cork: Mercier Press, 1971); F.S.L. Lyons *Ireland since the Famine* (London: Fontana, 1973) relevant sections; J. Lee *The Modernisation of Irish Society 1848-1918* (Dublin: Gill & MacMillan, 1973) Ch. 1; T.J. McElligot *Education in Ireland* (Dublin: Institute of Public Administration, 1966).
2. See P.J. Dowling *The Hedge Schools of Ireland* (Cork: Mercier Press, 1968)
3. Akenson *The Irish Education Experiment* Chapter 1
4. See the section on 'Deprived Children' in Chapter 6, pages   to   , for further discussion on the school attendance service.
5. Department of Education *Statistical Report 1976-77* (Dublin: Stationery Office, 1978) p. 29
6. *Irish Times* 21 October 1974
7. *Dáil Debates* Vol 308 (1978) cols. 75-8
8. See *Boards of Management of National Schools: Constitution of Boards and Rules of Procedure* pp 12-14
9. *Investment in Education* (Dublin: Stationery Office, 1965) pp 225-66
10. While some small rural schools were being closed or amalgamated, others were being established in the growing urban areas.
11. NESC Report No 19 *Rural Areas: Social Planning Problems* (Dublin: Stationery Office, 1976) pp 52-3
12. *Irish Times* 29 July 1976
13. *Irish Times* 8 February 1977
14. *Rules for National Schools under the Department of Education* (Dublin: Stationery Office, 1965) p. 8
15. *Investment in Education* p. 150
16. Department of Education *List of Recognised Secondary Schools 1978-79* (Dublin: Stationery Office, 1979)
17. Between 1966 and 1976 the numbers enrolled in all post-primary schools increased from 146,704 to 277,724, an increase of 89.3%. For

details of the increase in participation rates by age see A.D. Tussing *Irish Educational Expenditures — Past, Present and Future* (Dublin: Economic and Social Research Institute, 1978) Chapter 4

18. A.D. Tussing 'Labour force effects of 1967/68 changes in education policy in the Irish Republic' *Economic and Social Review* 7,3 (1976)

19. *Department of Education School Transport Scheme* Report of Study carried out by Hyland Associates Limited (Dublin: Stationery Office, 1974)

20. C. Murphy 'School transport levy not to be introduced — Wilson' *Irish Times* 21 June 1979

21. *Dáil Debates* Vol 316 (1979) col. 481

22. *List of Recognised Secondary Schools 1978-79* p. 20

23. J.H. Whyte *Church and State in Modern Ireland 1923-1970* (Dublin: Gill and Macmillan, 1971) p. 38

24. *Administration Yearbook and Diary 1980* (Dublin: Institute of Public Administration) pp 104-110

25. *Investment in Education* pp 154-68

26. *Reviews of National Policies for Education: Ireland* (Paris: OECD, 1969) Appendix IV

27. *Reviews of National Policies for Education: Ireland* Appendix IV

28. *Reviews of National Policies for Education: Ireland* Appendix IV

29. Steering Committee on Technical Education *Report to the Minister for Education on Regional Technical Colleges* (Dublin: Stationery Office, 1969)

30. Lyons *Ireland since the Famine* p. 93

31. *Commission on Higher Education 1960-67 Vol. 1, Presentation and Summary of Report* (Dublin: Stationery Office, 1967) p. 49

32. *Commission on Higher Education 1960-67* Vol. 1, p. 50

33. *Reviews of National Policies for Education: Ireland* Appendix IV

34. *Commission on Higher Education,* Vol. 2 pp 760-3

35. *Development for Full Employment* (Dublin: Stationery Office, 1978) p. 82. The teaching institutions funded by the HEA are the NUI, its constituent colleges, St Patrick's Maynooth, Trinity College, the Royal College of Surgeons in Ireland, The National College of Art & Design, NIHE, Limerick, and NIHE, Dublin.

36. *Observations of the Higher Education Authority on Paragraph 7.33 in the Green Paper 'Development for Full Employment',* (Dublin: Higher Education Authority, 1978) p. 4. McDonagh, K. in 'The way the money goes' *Oideas* 17 (1977) pp 33-4, points out that the unit cost of students in teacher training colleges is more than double that of university students

37. *Programme for National Development 1978-81* (Dublin: Stationery Office, 1979) p. 86

38. J. Sheehan *Future Enrolments in Third-level Education* (Dublin: Higher Education Authority, 1978)

39. *National Adult Education Survey: Interim Report* (Dublin: Stationery Office, 1970) p. 19

40. *National Adult Education Survey* p. 20

41. *Adult Education in Ireland* (Dublin: Stationery Office, 1973) p. 1

42. *Adult Education in Ireland* p. 64

43. *Discussion Document on an NCEA Award Structure for Recurrent Education* (Dublin: National Council for Educational Awards, 1978)
44. M. McGreil *Educational Opportunity in Dublin* (Catholic Communications Institute of Ireland, 1974)
45. McGreil *Educational Opportunity in Dublin*
46. *Investment in Education* p. 173
47. *Commission on Higher Education*, Vol. II, pp 760-764
48. J.P. MacHale 'The socio-economic background of students in Irish universities' *Studies* LXVIII/271 (1979)
49. P. Clancy and C. Benson *Higher Education in Dublin: A Study of some emerging Needs* (Dublin: The Higher Education Authority, 1979) pp 13-16
50. See S. Holland *Rutland Street — the Story of an Educational Experiment for Disadvantaged Children in Dublin* (The Hague: Bernard Van Leer Foundation and Oxford: Pergamon Press, 1979)
51. NESC Report No 12 *Educational Expenditure in Ireland* (Dublin: Stationery Office, 1976); McDonagh 'The way the money goes'; Tussing *Irish Educational Expenditures*
52. The extent of the difference in the current costs per pupil between the three levels may be gauged from the following figures for 1978: first level £224; second level (a) secondary, comprehensive and community schools, £413, (b) vocational schools £529; third level (including third level vocational) £1,341. *Dáil Debates* Vol. 316 (1979) col. 480
53. NESC *Educational Expenditure in Ireland* p. 20
54. E. Gibson 'The way the money goes — a reply' *Oideas* 18 (1977)
55. By 1978 the proportion of teachers who were members of religious orders was 12% at first level and 22% in secondary schools.
56. Tussing *Irish Educational Expenditures* p. 175
57. *Development for Full Employment* p. 82
58. *Programme for National Development* p. 86

Chapter Five: Health Services

1. For a discussion of the case for reduced public expenditure on health care in Ireland see S. Barrett 'Social and economic aspects of the health service' *The Irish Banking Review* (March, 1979)
2. See R.M. Titmuss *Commitment to Welfare* (London: George Allen and Unwin, 1973) pp 145-7
3. *The Health Services and their Further Development* (Dublin: Stationery Office, 1966) p. 16
4. B. Hensey *The Health Services of Ireland* 3rd edition (Dublin: Institute of Public Administration, 1979)
5. *The Health Services and their further Development*
6. In addition, there are a number of special advisory bodies attached to the Department of Health, see Hensey *The Health Services of Ireland* pp 48-50

7. The National Health Co uncil was established under the Health Act 1953 to advise the minister for Health on such matters affecting or incidental to the health of the people as may be referred to them by the Minister and on such other general matters (other than conditions of employment of officers and servants and the amount or payments of grants and allowances) relating to the operation of the health services as they think fit. The Council is reconstituted every two years.

8   *Report of the National Health Council 1977* (Dublin: Stationery Office, 1977) pp 20-1; Hensey *The Health Services of Ireland* also states (p.48) that 'For some time it has been recognised that, with the developing roles of the Comhairle and the health boards, the regional hospital boards are unnecessary.'

9. *Report of the National Health Council, 1975* (Dublin: Stationery Office, 1975) pp 15-21

10. *Dáil Debates* Vol. 289 (1976) col. 512

11. *Dáil Debates* Vol. 291 (1976) col. 1106

12. *Dáil Debates* Vol. 281 (1975) col. 60

13. *Programme for National Development 1978-81* (Dublin: Stationery Office, 1979) p. 84

14. *The General Practitioner in Ireland,* Report of the Consultative Council on General Medical Services (Dublin: Stationery Office, 1974) p. 45

15. Statistics used in this section are derived from *Reports of the General Medical Services (Payments) Board*

16. *Report of the Working Party on Prescribing and Dispensing in the General Medical Service* (Dublin: Stationery Office, 1976) p. 37

17. Health boards provide a dental service for persons with full eligibility under the Community Care Programme. Dental services for insured persons are provided under the aegis of the Department of Social Welfare. Both services are discussed in this section.

18. See *Plan for Development of Dental Services 1975-85* (Western Health Board, 1974)

19. *Report of the National Health Council, 1976* (Dublin: Stationery Office, 1976) p. 18

20. See P. Kaim-Caudle *Dental Services in Ireland* Broadsheet 1 (Dublin: Economic and Social Research Institute, 1969); *A Review of Irish Health Services: the Waterford Seminar Proceedings* Department of Health, (Dublin, 1975)

21. *Dental Service Report* Joint Working Party (1979)

22. See J.H. Whyte *Church and State in Modern Ireland 1923-1970* (Dublin: Gill and Macmillan, 1971); M. McInerney 'Noel Browne: church and state' *University Review* V,2 (1968)

23. *The Child Health Services* Report of a Study Group appointed by the Minister for Health (Dublin: Stationery Office, 1968) p. 16

24. *The Child Health Services* p. 16

25. Whyte *Church and State in Modern Ireland* p. 404

26. McInerney 'Noel Browne: church and state' p. 193

27. Department of Health *Statistical Information relevant to the Health Services*

1978 (Dublin: Stationery Office, 1978) pp 17-18. These figures do not include the numbers examined in the Dublin area and eligible children are those born in centres where developmental paediatric clinics are conducted. Assuming that all children in the Dublin area were examined then the number of children examined in 1976 represents approximately 60% of all children of six months.

28. *Statistical Information relevant to the Health Services 1978* p. 19
29. The seminar was convened by Brendan Corish, then Minister for Health, in Waterford in May 1975. The objectives of the seminar were 'to obtain a preliminary overall view of the state of the health services, to direct attention to the major problems which beset them, and to identify the key issues requiring further investigation and attention'. The seminar was representative of organisations involved in the health services.
30. *A Review of Irish Health Services* p. 34
31. For a breakdown of expenditure, number of home helps and beneficiaries by health board areas, see *Report on the Home Help Service* (Dublin: National Social Service Council, 1978) pp 16-17
32. *Report on the Home Help Service* pp 14-15
33. See *Statistical Information relevant to the Health Services 1978* p. 40
34. For evolution of Irish hospital system see *Outline of the Future Hospital System* Report of the Consultative Council on the General Hospital Service (Dublin: Stationery Office, 1968)
35. *Outline of Future Hospital System*
36. Department of Health *General Hospital Development Plan* (1975) p.1
37. *Irish Times* 21 October 1975
38. *Action Plan for National Reconstruction* Fianna Fáil Manifesto, General Election (1977) p. 25
39. Comhairle na nOspideal *Second Report* January 1976-December 1978, (Dublin, 1978) p. 24
40. Comhairle na nOspideal, *Second Report* p. 25
41. By 1975, the number of beds in psychiatric hospitals per 1,000 population had fallen to 4.8 and this was the highest of any member state of the EEC. *(Statistical information Relevant to the Health Services* (1978) p. 28)
42. *Report of the Commission of Inquiry on Mental Illness* (Dublin: Stationery Office, 1966) p. xv
43. *The Irish Psychiatric Hospital Census, 1971* (Dublin: Medico-Social Research Board, 1974)
44. This group does not include farmers but includes agricultural labourers, groundsmen and gardeners, labourers, other agricultural workers, foresters and forestry labourers and fishermen *(Census of Population 1971* Vol. IV)
45. *Report of Commission of Inquiry on Mental Handicap* (Dublin: Stationery Office, 1965)
46. For full details regarding these schemes see 'Summary of Health

Services' Department of Health (1979)

47. See NESC Report No 30 *Personal Incomes by County in 1973* (Dublin: Stationery Office, 1977)

48. In 1971 the percentage of the population aged 65 or over by health board area was as follows: Eastern 8.5%; Midland 11.7%; Mid-Western 11.6%; Southern 11.7%; North Western 14.9%; Western 14.2%

49. NESC Report No 38 *Universality and Selectivity: Social Services in Ireland* (Dublin: Stationery Office, 1978) pp 98-9

50. J. Curry 'Variation in the assessment of farm income in social administration' *Irish Journal of Agricultural Economics and Rural Sociology* 7, 1 (1978)

51. See NESC Report No 29 *Some Major Issues in Health Policy* (Dublin: Stationery Office, 1977) pp 43-7; NESC *Universality and Selectivity: Social Services in Ireland* pp 201-7

52. Under the terms of the *National Understanding for Economic and Social Development* (1979) agreed between government, employers and trade unions, the income limit for health eligibility was to be raised from £5,500 to £7,000. The limit was not raised but an interim scheme was introduced from 25 July 1979 (the date of ratification of the National Understanding) to 5 April 1980. Under this scheme a refund of hospital consultants' fees could be obtained from the VHI for people with an income of between £5,500 and £7,000 in the year ended 5 April 1979. The health contributions continued to be levied on income up to £5,500. In June 1980 the income limit was raised to £7,000.

53. All people, irrespective of income, paying social insurance contributions were entitled to assistance towards the cost of prescribed medical requisites in excess of £5 per month.

54. J.H. Whyte *Church and State in Modern Ireland* pp 298-299

55. For full details of VHI revised schemes see explanatory booklet available from VHI.

56. Voluntary Health Insurance Board *21st Annual Report and Accounts for the year 1 March 1977 to 28 February 1978* (Dublin) p. 1

57. NESC *Some Major Issues in Health Policy* p. 47

58. See *Report of the National Health Council 1974* (Dublin: Stationery Office, 1975) pp 6-7

59. See NESC *Some Major Issues in Health Policy* p. 46

60. Irish Medical Association 'The feasibility of a compulsory specialist and hospital insurance scheme as an alternative to the present Irish system: a discussion document' (Dublin, 1976)

61. Department of Health *Interim Report, Consultant Medical Staff Review Body* (1978) p. 2

Chapter Six: Welfare Services

1. *Statistical Information relevant to the Health Services* (1978) p. 12

2. *The Care of the Aged* (Report of an Inter-Departmental Committee) (Dublin: Stationery Office, 1968) p. 13

3. A.J. Reeves 'The social and medical needs of the aged' *Studies* (Winter, 1966) p. 343

4. See NESC Report No 17 *Statistics for Social Policy* (Dublin: Stationery Office, 1976) p. 48

5. In December 1977 there were 6,021 beneficiaries but the breakdown by category is not available. See *Report on Home Help Services* (National Social Service Council, 1978) pp 16-17

6. *The Care of the Aged* p. 34

7. Medico-Social Research Board *Admission to County Homes: A study of the Aged in Three Homes and Three Counties in Ireland Part I: Care of Aged* (Dublin, 1975) p. 81

8. Western Health Board *Psychiatric and Geriatric Services* (1974) pp 46-47

9. Department of Health *Statistical Information relevant to the Health Services* (1978) p. 59

10. *Training and Employing the Handicapped* (Dublin: Stationery Office, 1975) p. 12

11. For an excellent overview of services for handicapped people and policy issues see NESC Report No 50 *Major Issues in Planning Services for Mentally and Physically Handicapped Persons* (Dublin: Stationery Office, 1980)

12. Medico-Social Research Board *Census of the Mentally Handicapped in the Republic of Ireland 1974: Residential* (Dublin, 1976)

13. Medico-Social Research Board *Census of the Mentally Handicapped in the Republic of Ireland 1974:Non-Residential* (Dublin, 1976)

14. *Training and Employing the Handicapped* p. 22

15. *Statistical Information relevant to the Health Services* p. 62

16. *Training and Employing the Handicapped* p. 23

17. National Rehabilitation Board, *Annual Report and Accounts* (1976) pp 9-10 9-10

18. *Statistical Information relevant to the Health Services* p. 33

19. CARE *Children Deprived: The CARE Memorandum on Deprived Children and Children's Services in Ireland* (Dublin, 1972) p. 12

20. *Bunreacht na hÉireann* Article 42

21. *Some of our Children: A Report on the Residential Care of the Deprived Child in Ireland* Tuairim pamphlet No 13 (London, 1966)

22. *Reformatory and Industrial Schools Systems Report* (Kennedy Report) (Dublin: Stationery Office, 1970)

23. *Children Deprived*

24. *Report on Vital Statistics 1975* (Dublin: Stationery Office, 1979) p. 5

25. *Report of An Bord Uchtála for year ended 31 December 1977* (Dublin: Stationery Office, 1978) p. 3

26. *Reports on Crime* (annual) (Dublin: Stationery Office)

27. Department of Education *Statistical Reports* (Dublin: Stationery Office)

28. *School Attendance Department, County Borough of Dublin, Annual Report for year ended 30 June 1973* p. 1

29. See also W.P. Johnstone 'To mitch should be a social error, not a

criminal act' *Education Times* 24 January 1974

30.   At the 1978 annual general meeting of the ISPCC a motion to change the title of the organisation to the Irish Society for the Care of Children was defeated. *Irish Independent* 25 May 1978

31.   ISPCC *Annual Report* (1978) p. 3

32.   *Report of An Bord Uchtála 1977* p. 5

33.   *Report of An Bord Uchtála 1977* pp 7-8

34.   For further changes and developments see A.J. Shatter *Family Law in the Republic of Ireland* (Dublin: Wolfhound Press, 1977) Chapter 12

35.   Shatter *Family Law in the Republic of Ireland* pp 178-182

36.   V. Darling *Adoption in Ireland* CARE Discussion paper No 1, (Dublin, 1974)

37.   *Report of the Commission on the Status of Women* (Dublin: Stationery Office, 1972) p. 232

38.   *Progress Report on the implementation of the Recommendations in the Report of the Commission on the Status of Women* A report by the Women's Representative Committee (Dublin: Stationery Office, 1976) p. 27

39.   *Report on Crime 1976* p. 23

40.   *Kennedy Report* Appendix G

41.   *Kennedy Report* Chapter 10

42.   *Children Deprived* Chapter 12

43.   *Kennedy Report* p. 69

44.   *Children Deprived* p. 79

45.   *Children Deprived* pp 82-84; see also *Justice for Children: The Scottish System and its application to Ireland* CARE Discussion Paper No 2 (Dublin, 1974)

46.   *Kennedy Report* pp 2-3

47.   See *Dáil Debates* Vol. 276 (1974) cols. 619-25

48.   See CARE *'Who wants a children's prison in Ireland?'* (Dublin, 1978)

49.   See *Dáil Debates* Vol. 306 (1978) cols. 22-37, 147-158

50.   Also recommended in Tuairim pamphlet and CARE Memorandum

51.   *Task Force on Child Care Services: Interim Report* (Dublin: Stationery Office, 1975)

52.   Details regarding the activities of organisations referred to in this section and others may be found in the *Directory of Social Service Organisations* Third edition (Dublin: National Social Service Council, 1978)

53.   *Report of the Committee on Local Authority and Allied Personal Social Services* (Seebohm Report) (London: HMSO, 1968) p. 152

54.   In 1974 the then Minister for Justice, Patrick Cooney, established a committee under the chairmanship of Justice Denis Pringle to advise on the introduction of a comprehensive scheme of legal aid and advice in civil matters. *The Report of the Committee on Civil Legal Aid and Advice* was published in 1978 and recommended state aid for family legal problems as a minimum interim step in its proposals for the introduction of a comprehensive system of legal aid, intended to cover 75% of the population.

55. *The Voluntary Worker in the Social Services* (London: The Bedford Square Press of the NCSS and George Allen and Unwin, 1969) p. 24
56. R.A.B. Leaper in *Meeting Social Need/The Joint Effort of Statutory and Voluntary Bodies* (National Social Service Council, 1972) p. 11
57. *The Care of the Aged* pp 110-111
58. See K. Woodruffe *From Charity to Social Work in England and the United States* (London: Routledge and Kegan Paul, 1962) Chapter 2
59. Woodruffe *From Charity to Social Work* pp 50-51
60. H. Binchy 'Social services in modern Ireland' *Studies* 52 (1963) p. 177
61. *Dáil Debates* Vol. 297 (1977) col. 455
62. A. Lavan *Social Work Services in Tallaght* (Department of Social Science, University College, Dublin, 1975)
63. O. Stevenson 'Seebohm — seven years on' *New Society* 2 February 1978
64. *Proceedings of Social Service Councils Conference 1976* (Dublin: National Social Service Council, 1976)

Chapter Seven: Some EEC Comparisons

1. M. Shanks *European Social Policy, Today and Tomorrow* (Oxford: Pergamon Press, 1977) p. 3
2. *Social Action Programme* Bulletin of the European Communities, Supplement 2/74 (Brussels, 1974) p. 15
3. *Report on the Development of the Social Situation in the Communities in 1977* (Brussels, 1978) p. 42
4. *Report on the Development of the Social Situation in the Communities in 1977* p. 43
5. National Council of Social Service 'Look Europe' (October, 1977) p. 2
6. 'The future of social policy in the European Communities' A paper presented to the Rt. Hon. Roy Jenkins, President of the Commission of the European Communities and Henk Vredeling, Commissioner for Social Affairs, by the International Committee of the United Kingdom National Council of Social Service (February, 1977) p. 3
7. Shanks *European Social Policy* Chapter 8
8. E. James and A. Laurent 'Social security: the European experiment' *Social Trends* (London: HMSO, 1975) p. 27
9. R. Lawson and B. Reed *Social Security in the European Community* PEP, European Series No 23 (London, 1975) p. 23
10. M. Pechabrier 'Family support services — the French approach' *Social Studies* 2, 6, pp 636-7
11. James and Laurent 'Social security: the European experiment' p. 32
12. *Comparative Tables on the Social Security Systems in the Member States of the European Communities* 9th edition (Brussels, 1976) pp 108-9
13. *Comparative Tables on Social Security Systems* pp 110-3
14. James and Laurent 'Social security: the European experiment' p. 28
15. *Social Action Programme* p. 27
16. *Social Action Programme* p. 27

17. *The European Community's Social Policy* (Brussels: European Documentation, 1978) p. 38

18. See A. Maynard *Health Care in the European Community* (Croom Helm and University of Pittsburg Press, 1975)

19. James and Laurent 'Social security: the European experiment' p. 33

20. Lawson and Reed *Social Security in the European Community* pp 36-7

21. See Maynard *Health Care in the European Community*

22. A. Maynard 'Medical care in the European Community' *New Society* 28 August 1975

23. *Report on the Development of the Social Situation in the Communities, 1977* (Brussels, 1978) p. 129

24. *Social Indicators for the European Community 1960-75* (Brussels, 1977) pp 230-1

25. A.D. Tussing *Irish Educational Expenditures — Past, Present and Future* (Dublin: Economic and Social Research Institute, 1978) p. 164

26. See *Towards a European education policy* (Brussels: European Documentation, 1977)

Bibliography

General

Binchy, H. 'Social services in modern Ireland' *Studies* 52 (1963)

Coughlan, A. 'Public affairs: the social scene' *Administration* 23/4 (1975)

Aims of Social Policy Tuairim Pamphlet No 14 (Dublin, 1966)

Council for Social Welfare *Planning for Social Development* (Dublin, 1976)

A Statement on Social Policy (Dublin, 1973)

Kaim-Caudle, P. *Social Policy in the Irish Republic* (London: Routledge & Kegan Paul, 1967)

Comparative Social Policy and Social Security: A Ten Country Study (London: Martin Robertson, 1973)

Kavanagh, J. 'Social policy in modern Ireland' *Administration* 26/3 (1978)

Kennedy, F. *Public Social Expenditure in Ireland* (Dublin: Economic and Social Research Institute, 1975)

NESC Report No 8 *An Approach to Social Policy* (Dublin: Stationery Office, 1976)

NESC Report No 11 *Income Distribution in Ireland* (Dublin: Stationery Office, 1975

NESC Report No 19 *Rural Areas: Social Planning Problems* (Dublin: Stationery Office, 1976)

NESC Report No 25 *Towards a Soicial Report* (Dublin: Stationery Office, 1977)

NESC Report No 36 *Universality and Selectivity: Strategies in Social Policy* (Dublin: Stationery Office, 1978)

NESC Report No 37 *Integrated Approaches to Personal Income Taxes and Transfers* (Dublin: Stationery Office, 1978)

NESC Report No 38 *Universality and Selectivity: Social Services in*

Ireland (Dublin: Stationery Office, 1978)

NESC Report No 41 *Rural Areas: Change and Development* (Dublin: Stationery Office, 1978)

Report of the Commission on the Status of Women (Dublin: Stationery Office, 1972)

Second Progress Report on the implementation of the recommendations in the Report of the Commission on the Status of Women — Final Report of the Women's Representative Committee (Dublin: Stationery Office, 1979)

Whyte, J.H. *Church and State in Modern Ireland* (Dublin: Gill and Macmillan, 1971)

Dowling, B.R. and Durkan, J. (eds) *Irish Economic Policy: A Review of Major Issues* (Dublin: Economic and Social Research Institute, 1978)

Income Maintenance

Department of Social Welfare *Social Insurance for the Self-Employed — A Discussion Paper* (Dublin: Stationery Office, 1978)

A National Income Related Pension Scheme — A Discussion Paper (Dublin: Stationery Office, 1976)

Reports (triennial)

Farley, D. *Social Insurance and Social Assistance in Ireland* (Dublin: Institute of Public Administration, 1964)

Kaim-Caudle, P. *Social Security in Ireland and Western Europe* (Dublin: Economic and Social Research Institute, 1964)

Irish Pensions Schemes 1969 (Dublin: Economic and Social Research Institute, 1971)

Ó Cinnéide, S. 'The development of the home assistance service' *Administration* 17/3 (1969)

A Law for the Poor (Dublin: Institute of Public Administration, 1970)

'The extent of poverty in Ireland' *Social Studies* 1/4 (1972)

Sheehan, M. *The Meaning of Poverty* (Dublin: Council for Social Welfare, 1974)

Housing

Baker, T.J. and O'Brien, L.M. *The Irish Housing System: A Critical Over-view* (Dublin: Economic and Social Research Institute, 1979)

Department of the Environment *Current trends and policies in the field of housing, building and planning* (1978)
Quarterly Bulletin of Housing Statistics
Reports (annual)

Flannery, M. *Building Land Prices* (Birr: The Tribune Printing and Publishing Group, 1980)

Housing in the Seventies (Dublin: Stationery Office, 1969)

Kaim-Caudle, P. 'The economic and social cost of housing' *Administration* 22/3 (1974)
Housing in Ireland: Some Economic Aspects (Dublin: Economic and Social Research Institute, 1965)

McKeon, J. and Jennings, R. *Public Subvention to Housing in Ireland* (Dublin: An Foras Forbartha, 1978)

Meghen, P.J. *Housing in Ireland* (Dublin: Institute of Public Administration, 1964)

NESC Report No 14 *Population Projections 1971-86: The Implications for Social Planning - Dwelling Needs* (Dublin: Stationery Office, 1976)

NESC Report No 16 *Some Aspects of Finance for Owner-Occupied Housing* (Dublin: Stationery Office, 1976)

NESC Report No 23 *Report on Housing Subsidies* (Dublin: Stationery Office, 1977)

Pfretzschner, P. *The Dynamics of Irish Housing* (Dublin: Institute of Public Administration, 1965)

Report of the Committee on the Price of Building Land (Dublin: Stationery Office, 1974)

Education

Adult Education in Ireland (Dublin: Stationery Office, 1973)

Akenson, D.H. *The Irish Education Experiment* (London: Routledge & Kegan Paul, 1970)

Atkinson, N. *Irish Education, A History of Education Institutions* (Dublin: Allen Figgis, 1969)

Breathnach, A. 'Towards the identification of educational priority areas in Dublin' *Economic and Social Review* 7/4 (1976)

Clancy, P. and Benson, C. *Higher Education in Dublin: A Study of Some Emerging Needs* (Dublin: Higher Education Authority, 1979)

Commission on Higher Education (Dublin: Stationery Office, 1967)

Department of Education *Statistical Report* (annual)

Dowling, P.J. *A History of Irish Education* (Cork: Mercier Press, 1971)

Holland, S. *Rutland Street — The Story of an Educational Experiment for Disadvantaged Children in Dublin* (The Hague: Bernard van Leer Foundation; Oxford: Pergamon Press, 1979)

Hyland Associates Limited *Department of Education School Transport Scheme* (Dublin: Stationery Office, 1979)

Investment in Education (Dublin: Stationery Office, 1965)

MacHale, J.P. 'The socio-economic background of students in Irish universities' *Studies* LXVIII/271 (1979)

McDonagh, K. 'The way the money goes' *Oideas* 19 (1977)

McElligott, T.J. *Education in Ireland* (Dublin: Institute of Public Administration, 1966)

McGréil, M. *Educational Opportunity in Dublin* (Dublin: Catholic Communications Institute of Ireland, 1974)

National Council for Educational Awards *Discussion Document on an NCEA Award Structure for Recurrent Education* (Dublin, 1978)

NESC Report No 12 *Educational Expenditure in Ireland* (Dublin: Stationery Office, 1976)

Reviews of National Policies for Education: Ireland (Paris: OECD, 1969)

Tussing, A.D. *Irish Educational Expenditure — Past, Present and Future* (Dublin: Economic and Social Research Institute, 1978)

Health
Barrett, S. 'Social and economic aspects of the health service' *Irish Banking Review* March 1979

The Child Health Services — Report of a Study Group (Dublin: Stationery Office, 1968)

Comhairle na nOspidéal *Reports* (various)

Department of Health *The General Hospital Development Plan* (1975)

A Review of the Irish Health Services: the Waterford Seminar Proceedings (1975)

Statistical Information Relevant to the Health Services

Hensey, B. *The Health Services of Ireland* 3rd edition (Dublin: Institute of Public Administration, 1979)

General Medical Services (Payments) Board *Reports* (annual)

The Health Services and their Further Development (Dublin: Stationery Office, 1966)

The General Practitioner in Ireland — Report of the Consultative Council on General Medical Practice (Dublin: Stationery Office, 1974)

Kaim-Caudle, P. *Dental Services in Ireland* (Dublin: Economic and Social Research Institute, 1969)

Medico-Social Research Board *Reports* (annual)

National Health Council *Reports* (annual)

NESC Report No 29 *Some Major Issues in Health Policy* (Dublin: Stationery Office, 1977)

Outline of the Future Hospital System — Report of the Consultative Council in the General Hospital Services (Dublin: Stationery Office, 1968)

Report of Commission of Enquiry on Mental Handicap (Dublin: Stationery Office, 1965)

Report of Commission of Enquiry on Mental Illness (Dublin: Stationery Office, 1966)

Report of the Working Party on Prescribing and Dispensing in the General Medical Service (Dublin: Stationery Office, 1976)

Survey of Workload of Public Health Nurses (Dublin: Stationery Office, 1975)

Training and Employing the Handicapped (Dublin: Stationery Office, 1975)

Voluntary Health Insurance Board *Reports* (annual)

Welfare Services

An Bord Uchtála *Reports* (annual)

CARE *Children Deprived: The CARE Memorandum on Deprived Children and Children's Services in Ireland* (Dublin, 1972)

Justice for Children: The Scottish System and its Application to Ireland (Dublin, 1974)

'Who wants a children's prison in Ireland' (Dublin, 1978)

The Care of the Aged — Report on an Inter-Departmental Committee (Dublin: Stationery Office, 1968)

Darling, V. *Adoption in Ireland* (Dublin: CARE, 1974)

Lavan, A. *Social Work Services in Tallaght* (Dublin: Department of Social Service, University College, 1975)

Mollan, C. *Children First* (Dublin: Arlen House, 1979)

National Social Service Council *Directory of Social Service Organisations* 3rd edition (Dublin, 1978)

    Meeting Social Need/The Joint Effort of Statutory and Voluntary Bodies (Dublin, 1972)

    Proceedings of Social Service Councils Conference (Dublin, 1976)

    Report on Home Help Service (Dublin, 1978)

Reformatory and Schools Systems Report (Dublin: Stationery Office, 1970)

Report of the Committee on Civil Legal Aid and Advice (Dublin: Stationery Office, 1978)

Scheme of Civil and Legal Aid (Dublin: Stationery Office, 1979)

Shatter, A. *Family Law in the Republic of Ireland* (Dublin: Wolfhound Press, 1977)

Task Force on Child Care Services — Interim Report (Dublin: Stationery Office, 1975)

EEC

Comparative Tables on the Social Security Systems in Member States of the European Communities 9th edition (Brussels: EEC, 1976)

James, E. and Laurent, A. 'Social security: the European experiment' *Social Trends* (London: HMSO, 1975)

Lawson, R. and Reed, B. *Social Security in the European Community* (London: PEP, 1975)

Maynard, A. *Health Care in the European Community* (London: Croom Helm, 1975)

Report on the Development of the Social Situation in the Communities (Brussels: EEC, annual)

Shanks, M. *European Social Policy, Today and Tomorrow* (Oxford: Pergamon Press, 1977)

Social Action Programme (Brussels: EEC, 1974)

Social Indicators for the European Community 1960-75 (Brussels: EEC, 1977)

Index

ADAPT 216
adoption 205, 208-210, 212
Adoption Acts (1952 to 1976) 208-9
Adoption Board 208
adult education 130-3, 141
Adult Education in Ireland (1973) 131-2
adult dependant's allowance 32
adults: eligibility for dental services
    161-2; eligibility for health services
    178-186; handicapped 198-203
Aims of Social Policy (1966) 12
aged *see* elderly
agricultural workers *see* farm labourers
Agriculture, Department of, and
    housing 62
alcoholism 205, 215
allowance *see* adult dependant's,
    children's, deserted wife's, dis-
    abled person's maintenance,
    domiciliary for handicapped child-
    ren, electricity, infectious diseases
    maintenance, prisoner's wife's,
    supplementary welfare, unmarried
    mother's
All Our Children (1969) 94
ALLY 13, 216
ALONE 13
Aontas 133
appeals system for income mainten-
    ance schemes 39-40, 48-50
apprentices 115
army staff, housing for, 75
assistance *see* home, small-
    holder's, social, unemployment
assistance officers 156
Association of Secondary Teachers
    of Ireland and community schools
    119-120
assurance companies and house
    purchase loans 81-4
ASTI *see* Association of Secondary
    Teachers of Ireland
Athlone: regional technical college in,
    121; mentioned 100
aural treatment 165-6, 179-180
Aves Report 216-217

Baker, T.J. and O'Brien, L.J. 87-8
banks and house purchase loans 63,
    64, 81-3
Barry, Peter, Minister for Education,
    on closure of small schools 106
battered wives 216
Belfast: Queen's College 123;

Queen's University 124; teacher
    training college in 97
Belgium: EEC membership 224;
    health services 235, 236-7;
    housing 77, 241, 242; income
    maintenance 232; school leaving
    age 245
benefits 10-11 *see also* deserted wife's,
    disability, marriage, maternity,
    occupational injuries, pay-related,
    treatment, unemployment
Benelux countries and income main-
    tenance 232
birth rate and social service provisions
    2, 189-190, 231
the blind 197
blind pension 31, 52; appeals 48-51;
    electricity allowance 42-3; free
    television licence 42; free travel 42;
    means test 33-4; medical card 178-9
    see also prescribed relative
    allowance
boarding out *see* fosterage
Boarding Out of Children Regulations
    (1954) 92
An Bord Uchtála 208
borough council members on health
    boards 150
boroughs, pension committees in, 50
Bray VEC 114
Britain: community care for elderly
    191; education 136, 244-6 *passim;*
    EEC membership 224; health
    services 145, 146, 154, 236-8 *passim;*
    housing 242; income maintenance
    227-232 *passim;* and Irish
    social services 6; National
    Society for the Prevention
    of Cruelty to Children 208;
    politics and social policy 5;
    rent control 85; Seebohm report
    19, 216, 221; social work 220,
    222; TCD students from 126;
    voluntary organisations 215
Browne, Dr Noel: (Minister for
    Health) and mother and child
    scheme 162-164
building societies and house purchase
    loans 63, 81-4
Burke, Richard: (European Com-
    missioner for Consumer Affairs,
    Transport, Taxation and Relations
    with European Parliament) 224;
    (Minister for Education) primary

school amalgamations 106; primary school joint management committees 100; university reorganisation 126-7; vocational school boards of management 115

capitation grants for secondary schools 109-110
CARE 6, 204, 215; and Loughan House 213; memorandum on deprived children 204 , 212
The Care of the Aged (1968) 191, 194-6 218
Carlow, regional technical college in, 121
Carraroe, comprehensive school in, 117.
Carysfort College *see* Our Lady of Mercy
casework 208, 220, 222-4
Catholic Church: and Council for Social Welfare 12-13; education 95; mother and child scheme 165-6; national schools 96-7, 99-104; social teaching of 4-5; universities 123-6; VECs 115 *see also* religious orders
Catholic Primary School Managers' Association 102, 103
Catholic Protection and Rescue Society (Adoption Society) 219
Catholic University 123-4
Cavan (County) medical card holders in, 182
Census of Population: (1881) cottiers' dwellings 63; (1961) privately let dwellings 84-5; (1971) age of dwellings 67, 88; educational levels 130; privately let dwellings 84-5
Central Remedial Clinic 202
cerebral palsy 177
Charity Organisation Society 220
CHERISH 216
chief medical officer and housing allocations 75
Child Health Council 163
Childers, Erskine: (Minister for Health) and NSSC 219
children: and dental services 160-1; deprived 189; 203-214; handicapped 44, 92, 200, 203; and health services 2, 156, 162-166, 168; and mental health care 174, 177-8, 222; social services for 6
Children Act (1908) 211
children's allowance 2, 38, 40-42, 46; expenditure on 4, 52; fraudulent claims 56; and rent assessment 92
Children's Court, Dublin 211-212

children's hospitals 222
choice of dentist scheme 162
choice of doctor scheme 7, 10, 146, 156-7, 180
Christian Brothers and national schools 96
Christus Rex see *Social Studies*
Church of Ireland: national school, Dalkey 108; primary school patronage 104 .
Church of Ireland College of Education 97
CIE *see* Córas Iompair Éireann
Clancy, P. and Benson, C. 135
Cluskey, Frank: (Parliamentary Secretary to Minister for Health and Social Welfare) 5-6; and fraudulent claims to income maintenance 57; and NCPSCP 21; and Social Welfare Act (1975) 39
Coalition Government (1973-77) 5-6
civil servants: health care in France 239; housing for 75; social insurance for 27, 28; social security in EEC for 228
coal 44
co-educational: community schools 120; vocational schools 116
Cold Comfort Campaign 44
Collins, Gerard: (Minister for Justice) and Loughan House 214
Commission of Enquiry on Mental Handicap (1965) 175-6
Commission of Inquiry on Mental Illness (1966) 173-4
Comhairle na nOspidéal: and GHDP 171-3; role of 150-1
Commission on Higher Education (1967) 125-128 *passim*, 135
Common Market *see* European Economic Community
the community: and adult education 132, 134; and care of deprived children 207-214; and care of elderly 2, 191-4, 197; and care of mentally handicapped 178, 202; and care of mentally ill 175-6, 193; and community schools 120, 143; and doctors 190; and home help service 2, 170; and housing 61-2; and poverty 21-2; and primary schools 105-7; and social services 1, 5, 6, 9; social work in 224-5; and VEC's 115-6
Community Care Programme 157-170 223
community facilities in housing estates 91-2
community health centres 172

community hospitals 174
community information centres 48
community schools 10, 95, 118-120, 139-142
comprehensive schools 10, 95, 116-118
Comptroller and Auditor General 142
Colley, George: (Minister for Education) amalgamation of secondary and voluntary schools 119-120; (Minister for Finance) index linked social welfare payments 54; social welfare means test 38
Connacht: housing 79; secondary schools 111
Conservative Party 5
consultants: Comhairle na nOspidéal and 51; and free hospitalisation scheme 187-8; and General Hospital Service 171, 185
contributions: for health services 177, 181-5; and maternity service 164; none for mother and child scheme 163; to Redundancy Fund 45; to social insurance fund 15-16, 23, 26, 27-8, 50-51, 55-8 *passim*
Constitution of Ireland (1937) the family 203-4 *see also* referendums
'continuation' education 115
Cootehill, comprehensive school in, 117
Córas Iompair Éireann 42
Corish, Brendan: (Minister for Health and Social Welfare) and Community Care Programme 155; and free medicine 186-7; and GHDP 170; and regional health board system 152
Task Force on Child Care 214
Cork: adult education in 131; health authority in 148; hospital services in 172; income-related rents in 70; medical teaching centre 169; patronage of national schools 104; Protestant comprehensive school in 118;
Queen's College in 123; regional technical college in 121; Rehabilitation Institute centre in 200; technical education in 115; University College 122, 124, 126-7
Cork Regional Hospital Board 151
COS *see* Charity Organisation Society
Costello, John A.: (Taoiseach) and mother and child scheme 163
Coughlan, A. 5, 7, 12
Council of Ministers (EEC) 224; and SAP 21. 225-6

Council for Social Welfare: aims and functions 12-13; and poverty 20-21, 42; social welfare reforms 47
county borough councils: and health boards 150; and housing 61; and school meals 43;
county boroughs: school attendance committees 98, 206; VECs 114
county councils: and health boards 150; and health services 147; and housing 62; and local health advisory committees 151
county health advisory committees 151, 172
county homes 194-5, 196 *see also* geriatric hospitals
county hospitals 169, 170, 172
county manager/management and health services 147, 150, 151
counties: distribution of elderly 190; education committees proposed 132; health services organisation 148, 151-2, 169; pension committees 50; VECs 114
courts: children and the 210-212; and school attendance 98, 206
CRC *see* Central Remedial Clinic
crèches *see* day care facilities
criminal responsibility, age of, 212
curative medicine 155, 174
cystic fibrosis 177
Dáil Éireann: all-party committee on health services 152; mentioned 57
Daingean (County Offaly) boys' reformatory school 213
Dalkey School Project 108
Darling, V. 209
day care facilities: children 156, 210; mentally handicapped 176, 198-200 mentally ill 174
death grant 23, 25, 44
democracy: and education 94; and EEC institutions 227; and social change 23; and social legislation 6; and state housing 60
demographic structure: and education 2; the elderly 189-191; family benefits in EEC and 231; housing output 2, 66, 68-9; income maintenance 2; primary schools and 104-6; and poverty 19; secondary schools 112; self-employed 28-30
demountable dwellings 69, 193
Denmark: education 244-248 *passim;* EEC membership 224; health services 236, 238; income maintenance 227, 229, 231

denominationalism: and adoption
209; first level education 96-9
passim, 108; second level education 116; third level education
124-7; voluntary welfare agencies
217

dental services 145, 156, 160-162,
166, 180

dentists: and Community Care Programme 156, 161-2; members of
health boards 150

dependency ratio 2-3, 16-17, 19

deserted parents 216

deserted wife's allowance 30, 32;
means test for 34; and medical card
179

deserted wife's benefit 10, 23, 28; and
electricity allowance 42; and free
television licence 42

developed countries: demographic
features of 185; education in 134;
income maintenance 15-16

developing countries, unemployment
assistance in, 31

developmental paediatric clinics 165

Development for Full Employment (1978)
4, 41-2, 129

Dignan, Dr John, Bishop of Clonfert 11-12, 26

Director of Community Care 156

*Directory of Social Service Organ-
isations* (1978) 218

disabled persons, housing for, 67, 69

disabled person's maintenance allowance 44, 198; free travel 42;
medical card 178-9; rent assessment 92

disability benefit 23, 26, 27, 37, 52;
appeals over 48; fraudulent claims
57; rent assessment 91

dispensary system 7, 147, 156-7, 176;
maternity care under 162-3

district hospitals 170

district justices and young offenders
212

doctors: and child health services
162-3, 165, 166; and Community
Care Programme 170-171; and
General Hospital Programme 170-
171; and General Medical Service
156-8, 179, 180, 188; and health
boards 150; and health services
in EEC countries 236-9; and local
health advisory committees 151;
and Special Hospital Programme
174 *see also* consultants, psychiatrists

dole *see* unemployment assistance

Donnison, Professor David, on social
policy aims 8

domiciliary allowance for handicapped
children 44

Drogheda VEC 114

drugs 177, 187; under choice of
doctor scheme 157-160

DSP *see* Dalkey School Project

Dublin: adult education 130; Children's Court 211-212; Community
Care Programme 158; community
schools 120; education advisory
council 140; FLAC 13; free post-
primary education scheme 112;
health authority 149-150; hospital
services 172, 174; housing 63, 66-7,
85; Juvenile Liaison Officer Scheme
in 212; NIHE 122; NSPCC in
210; population 3; Protestant comprehensive schools 118; Rehabilitation Institute centre 202;
residential centres for children
216; Samaritans 13; School Attendance Department 207-8; school
management committees 102; secondary schools 109; Simon Community 13; teacher training colleges
97-8; technical education 116;
University College 124-9 *passim,*
132, 136-7

Dublin: (County) health functions
148: housing 75; (County Borough
health functions 148; housing 75

Dublin: (Ballyfermot) educational
standards 134; (Ballymun) housing
66, 90; (Crumlin) housing 65;
(Dalkey) interdenominational
primary schools 108; (Darndale)
housing 90-91; (Finglas) special
school 213; (Firhouse) inter-
denominational primary school 108;
(Killiney) educational standards
134; (Kill-o'-the-Grange) educational standards 134; (Lusk) special
school 213; (Marlborough Street)
training schools and model school
96-7; (Marley Grange) inter-
denominational primary school
108;;
(Rutland Street) educational project
136; (Tallaght) social work in 222

Dublin University 123, 126-128

Dublin Regional Hospital Board 151

Dublin Institute of Technology 120

Dublin, Archbishop of: patronage of
national schools 104; and Catholics
at TCD 125-6

Dundalk Regional Technical College
121

Dun Laoghaire Borough: housing 75; VEC 114

Dwellings for Labouring Classes (Ireland) Act (1860) 63

dynamisation and social security payments 232-3

Eastern Health Board 148; community care areas 156; medical card holders 180; mentally handicapped 198; mentally ill 175

economy: and education 94-5, 112; and housing 65-6; and SAP 225-6; and social services 3-4, 9-11

Economic and Social Research Institute 12

education 1-2, 5, 10, 16, 94-144; EEC comparisons 244-9

Education, Department of: adult education 132; *All Our Children* 94; community schools 139-142; comprehensive schools 18; free post primary education scheme 111; model schools 102; national schools 97-8; national schools for handicapped children 200; NIHE, Limerick 122; primary schools joint management committees 102-4; nationalisation of primary schools 104, 106; regional technical colleges 109-111, 113; secondary schools 109-111, 113; Thomond College 122; vocational schools 115

Education, Minister for: community schools 119; national schools 97; NCEA 122; vocational schools 114, 116

the elderly: dental services 160; home help service 168; housing 68, 69, 93-4; medical cards 180; welfare services for 3, 13, 189-196;

electricity allowance 38, 42, 193

Electricity Supply Board 42

eligibility for: choice of doctor scheme 156-8; dental services 160-161; developmental paediatric clinics 165; health services 146, 153-4, 176-188; home help service 167; social assistance *see* means test

emigration: and housing 2, 65, 78; and mental illness 173

employees: social insurance contributions 10-11, 15-16, 23-5, 51, 55-6, 229; health insurance contributions in EEC countries 233-6

employers: children's educational

opportunities 111, 134-5; and mental illness 174-5; social insurance contributions 15-16, 23-4, 50-51, 55-6; and social security schemes in EEC countries 227-9

employment: in SAP 225-6; in Treaty of Rome 225; *see also* unemployment

Employment Appeals Tribunal 45

Environment, Department of: certificate of reasonable value of house 78; housing 61; local authority house purchase schemes 73, mentioned 85, 90

Environment, Minister for, and National Building Agency 75

epilepsy 178

equal pay, EEC directive on, 14, 226

equality of opportunity: in education 94-5, 111-113, 116-117, 127-8, 133- 9 *passim;* in housing 61, 87-88; objective of voluntary work 217; poverty and 22; and social policy in EEC 226; and social policy in Ireland 7-9 ·

ESB *see* Electricity Supply Board

ESRI *see* Economic and Social Research Institute

essential repairs scheme 68, 79, 193

Europe: declining birth rates 190; free legal aid services in 216; housing stock in 88 *see also* European Economic Community

European Commission 13-14, 21, 224, 226-7·

European Court of Justice 224

European Economic Community: birth rate 2; dependency ratios 2, 15-16; dentists in 161; directives 224; economic and monetary union 225; Economic and Social Committee 224; education 130, 244-9; health services 154, 233-240; housing 76-7, 240-243; handicapped 203; income maintenance 51, 227-233; membership of 224; NCPSCP and 21-22; recommendations 224; regulations 224; SAP 21, 225-7; social policy in 13-14, 225-7

European Parliament 224

European Social Fund 203

exchequer *see* government

'The extent of poverty in Ireland' (S. Ó Cinnéide) 12, 20

the family: and Community Care
Programme 156; children and
203-6, 213; domiciliary services for 194; and educa-
tion 95; in France 231;
home help services 168;
housing and 60-61, 67-8, 74-5,
87, 241; income mainten-
ance 15, 40; and the men-
tally ill 174; and poverty 19;
social responsibilities of 4;
social work with 208, 220-2 *passim;*
welfare of 8
family allowance in EEC countries
231-2
family (child) benefit in EEC
countries 227
family centres 208
Farley, D. 40
farm labourers: illiteracy 132;
medical cards 180; mental illness 175; social insurance
contributions 27; unemployment assistance 31
farmers: children's educational
opportunities 128; contributions to
health services 154; eligibility for
health services 176-7, 180, 183,
185; health insurance in Luxembourg and 236; housing 62, 63, 77,
79; illiteracy 132; small holder's
assistance 32, 34, 58-9; social
insurance and 26, 28; social
security in EEC countries and 228
Faulkner, Patrick, Minister for
Education, and community
schools 119
Fianna Fáil: county hospitals 172;
index-linked social welfare payments 54; mother and child scheme
164; political ideology 5
Finance Acts: (1974) 81; (1979) 58
Finance, Minister for, and house
purchase loans 82
Fine Gael: Loughan House 213;
political ideology 5
fishermen and mental illness 175
Fitzgerald, Professor Patrick, 170
Fitzgerald Report 170-173
FLAC *see* Free Legal Advice Centres
Flanagan, Seán, Minister for Health,
and GHDP 170
flats 1, 69, 77
fluoridation of water 160
footwear scheme 38, 44
fosterage 205, 210, 212
Foundation Certificate 133
Foundation for Improved Living
Conditions 226

France: education 245; health services
236-7; housing 231; 241-2; income
maintenance 231-2
fraud and income maintenance
schemes 4, 55-9
free health services 145, 146, 186-7;
eligibility for 176, 183; hospitalisation 10
Free Legal Advice Centres 13, 215-
216
free post-primary education scheme:
future of 138-9;
introduction of 3, 5, 10, 95, 110,
111-113; school leaving age and
132, 134; and third level enrolments 129;
free television licence 38, 42, 193
free transport: primary school pupils
105-6;
secondary school pupils 112-113
free travel 38, 42, 193
fuel scheme, 37, 43-4

Gaeltachta, Roinn na, and housing
62
Gaeltachta: housing grants 62;
school meals 43
Galway Regional Hospital Board 151
Galway: adult education 131;
future hospital services in 172;
Queen's University in 123;
regional technical college in 121;
University College 122, 124, 126-
7; VEC 114
Garda Review and Loughan House 214
Garda Síochána: and unemployment
certificates 46; housing for 75;
juvenile liaison officers 210-211;
school attendance officers 98, 206
gas 44
general hospitals 168-170, 172; elderly
in 194, 196; psychiatric units 174;
social work in 222
General Hospital Development Plan
171-3
General Hospital Programme 168-173
General Medical Card 160, 162, 178-
181
General Medical Service 156-160
general medicine and psychiatry 174
general practitioners: Community
Care Programme 156; General
Medical Service 156-160, 179;
hospital services 170; medical
screening of children 164-6;
mentally ill 174
geriatric: assessment units 196;
hospitals 196; social workers
220

Germany: dentists in 161;
  health services 235, 237;
  housing 77, 241-2;
  income maintenance 227, 231-2
GHDP *see* General Hospital Development Plan
Glenties, comprehensive school in,
  117
government expenditure: (education)
  adult education 132-3; community
  schools 119, 120; comprehensive
  schools 118; first level 95, 99,
  102, 136-9; NIHE, Limerick 122;
  second level 95; 136-9; secondary
  schools 109, 110; universities 126,
  128-9, 136-9; vocational schools 115;
  (health services) 148, 152-3; (housing) 64, 65, 74, 76; local authority
  housing 70; grants 78-9; income tax
  relief 80-81; stamp duty 81; housing
  subsidies 86-7; (income maintenance) 15-16, 50-52; cheap footwear
  scheme 44; cheap fuel scheme 44;
  supplementary welfare allowance
  40; (social services provision) 1,
  3-4, 9, 11
government policy: (education) amalgamation of TCD and UCD 126-7;
  denominationalism in primary 97-8,
  108; equality of opportunity 94-5,
  113-4; free post primary scheme
  111-113; higher education grants
  127-8; rationalisation of primary
  schools 104-6; technical education
  115-6, 118, 120; (health services)
  care of mentally handicapped 176;
  care of mentally ill 173-4; Community Care Programme 155, 191;
  General Hospital Programme 170-
  173; mother and child scheme
  162-4; regional health boards
  147-8, 151-2; (housing) 60-61;
  factors in planning 67-9; owner-
  occupation 78; housing estate facilities 90-91; (income maintenance) poverty 21-22; social assistance 15-16; social insurance 15-16;
  (social service provisions) 4-11;
  (welfare services) growing role of
  state 189, 215; care of deprived
  children 204; care of elderly 191;
  care of handicapped 191, 199-200,
  202-3
gross national product 1, 9
ground rent 62
Group Certificate 141
group homes for children 212-213
'group solidarity' and social security
  coverage 229
group work 222-3

the handicapped: the Church and
  services for 5; and EEC 225, 226,
  232; home improvement grants for
  79; welfare services for 196-203 *see
  also* mentally, physically
Haughey, Charles, Minister for
  Health and Social Welfare and
  eligibility for health services 181, 188
HEA *see* Higher Education Authority
Health Act (1947) 162-4
Health Act (1953) 10, 164, 176
Health Act (1970): day nurseries 210;
  eligibility for health services 176,
  178, 188; reorganisatin of health
  services 10, 148, 150-151, 156,
  164-7 *passim*
health boards *see* regional health
  boards
health contributions 153-4
Health Contributions Act (1971) 153
Health (Corporate Bodies) Act (1961)
  202
Health, Department of: child care services 214; establishment of 9, 147,
  148; income maintenance schemes
  44; and medical consultants 187;
  and voluntary public hospitals 169;
  mentioned 151, 161, 180
health education 146, 161-2
health inspectors 156
health insurance 10, 185-6, 187; in
  EEC countries 233-240
Health, Minister for: care of aged
  191; and Comhairle na nOspidéal
  151; and Community Care Programme 155, 157, 158, 161, 164;
  eligibility for health services 178;
  and hospitals Commission 153; and
  Hospitals Trust Fund 153; and NRB
  203; and regional health boards 150
health services 1, 3, 10, 16, 145-188;
  in EEC countries 233-240
Health Services (Financial Provisions)
  Act (1947) 152
*The Health Services and their Further
  Development* (1966): choice of doctor
  scheme 156-7; financing of health
  services 152; government policy
  145; regionalisation of health
  services 148, 152
health visitors 163
hearing aids 166
Hensey, Dr Brendan, 147
higher income group: and adult
  education 132; eligibility for

health services 177, 185-6; and income tax 16; maternity services 164

Higher Education Act (1971) 128

Higher Education Authority: functions 128-9; and NCEA 122; and NIHE 121; university re-organisation 127

High Court and designation of building land 69

higher education grants 10, 127-8, 135

Hillery, Dr Patrick: (European Commissioner for Social Affairs) 224; (Minister for Education) comprehensive schools 116-7; regional technical colleges 120

home assistance 7, 11, 38-40, 59

home help service 11, 156, 166-8, 194

homelessness 13, 60, 74

Hospitals Commission 153

hospital services: acute medical care 148, 170-171; beds 155, 169, 170; equipment 170; in patient treatment 170, 183, 186; length of stay 170; location of 146, 148, 168-173; non-acute medical care 70; out-patient treatment 168, 170, 183, 186; staff 170, 187; teaching in 170; x-rays 183

Hospitals Trust Fund 153

house: building programmes 2, 9-11, 64-7; building standards 61, 79; demolition 64; evictions 74, 78; mortgages 74, 80-81

House of Commons and Irish primary education (1831) 96

housing: age of 88; amenities 89-90; in EEC countries 240-244; estates 64-7, 90-91; and life expectancy 146; land for 64, 69, 81; over-crowding 60, 67-8, 69, 74-5, 88-9, 107-8, 205; unfit for habitation 63, 67, 73, 74-5

housing grants: for building 3, 62-5, 78-9; for improvement 62, 79; for reconstruction 79; for sanitation 79

housing loans: for improvement 62;for purchase 62, 63, 65, 74, 79, 81-4

housing subsidies: for local authority house rents 70, 86; for local authority low rise mortgage scheme 74; for private rented sector 87-8; for urban housing 62

Housing Acts: (1919) 63; (1924) 64; (1931 and 1932) 64; (1957) 193; (1962) 193; (1966) 67

Housing (Amendment) Acts (1948 to 1952) 65

Housing: Progress and Prospects (1964) 66

Housing in the Seventies (1969) 60, 66

Housing of the Working Classes (Ireland) Act (1908) 62

Housing of the Working Classes Act (1890) 62

'humanisation' of work 225-6

humanitarianism and social policy 7-8

human rights and poverty 20

Hyland Associates Limited 113

ICTU *see* Irish Congress of Trade Unions

ideology and social policy 4-6, 7-9; in EEC 226

illiteracy 97, 131-2

illegitimate children: adoption 209; care of 205

immunisation 145, 156

income maintenance 15-59; dependants on.1, 215; demographic changes and 2-3; and the elderly 192-3; in EEC 227-233

income tax: allowance for children 41-2; personal allowances 11; and provision of income maintenance schemes 2-3, 15-16, 50, 229; relief on interest element of house mortgages 60-61, 78, 80-81, 86; relief on interest element of life assurance payments 80-81; VHI payments deductible from 186 *see also* contributions

Independence: health services before and after 6-7, 147, 169

index linking and income maintenance payments 52-55

the individual: Community Care Programme 156; education 94-5, 136; as focus of social work 220-223; health services 145, 150; housing 87; income maintenance 15; poverty 17-19; social services for 1; subsidiarity 5, 163

industrial development: housing needs 61-2, 68, 75, 78; social services and 7; technical training for 115, 121

industrial schools: and deprived children 212, 213; and school attendance 98, 206

Industry, Commerce and Tourism, Department of: and housing 62; mentioned 46

inequality *see* equality of opportunity

infant welfare services 179, 183, 187
infectious diseases 156, 177
infectious diseases maintenance
  allowance 44, 178-9
inflation: cause of social friction 227;
  effects on social expenditure 11;
  health services 151, 167, 178;
  house purchase loans 79-80; income
  maintenance payments 53, 232; old
  age pensions 193
information, access to: income maintenance 47-8; social services 219;
  community workers and 223
insurance companies and house
  purchase loans 63
Insurance (Intermittent Unemployment) Act (1942) 25
Intermediate Education Act (1878)
  109
Intermediate Education (Amendment)
  Act (1924) 109
Intermediate Education Board 109
Intermediate Certificate 109, 138,
  141; and vocational schools 116
intermittent unemployment (wet-time)
  insurance 23, 25, 27-8
Inter-Party Government (1948-51)
  162-4
INTO *see* Irish National Teachers'
  Organisation
invalidity pensions 23, 25, 198; in
  EEC countries 231; electricity
  allowance 42; free television licence
  42; free travel 42
Investment in Education (1965) 10, 94;
  community schools 118; comprehensive schools 116; free post-primary
  education scheme 111; primary
  school rationalisation 105; participation at third level 127, 134;
  technical education 121
Irish Army Pension Act 34
Irish Association of Social Workers
  213
Irish Congress of Trade Unions:
  campaign on long-term benefit payment increases 34, 232; and taxing
  children's allowance 42
Irish Dental Association 161
Irish Education Act (1892) 98
*Irish Educational Expenditures — Past,
  Present and Future* (1978) 12
Irish Free State: and denominational
  education 97; housing policy 64;
  and secondary schools 110; and
  social services provision 25
Irish Housing Fund 62
Irish Insurance Commissioners 45

the Irish language: matriculation in
  125; in schools 102
Irish Local Government Board 147
Irish Medical Association: 'free'
  health service 187;
  mother and child scheme 163
Irish National Teachers' Organisation
  and joint management committees
  102-4 *passim*
Irish Poor Law Commissioners 147
Irish Society for the Prevention of
  Cruelty to Children 205, 208, 213,
  217
The Irish Times on GHDP 172
Irish Universities Act (1908) 124-5
ISPCC *see* Irish Society for the
  Prevention of Cruelty to Children
Italy: education 245; health services
  236-238 *passim;* housing 241
itinerants 9, 214, 215

James, E. and Laurent, A. 229
jargon *see* terminology
Jesuits and Catholic University 124
job creation 4
Justice, Department of: ground rent
  52; rent control 62; unemployment
  certificates 46
juvenile courts 211-212
Juvenile Liaison Officer Scheme 210-
  211

Kaim-Caudle, P.A.: housing subsidies
  85; *Social Policy in the Irish
  Republic* 12; social security 15;
  social services 1
Kavanagh, Professor James, 20
Kennedy, Eileen, District Justice, 204
Kennedy, Finola: appeals on old age
  pensions 49-50; children's allowance
  41; social policy aims 7-8; social
  policy phases 9-11
Kennedy Report 204, 212-214 *passim*
Kenny Report 69
Kildare (County): community care
  area 156; elderly in 190
Kildare Place Society 96
Kilkenny: conference on poverty 20;
  social service council 218, 223

Labour, Department of, and redun-
  dancy payments scheme 45
Labourers (Ireland) Act (1883) 63
Labour Party (Britain) 5
Labour Party and Loughan House
  213
Land Acts 77
landlords: rural housing 63; privately

rented accommodation 85, 87
A Law for the Poor (S. Ó Cinnéide) 12
Lawson, R. and Reed, B. 229
Leaper, R.A.B. 6, 217
Leaving Certificate 109; and community schools 141; and regional technical colleges 121; and university grants 128; and vocational schools 116
Legitimacy Act (1931) 209
Leitrim (County): elderly in 190; population density 3; no developmental paediatric clinic in 165
Lenihan, Brian: (Minister for Education) adult education 131; equal opportunity in education 94
Letterkenny Regional Technical College 121
life expectancy 146, 189
life assurance and income tax relief 80-81
Limerick (City): health authority in 148; hospital services in 172; NIHE 121-2; Rehabilitation Institute centre in 200; social service council 218; Social Service Councils conference in 222; teacher training college 97; technical education in 115; VEC 114
local authorities: expenditure on social services 1; (education) adult 132; community schools 142; higher education grants 127-8; provision of school sites 99, 104; school attendance committees 98, 206; vocational schools 114-116; university scholarships 125; (health services) expenditure on 152; hospitals 169; maternity care 162; provision of 147-8; school medical examination service 165; (housing) building 60-61, 64-7 *passim*, 69-70; for the elderly 193-4; essential repairs scheme 68, 79; finance for 70; land for 69; loans for building 64; loans for improvements 79; loans for purchase 63, 73-4, 79-80, 82; low rise mortgage scheme 74; and NBA 61, 75; rates remission on new housing 80; rented accommodation 58, 69, 70-73, 74-5, 85; special housing problems 65, 69; (income maintenance) cheap footwear scheme 44, 46; cheap fuel scheme 43, 46; home assistance 39; pension committees 50; school meals 43; (welfare services) 215

Local Authority (Higher Education Grant) Act (1968) 128
Local Government Board for Ireland 63
Local Government, Department of, 147-8 *see also* Environment, Department of
Local Government and Public Health, Department of, 46, 147
Local Government and Social Welfare Minister for, 191
local taxation: abolition of, on private dwellings 11, 80; and finance for housing programmes 70; and health services 152; remission of, on grant-aided houses 64, 78 80; and school meals 43; and supplementary welfare allowance 40
London: Charity Organisation Society in 220; Department of Social Science and Administration, LSE 220; University of 123
long-term sickness benefit 198
Loughan House (County Cavan) 213-4
Louvain University and Catholic University 124
lower income group: and education 127-8, 133, 136; eligibility for health services 176; and house purchasing 79-80; and maternity care 164
Luxembourg: health services 236-7; income maintenance 232
Lyons, F.S.L. 123

McDonagh, K. and public expenditure on education 133-6 *passim*
McKinsey and Co., report on management of health services, 150, 156
McGreil, M., equality of opportunity in education 134-5
MacHale, Dr John, Archbishop of Tuam, and national schools 96
maintenance subsidies for schools 99, 102
managers: children's educational opportunities, 111, 135; and mental illness 175; and SAP 225
manual workers: children's educational opportunities 128; eligibility for health services 181; wet-time insurance for 25
market forces: education 94; health services 145; housing 60, 82; rents 85

marriage benefit (1929) 25
marriage rate: and mental illness 173; and social services provision 2
married couples: and adoption 209; and housing 11, 68, 69, 75, 87; and social assistance means test 35; and social services 8
married persons and eligibility for health services 188
mass dismissals, EEC directive on, 226
maternity benefit 23, 26; (allowance) 25, 26; (cash grant) 180
mortgages 74
maternity home 164
maternity hospitals 168
maternity services 162-4; eligibility for 179, 183; VHI and 185-6
Maynooth *see* St Patrick's College
Mayo (County), medical card holders in, 180
meals on wheels 156, 194
means test: for full eligibility for health services 176, 178; for higher education grant 128; for home improvement grants 79; none for mother and child scheme 163; for Protestant secondary pupils 111; for social assistance schemes 16, 23, 31, 28, 33-8, 48, 50, 192-3
Meath (County), medical card holders in, 180
medical: appliances 157, 177, 179; card *see* General Medical Service Card; hospital 168; officers of health 198; prescriptions 157-8; services 145, 148; social workers 220
Medico-Social Research Board: and care of mentally handicapped 174, 197-8; and county homes 195
medicines: and choice of doctor scheme 157-8; free 177-8, 179
men: and first level education 130; social insurance contributions 27; unemployment assistance 31
mental hospitals 174
Mental Treatment Acts 199
mentally handicapped: census of 197-9; rehabilitation of 200-203; schools for 102; services for 199-200; Special Hospital Programme and 173, 175-6, 177-8
mentally ill: community care for 191, 197, 199; rehabilitation of 202;
Meath (County), medical card holders in, 180
medical: appliances 157, 177. 179;

card *see* General Medical Service Card; hospital 168; officers of health 198; prescriptions 157-8; services 145, 148; social workers 220
Medico-Social Research Board: and care of mentally handicapped 174, 197-8; and county homes 195
medicines: and choice of doctor scheme 157-8; free 177-8, 179
men: and first level education 130; social insurance contributions 27; unemployment assistance 31
mental hospitals 174
Mental Treatment Acts 199
mentally handicapped: census of 197-9; rehabilitation of 200-203; schools for 102; services for 199-200; Special Hospital Programme and 173, 175-6, 177-8
mentally ill: community care for 191, 197, 199; rehabilitation of 202; Special Hospital Programme and 173-5, 178;
middle income group: eligibility for health services 176; and maternity care 164
Midland Health Board 148; mentally handicapped in area 197
midwives 162, 164
migrant workers in EEC 225, 226
migration: and elderly 3, 190; and housing 68; and mentally handicapped 198; and workers in EEC 226 *see also* emigration
'Million Pound Scheme' 64
miners and social security coverage in EEC countries 228, 239
mobile homes 193
model schools 96, 102
mortality rate: in France 231; amongst infants and mothers 163; and social services 2
Mortgages 74
Mother and Child Scheme 4-5, 162-4
mothers: expectant 162, 164, 180; nursing 162, 180
motor taxation 11
multiple sclerosis 178
municipal boroughs and Irish Education Act (1892) 98
Murphy Report 131-4

National Association of School Attendance Officers 207
National Association of Tenant's Organisation, rent strike (1973), 71
National Board of Education,

Commissioners of, 96-99, 108

National Building Agency 61, 75-6

National College of Physical Education *see* Thomond College

National Council for Educational Awards: establishment and role of 122, 127; and recurrent education 133

National Committee on Pilot Schemes to Combat Poverty 21-22, 223

National Economic and Social Council: and closure of small, rural schools 105-6; and educational expenditure 136; and housing requirements 67, 73, 86; and income maintenance schemes 17, 42, 54; study of social aims and policy 8; role of 12

National Health Council: and organisation of health services 151; and public dental service 161

National Health Service (Britain) 146, 237

A National Income-Related Pension Scheme 29-30

National Institute for Higher Education: Dublin 122; Limerick 121-2

National Health Insurance Society 12, 26, 46

National Health Insurance Act (1933) 46

National Insurance Act (1911) 23, 45

A National Partnership (1974) 53

National Rehabilitation Board 202-3

national schools: 96-8, 99-108; and dental services 160; and free school meals 43; and health examinations 165; teachers 96-107 *passim*

National Social Service Council: community information centres 48; functions of 13, 218-220; and home help services 168; and tax on children's allowance 42

National Society for the Prevention of Cruelty to Children 208

National Understanding for Economic and Social Development 54

National University of Ireland 122, 124-7

NCEA *see* National Council for Educational Awards

NCPSCP *see* National Committee on Pilot Schemes to Combat Poverty

NESC *see* National Economic and Social Council

The Netherlands: education 244-5, 247; health services 233, 237; housing 242; income maintenance 229, 232

Newman, Dr John Henry, and Catholic University 124

Nevin, Monica, and survey of UCD students 127-8, 134-5

NHS *see* National Health Service

NIHE *see* National Institute for Higher Education

non-manual workers: children's educational opportunities 128, 135; and eligibility for health services 181

North Eastern Health Board, medical card holders in area, 180

North Western Health Board 148, 151; mentally handicapped in area 198

Northern Ireland 20

Norway, primary schools in, 105

NRB *see* National Rehabilitation Board

NSSC *see* National Social Service Council

NUI *see* National University of Ireland

numeracy 131

nurseries *see* day care facilities

nurses: and Community Care Programme 156; and maternity care 162-4; members of health boards 150; and mentally ill 174; and school health examinations 166

nursing homes 186

nutrition and life expectancy 146

occupational injuries benefit 23, 25-8 *passim;* appeals 48

occupational therapy 202-203

Ó Cinnéide, Séamus, and poverty 12, 20, 39

O'Connor, Sean: (Secretary of Department of Education) and primary schools joint management committees 102

oil crisis (1973-4): and SAP 226; and school transport 106; and state maintenance subsidies to primary schools 102

Oireachtas 47

old age (care) allowance and medical card 178-9

Old Age Pension Act (1908) 31, 50

old age pensions 59, 215; appeals system 48-9; in EEC countries 231; electricity allowance 42; free television licence 42; free travel 42; qualifying age 4, 17, 25, 32,

192; rates of payment 11, 54; supplemented by home assistance 39 *see also* the elderly, prescribed relative allowance;

old age contributory pensions 10, 23, 25, 29, 52, 59, 192

old age non-contributory pensions 30-31, 52, 192; and cheap fuel scheme 43; means test 34-5, 192; medical card 178-9 *see also* adult dependant's allowance

O'Malley, Donogh: (Minister for Education) amalgamation of TCD and UCD 126; free post-primary education scheme 5, 111; steering committee on technical education 121

open prison 213

open society 6, 8-9

open employment 200-202

ophthalmic services 166, 180

ophthalmologists 155

orphan's contributory pension 23-6 *passim*, 28

orphan's non-contributory pension 30, 35, 178-9

Our Lady of Mercy (Carysfort) College, Blackrock 97

owner-occupation 76-84; in EEC countries 242

para-medical services 156

parents: and children's health 163, 166; and community school boards of management 120; no contributions to primary school maintenance 104; and private, primary school fees 99; and school attendance 98, 132; and primary school management committees 102, 104, and school representative organisations 95; and VECs 155

Paris, EEC summit (1972), 225

the parish and primary education 104

parkinsonism 178

PAYE *see* income tax

pay-related benefits 16, 26

Peel, Sir Robert, and Queen's Colleges, 123

pension committees 50

pensions 2, 6; *A National Income-Related Pension Scheme* 29-30; rent assessment and 92 *see also* blind person's, invalidity, old age, orphan's, retirement, self-employed, widow's

Pfretzschner, Paul, and owner-occupation 77-8

pharmaceutical chemists: choice of doctor scheme 157; members of health boards 150

Philbin, Reverend Dr William, Bishop of Down and Connor, on NUI and TCD 125

physically handicapped 189, 197; rehabilitation of 200, 203; schools for 102

physiotherapy 202

Planning for Social Development (1976) 12

politicians/politics: ideology 5-6; and Social Welfare Acts 47 *see also* individual politicians, political parties

polio victims, rehabilitation of, 202

Poor Law Commission (1927) 25

Poor Law (Ireland) Act (1838): and health services organisation 147, 169, 194-5; and social assistance schemes 31, 32, 38, 39 *see also* workhouses

Pope Gregory XVI and national schools 96

population and: adult education 131; Community Care areas 156; dental services 160-161; eligibility for health services 176-7; health board areas 148; hospital locations 170-172; housing 65, 67; housing in EEC 240; illiteracy 97; income maintenance schemes 17; medical cards 180; mentally handicapped 198; participation in education 95, 112, 129-30, 138; psychiatric beds 173; school attendance in EEC countries 245; social services provision 1-3, 10 *see also* demographic structure

Posts and Telegraphs, Department of, and income maintenance payments 46

poverty: Catholic Church and 5, 13; and children's allowance 41-2; definition of 17-21; delinquency and 205; EEC and 20, 226, 229, 231; government policy on 8, 21-3; and housing 60; and redistribution of income 15

pre-schools, therapeutic, 208

prescribed relative allowance 38, 42-3

pressure groups: and rediscovery of poverty 20; and social services 6, 215-6

preventive: dentistry 162; medicine 145, 147, 155-6, 166, 174

Primary Certificate 105

primary schools: buildings 96, 99; books 96; compulsory attendance 98-9, 136, 138, 206-8; enrolment and class size 107-8; inspections 96; management and finance 99-104; rationalisation 104-106; transition to secondary school 113

prison, children and, 206, 212-3

prison officers and Loughan House 213

Prisoners' Rights Organisation and Loughan House 213

prisoner's wife's allowance 30, 32; means test 35

private health insurance: in EEC countries 233-6 *see also* VHI

private sector housing: 1, 60, 61, 63-4, 65, 74; co-operative schemes 75; owner-occupation 76-84, 86-88; rented 84-6, 87, 88

private/semi-private hospital accommodation 185-6, 187

private hospitals 168-9, 185-6; in EEC 238

private nursing homes 194

private practice: dental 161; medical 156-7, 163, 186-8

private primary schools 99

private secondary schools 95, 110, 113

professional groups: children's educational opportunities, 11, 134-5

Programme for National Development 1978-81: and health 155; and taxation of children's allowance 42; and third level education 129, 139

Probation of Offenders Act (1907) 56

Protestant: comprehensive schools 117-8; primary schools 99; secondary schools 111

Protestants: and Royal University 123; and TCD 125

ion licence 42; free travel 42; means test 33-4; medical card 178-9 *see also* prescribed relative allowance

psychiatric hospitals: and elderly 194; and mentally handicapped 197; and mentally ill 173-4; social work in 222

Psychiatric Hospital Census (1971) 174

psychiatric social worker 174, 220

psychiatrists 21, 173, 174

psychologists 174

Public Assistance Act (1939) 39-40

public health nurses 156, 198

public hospitals 6, 169-170, 177

Public Hospitals Act (1933) 153

Public Social Expenditure in Ireland (1975) 7

Queen Elizabeth I and TCD 123

The Queen's College 123, 124, 125

railwaymen and health care in France 239

Red Cross hospitals in EEC countries 238

redundancy 27, 44-5

Redundancy Fund 45

Redundancy Payments Acts (1967, 1969 & 1979) 44-5

redundancy payments scheme 44-5

Redundancy Payments (Weekly Payments) Order (1976) 58

Reeves, A.J., and old age 191

referendum: on entry to EEC 224; on university senators 127

reformatory schools 212-3 *see also* special schools

Reformatory Schools Act (1858) 212

regional health board(s): 10, 146, 239; and adoption 209, 210; care of deprived children 210; cheap footwear scheme 44; chief executive officer of 150, 178; and Community Care Programme 156; day-care facilities for children 210; and dental services 161; developmental paediatric clinics 165; disabled person's maintenance allowance 44, 198; domiciliary allowance for handicapped children 44; efficiency of 151-2; and fosterage 210; and fuel schemes 44; and General Hospital Programme 168; and GHDP 172; and health contributions 153; and home assistance 39; and home help service 166-7, 194; hospitals 169-170; infectious diseases maintenance allowance 44; and local health advisory committees 151, 172; meals on wheels 194; medical cards 178-181, 193; membership of 150; and mentally handicapped 173, 176, 197-8, 199; and mentally ill 173, 175; and pharmaceutical chemists 157; rehabilitation of handicapped 202-3; school health examinations 165; social work services 208, 221, 223; and voluntary hospitals 153; and voluntary

welfare agencies 218
regional hospital boards 150-1, 172
regional technical colleges 10, 95,
   108, 120-121, 130
rehabilitation: of elderly 196; of
   handicapped 200-203; of mentally
   ill 174
Rehabilitation Institute 200-201
Relate 220
religious orders: and care of handicapped 199; and community
   schools 119-120; and education 5;
   and hospitals 5; and industrial
   schools 212, 216; and primary
   education 96, 99, 137; and
   reformatory schools 212, 216; and
   secondary education 110, 111, 137
   see also individual religious
   orders
Rent Restrictions Acts (1960 and
   1967) 85
rents: control of 62, 85, 87-8;
   local authority 70-73, 91-3
*Report of the Commission on the
   Status of Women* 33, 210
*Report of Commission of Inquiry on
   Mental Handicap* (1965) 175-6
*Report of the Commission of Inquiry
   into Mental Illness* (1965) 12, 173-4
*Report of the Consultative Council on the
   General Hospital Services* (1968) 151
*Report on the Industrial and Reformatory
   Schools System* (1970) 12
Report on University Reorganisation
   (1972) 127
residential centres: for deprived child-
   ren 204, 205-6, 210, 212-4; for
   handicapped 197-8, 199-200;
the retired and health contributions
   153
retirement pension 23, 25, 27; electricity allowance 42; free television
   licence 42
RETOS (Shannon) 202
Revenue Commissioners 46, 154
roads 16
Roscommon (County), no developmental paediatric clinic in, 165
Royal College of Surgeons in
   Ireland 122
Royal Commission (1906-7) 125
Royal University 123, 124
*Rules of National Schools under the
   Department of Education* 97-8, 108
rural areas: choice of doctor scheme
   in 157; comprehensive schools in
   116-7; domiciliary services for
   elderly in 194; elderly in 190;

essential repairs scheme 68, 79,
   193; free school transport scheme
   in 112-3; house purchase scheme in
   73; housing amenities in 89; housing conditions in 89, 243; housing demand in 63, 65, 68; housing for elderly 68, 193; illiteracy
   in 131; medical screening of children in 165; mental illness in 173;
   number of primary schools in 104-
   6; poverty in 21; school attendance
   in 98; social services provision in
   3, 9 *see also* urban areas
Ryan, Dr James, Minister for Health,
   and mother and child scheme 164
Ryan, Richie, Minister for Finance,
   on social insurance contributions
   51

St Patrick's College, Maynooth, 122,
   124, 127
St Patrick's, Drumcondra, 97
St Patrick's Institution 213
St Vincent de Paul, Society of 21,
   215, 217
Salaried employees: children's educational opportunities 111, 135; and
   health insurance in EEC countries
   234-6; and mental illness 175
Samaritans 13, 215
SAP *see* Social Action Programme
sanitation 89, 145-6
schizophrenia 175
school attendance 98-9, 206-7
School Attendance Act (1926) 98-9,
   206-7
school books: 96, 112
school buildings 96, 99, 110, 137
school leaving age 99
school meals 38, 43
schools *see* community, comprehensive
   national, primary, secondary,
   vocational
Secondary Education Committee 111
secondary schools: 95, 108-113; and
   adult education 133; and comprehensive schools 117; and vocational
   schools 116, 118-119, 120, 140
Seebohm Report 19, 216, 221
self-employed; and health contributions 153, and health insurance
   in EEC countries 234-6; and rent
   assessment 91; and social insurance
   14, 26, 28-30, 229-231
semi-skilled workers, children's
   educational opportunities, 111, 135
SFADCo *see* Shannon Free Airport

Development Company
Shanganagh Castle (County Dublin) 213
Shanks, M., and EEC social policy, 225, 227
Shannon Free Airport Development Company 62
Shannon: comprehensive school at 117; RETOS centre at 202
Shatter, Alan, on adoption 209
Sheehan, J., on 3rd level education 130; on educational expenditure 136
Sheehan, M., on poverty, 20-21
sheltered employment 176, 189, 202-3
Shelton Abbey (County Wicklow) 213
Sick and Indigent Roomkeepers' Society 217
sickness benefit 6, 23-4, 45, 215
Simon Community 13
Sinfield, A. 20
single mothers and ALLY 13
single persons: and health services 188; and housing 87
single woman's allowance 31, 32-3; means test for 33-6 *passim*
skilled workers and wet-time insurance 27
Sligo: regional technical college in 121, VEC 114
slums 60, 62, 64
Small Dwellings Acquisition Act (1899) 63
smallholder's assistance 11, 32; means test for 34-5, 58-9
Social Action Programme (EEC): aims and implementation 225-227, 233; and poverty in Ireland 21
social assistance 30-38; in EEC countries 229-231; finance for 50-52 rates of payment 52-55; and rent assistance 92
Social Fund (EEC) 226
social insurance: 10-11, 16, 23-30; administration of 45-6; in EEC countries 227-232 *passim;* finance 50-52; fraud 55-9; rates of payment 52-5
Social Insurance for the Self-Employed (1978) 14
Social Policy in the Irish Republic (1967) 12
'Social Security' (Dr John Dignan) 12
social security 15, 226
Social Service Councils 22, 218-219; conference in Limerick 222-3
Social Services Act (1970) 221

Social Studies 13
Social Welfare Act (1952) 46, 47, 51
Social Welfare (Children's Allowance) Acts 92
Social Welfare (Consolidation) Bill (1976) 47
Social Welfare, Department of: dental panel 160; establishment and organisation of 9, 46, 47-8, 147; finance for 51; and fraudulent claims 59; and income maintenance schemes including special schemes for elderly etc. 15, 38, 42, 43, 44, 193; and means test 33; and redundancy payments 45; and social assistance 23, 28, 30; and social insurance 6, 23, 28-30
Social Welfare, Minister for: and assistance 40; and National Health Insurance Society 46; and supplementary allowance 39
Social Welfare (Supplementary Welfare Allowances) Act (1975) 38-40
social work: 220-223; with deprived children 205, 208
social workers: and Community Care Programme 156; and mentally ill 174; and poverty projects 21; and Social Service Councils 219; training of 13, 47, 220
socio-economic groups *see* higher, lower andmiddle income groups
social policy: in EEC 225-7; in Ireland 6-14
South Eastern Health Board 172
Special Hospital Programme 155, 173-6
special schools 205-6, 212-4
special national schools (for handicapped) 102, 200
specialised hospitals 172
spectacles 166
speech therapy 203
spina bifida 178
stamp duty 81
stamps (supplementary insurance) 27
standard of living: and income maintenance 16, 23, 30, 41, 54, 232-3; and Irish social policy 8; and SAP 225; and Treaty of Rome 225; and young offenders 212
Stanislaus, Sister 223
Statement on Social Policy (1973) 9, 12, 47, 55
Steering Committee of Technical Education 121, 122
strikers and supplementary welfare

allowance 40
students: and supplementary welfare allowance 40; and university fees 129, 137;
Studies 13
'subsidiarity' 5, 163
Summary of Social Insurance and Assistance Services 48
supplementary unemployment fund 28
supplementary welfare allowance: 7, 11, 21, 34, 38-40; and cheap footwear scheme 44; and cheap fuel scheme 43; and rent assessment 92
surgical hospitals 168

Tallaght Welfare Society 222
Task Force on Child Care Services 214
taxation *see* income tax
teacher training college 96-7, 130, 137, 139
teachers: forecast of needs for 137; salaries 96, 99, 109-110, 111, 117, 137; and social insurance coverage 28; unionisation of 95; and VECs 115 *see also* ASTI, national schools, TUI
Teachers' Union of Ireland 119
'technical' education: second level 137-8; third level 120-122; in vocational schools 115
tenants: local authority 69-75 *passim;* in nineteenth century 63; private 84-8 *passim*
terminology, simplification of, by Department of Social Welfare 48
Thomond College, Limerick 122
Thurles, Synod of 123-4
Toghermore Centre (Tuam), rehabilitation centre at, 202
Towards Better Health Care — Management in the Health Board 150
trade unions: and regional technical colleges 121; and social security schemes in EEC 229 *see also* ICTU
Tipperary (South), general hospital in, 172
Town Commissioners and provision of school meals 43
Townsend, P., on poverty 17
training: of handicapped 200-203; of social workers 220-221; of teachers 96-7, 130, 137, 139
Training and Employing the Handicapped 198, 200, 203
Tralee: regional technical college in 121; VEC in 114

travelling people *see* itinerants
treatment benefit 23
Treaty of Rome: 224; social provisions in 225; and SAP 226
Trinity College, Dublin 122, 123, 125-7
Tuam: Dr John MacHale, Archbishop of, and national schools 96; rehabilitation centre at Toghermore 202
tuberculosis and living accommodation 74
TUI *see* Teachers' Union of Ireland
turf 44
Tussing, A.D., on education 12, 136, 137-9

Unemployment Assistance Act (1933) 31
unemployment assistance 30, 31-32, 46; appeals 48; cheap fuel scheme and 43; fraudulent claims 56-7; means test for 33-8 *passim;* and medical card 180; qualification certificate for 31, 48; and women 33 *see also* smallholder's assistance
unemployment benefit 6, 23, 26, 27, 46, 52; appeals 48; before 1911 45, 215; in EEC countries 231; fraudulent claims 56-7; medical card 180; rent assessment 91 *see also* redundancy payments scheme
unemployment: conditions in schools in areas of 107-8; in EEC countries 226; effects on children 205; mental illness and 173; social provisions for 2-3, 3-4, 11, 17
United Kingdom *see* Britain
United Kingdom National Council of Social Service, International Committee, 226-7
United States of America, health services in 145
universal coverage: children's allowance 40; hospitalisation 186-8, 223
universal suffrage 7
University College *see* Cork, Dublin, Galway
University Education (Ireland) Act (1879) 123
university sector education 122-130
the unmarried and mental illness 175
unmarried mothers, voluntary agencies for 13, 216
unmarried mother's allowance 32; means test for 34-5
unmarried mother's benefit 10
unskilled workers: children's educational opportunities 111, 135; and

wet-time insurance 27
urban areas: cheap fuel scheme 43;
child welfare services 163;
community facilities 90-1; the
elderly 190; health clinics 164;
housing amenities 89; housing
conditions 75, 88-9, 242; housing
demands 62-8 *passim,* 78; housing
land 69; house purchase schemes
73; juvenile liaison officer scheme
211; meals on wheels 194; medical
screening of children in 165;
national schools in 106-7; poverty
21; preventive health services 147;
Rehabilitation Institute Centres in
200; rented accommodation in 75,
85; secondary schools 109, 113;
social services in 3, 9; voluntary
public hospitals 169 *see also*
rural areas
urban district: (areas) pension committees in 50; (councils) and health
services 147; and housing 62; and
school meals 43

vaccination 156
Vatican Council II 5
VEC *see* Vocational Education
Committee
VHI *see* Voluntary Health Insurance
Board
Vocational Education Act (1930) 114-
6 *passim*
Vocational Education Committees
114; and adult education 131; and
community schools 119, 120, 141;
and comprehensive schools 118;
and regional technical colleges 121
vocational guidance experts 21
vocational schools 114-6: and community schools 118, 120, 141;
and comprehensive schools 117; and
secondary schools 116
voluntary adoption societies 208
Voluntary Health Insurance Act
(1957) 10, 185
Voluntary Health Insurance Board
10, 185-6, 187
voluntary hospitals 168-170, 185;
finance for 153, 169
voluntary organisations: adult education 131; and community schools
141; day care facilities for children 210, 216; home help service
167, 194; hospitals run by 151;
housing for elderly 193; and maternity care 162; meals on wheels
194; mentally handicapped 173,

176; physically handicapped 194,
199, 200-203; and social welfare
services 151, 189, 214-216, 220,
221
Vredeling, Hank, European Commissioner of Social Affairs 226

wage earners: and health insurance
in EEC countries 233-236; and
medical cards 180; pension for
widows of 25
War of Independence, pensions and
allowances arising from service in
34
Waterford (City): health authority in
148; regional technical college in
121; seminar on Irish health
services in 166; teacher training
college in 97; technical education in 115; VEC in 114
water supply, 3, 89
Waugh, Benjamin, 208
wealth tax 11
welfare homes for elderly 196
welfare services 189-223
Western Health Board: and Galway
Regional Hospital Board 151; and
home help service 167; and
medical card holders 180; and
mentally handicapped 197-8; and
mentally ill
175; report on psychiatric and
geriatric services in area 195
Westminster 47
wet-time insurance *see* intermittent
unemployment insurance
Wexford VEC 114
Wicklow (County), community care
area 156
widowers and adoption 209
widows and adoption 209
Widows' and Orphans' Pension Act
(1935) 25
widow's contributory pension 23, 25,
26, 28, 52, 55; electricity allowance 42; free television licence 42
widow's non-contributory pension 30,
55; cheap fuel scheme 43; means
test 34-5; and medical card 179
Wilson, John, Minister for Education: and adult education 133;
and NCEA 127; and
university fees 129
women: and home help service 167;
illiteracy among rural 132; level
of education among 130; minority
group 9, 225; and social security
provisions 14, 25, 27, 33

Women's Aid Society, Irish 216
The Work of Justice (1977) 5
workhouses: and hospital system
6-7, 147, 169, 194; social workers
becoming modern 223 *see also*
Poor Law
working conditions: in SAP 225; in
Treaty of Rome 225
workman's compensation scheme
(1897) 25
World War II: cheap fuel scheme
started during 43; family allowance in France since before 231;
health services since 152; and
housing 65, 88, 242; increasing
affluence since 20; Irish social
policy since 7-11

x-rays 183

young: and European economic
expansion 225; offenders 210-214;
and unemployment 226